Faith-Integrated Being, Knowing, and Doing

A Study among Christian Faculty in Indonesia

Sarinah Lo

© 2020 Sarinah Lo

Published 2020 by Langham Academic (Previously Langham Monographs)
An imprint of Langham Publishing
www.langhampublishing.org

Langham Publishing and its imprints are a ministry of Langham Partnership

Langham Partnership
PO Box 296, Carlisle, Cumbria, CA3 9WZ, UK
www.langham.org

ISBNs:
978-1-83973-052-8 Print
978-1-83973-077-1 ePub
978-1-83973-079-5 PDF

Sarinah Lo has asserted her right under the Copyright, Designs and Patents Act, 1988 to be identified as the Author of this work.

All rights reserved. No part of this publication may be reproduced, stored in a retrieval system or transmitted, in any form or by any means, electronic, mechanical, photocopying, recording or otherwise, without the prior written permission of the publisher or the Copyright Licensing Agency.

Requests to reuse content from Langham Publishing are processed through PLSclear. Please visit www.plsclear.com to complete your request.

Scriptures taken from the Holy Bible, New International Version®, NIV®. Copyright © 1973, 1978, 1984, 2011 by Biblica, Inc.™ Used by permission of Zondervan.

British Library Cataloguing-in-Publication Data
A catalogue record for this book is available from the British Library.

ISBN: 978-1-83973-052-8

Cover & Book Design: projectluz.com

Langham Partnership actively supports theological dialogue and an author's right to publish but does not necessarily endorse the views and opinions set forth here or in works referenced within this publication, nor can we guarantee technical and grammatical correctness. Langham Partnership does not accept any responsibility or liability to persons or property as a consequence of the reading, use or interpretation of its published content.

To my husband and daughter, with deep thanksgiving for your ceaseless encouragement and support. To my parents, with deep gratitude for your faithfulness in upholding us in your prayers.

Give thanks to the LORD, for he is good.
His love endures forever.
~Psalm 136:1

Contents

List of Tables and Illustrations xi

Abstract xiii

Acknowledgments xv

Chapter 1 1
Introduction
    Researcher's Stance and Story 1
    Background of the Study 4
    Problem Statement 7
    Purpose of the Study 9
    Research Questions 9
    The Significance of the Study 10
        Theoretical Significance 10
        Practical Significance 10
    Definition of Terms 11

Chapter 2 13
Literature Review
    Historical Background of the Integration of Faith and Learning 13
        The Relationship between Faith and Learning in
            Different Eras 14
        The Disestablishment of Protestantism in the United States
            Educational System 16
        The Response of Christian Scholars to the Secularization of
            the Academy 21
        The Reawakening of Christian Scholarship and the
            Beginning of the Integration of Faith and
            Learning Movement 23
    Biblical and Theological Foundations for the Integration of
        Faith and Learning 25
        Creation 25
        Fall 27
        Redemption 30
        Restoration 32
    Theological and Educational Necessity for the Integration of
        Faith and Learning 34

The Multifaceted Definition of the Integration of Faith
and Learning 36
The Debate over the Semantic Use of "Integration" 39
Theoretical Approaches to the Integration of Faith and Learning 41
Integrative Strategies and Methodologies 45
Loci of Integration 48
    Teachers..49
    Curriculum...50
    Pedagogy 51
    Beyond the Classroom 53
Empirical Studies on the Integration of Faith and Learning 54
Challenges in Implementing Faith-Integrated Learning 60
    Gaps between Belief and Practice...60
    Insufficient Practical Knowledge and Experience 61
    Lack of Institutional Support and Resources...............................62
    Contemporary Western Culture of Mind....................................63
Summary 65

Chapter 3 69
Methodology
Research Design..69
Purpose Statement 70
Research Questions...70
Population and Sample Selection 70
Description of Participants...71
Higher Education in the Indonesia Context.......................................72
Data Collection 77
Data Analysis 78
Translation-Related Issues 78
Transferability...80

Chapter 4 81
Findings
Descriptions of Professoriate Roles in Indonesian Higher
    Education Contexts...81
    Tridharma: Trilogy of Higher Education 81
    Struggles to Keep the Trilogy in Harmony 85
Section 1: The Integration of Faith and Teaching Vocation 86
    Faith Gives a Strong Sense of Calling...86
    Faith Gives Purpose and Meaning to Faculty's Work...................99
    Faith Provides Moral and Ethical Guidance 106

   Faith Gives a Strong Work Ethos 108
   Faith Gives Strength in the Face of Adversity 122
   Faith Gives Desire for Personal Growth 145
  Section 2: The Integration of Faith and Academic Disciplines 161
   Approaches to the Integration of Faith and Learning 161
   Response to Conflicts between Faith and Learning 171
  Section 3: The Integration of Faith and Educational Practices 174
   "Spontaneous" Integration 174
   Faith Gives Principles to "Give the Best" and
    "Help Students Learn Best" 176
   Modeling an Exemplary Life 187
   Building Positive Relationships with Students 189
   Cultivating Christian Practices, Values, and Character 195
   Explicit Evangelism 202
 Summary of the Findings 203

Chapter 5 207
 Discussions and Implications
 Discussions 207
  Faith-Integrated Being 207
  Faith-Integrated Knowing 215
  Faith-Integrated Doing 223
 Implications for Practice 228
  Proposing a New Terminology: "Faith-Integrated
   Being-Knowing-Doing" 228
  Professional Development Formation 230
  Developing a Support Structure 233
 Suggestions for Further Research 235
 Conclusion 236

Appendix 1 239
 Informed Consent Form

Appendix 2 241
 Interview Protocol

Bibliography 245

List of Tables and Illustrations

Table 1. Participants and Types of Institution 72

Figure 1. Six Aspects of Faith-Integrated Being 87

Figure 2. Eight Approaches to Faith-Integrated Knowing 162

Figure 3. Two-Domain, One Source (BS1) 164

Figure 4. Six Aspects of the Integration of Faith and Educational Practices 175

Figure 5. Summary of the Findings 205

Figure 6. Model of Faith-Integrated Being, Knowing, and Doing 229

Figure 7. Basic Professional Development for the Integration of Faith and Learning 231

Figure 8. Support Structure for Christian Faculty 234

Abstract

Most studies of the integration of faith and learning focus on cognitive aspects of the integration and are conducted in the North American contexts. This qualitative study attempts to approach the integration of faith and learning holistically, including faith-integrated being, knowing, and doing among Christian faculty in Indonesian higher education contexts. The study focused on three areas of integration: faith and vocation (being), faith and academic disciplines (knowing), and faith and educational practices (doing). Thirty-six participants were purposely selected and data was collected using a semi-structured interview.

The findings of this study reveal that Christian faculty members in Indonesia have a strong emphasis on their faith-integrated *being* but less on their faith-integrated *knowing* and *doing*. Faith-integrated *being* is manifested in the participants' conviction of their vocation as faculty members; the purpose and meaning of work; work attitude, ethics, and performance; desire for personal growth; and resiliency in the face of adversities. Faith-integrated *knowing* does not occur substantially in the academic discipline of the participants. However, faith does make a difference in their scholarly pursuits by providing ethical and moral guidelines, shaping their attitudes and interpersonal relationships, and directing the purpose and application of their academic studies. Faith-integrated *doing* also does not occur at a substantial level. Faith is integrated in classroom practices through spontaneous integration, cultivating Christian practices and values, living out exemplary lives, and building authentic relationships with students.

In sum, the integration of faith and learning for most Christian faculty members in Indonesia is centered on cultivating pietistic lives and practices. For a substantial and foundational integration to occur, this study suggests

Christian faculty members in Indonesia need to be willing to be equipped with biblical-theological and philosophical foundations, educational theories and practices, critical reflective practices, and a structure of support which includes personal growth, a community of believers, and a community of academics. In addition, this study proposes a new terminology of "faith-integrated being-knowing-doing" to replace current semantic use of "the integration of faith and learning" that overemphasizes the cognitive domain and creates ambiguity and dualistic thinking.

Acknowledgments

This journey would not have been possible without the support of the company of saints. To my family, Philip and Sarah, thank you for encouraging me to embark on this doctoral journey and for your tireless support along the way. I am deeply grateful to Trinity Evangelical Divinity School (TEDS) for providing me with the Waybright scholarship. Special thanks to Dr. Donald Guthrie for your untiring support, guidance, and wisdom that help me to trust the *process*. Special thanks to Dr. James Moore for your guidance, insights, and invaluable feedback.

I owe a debt of gratitude who have contributed to the research process and the final product of this dissertation. To Christian faculty members in Indonesia, thank you for your participation in this study and allowing your stories to be part of this research. To Jim Bradley and Barbara Hampton, I am deeply grateful for your friendship and for proofreading my writing.

Special thanks to the Langham Publishing team, especially Luke Lewis, Vivian Doub and Brian Kramer, who have been instrumental in publishing this work.

I am grateful for all my EDS/ICS professors for modeling great teaching and showing me what it means to be a dedicated scholar-practitioner, each in their own unique way: Dr. Deborah Colwill, Dr. Donald Guthrie, Dr. James Moore, Dr. Camile Bishop, Dr. Peter Cha, Dr. James Plueddemann, Dr. Mimi Larson, and Dr. Tasha Chapman. My deep appreciation to Dr. Ng Peh Cheng, Dr. Siew Yau Man, Dr. David I. Smith, Dr. Jan Simonson, and Dr. Jo Kuyvenhoven for enhancing my Christian education formation prior to my study at TEDS. I am also grateful for my EDS colleagues for being a hospitable community of learners. Thank you so much to Elizabeth Bjorling-Poest, Jody Craiglow, Taina Luhtala, Yulee Lee, Suzie Sang, Tina Lau, Sutrisna Harjanto,

Kags Ndehiu, LaTonia Winston, Michael Mauriello, and many others. To my prayer warriors and friends at Church of Servant CRC, particularly the BES body, thank you for upholding me with your prayers and words of encouragement. Finally, thanks be to God for all his kindness and providence.

Ad Memoriam Dei Gloriam!

CHAPTER 1

Introduction

Researcher's Stance and Story

In a qualitative study, the human instrument is not free from biases. To maintain integrity, the researcher needs to move through the process of critical reflection to identify his or her experiences, worldview, and underlying assumptions that relate to the study at hand.[1] The following is my researcher's stance that will provide readers with a better understanding of how I "might have arrived at the particular interpretation of the data."[2]

I was born and raised in a devout Buddhist family, sent to public schools and instilled with Islamic teachings, then exposed to Christianity in grade 8 through the only Christian teacher at my middle school, and converted to Christianity at the age of sixteen. Since then, my new-found faith has shaped me and my purpose of life in a different direction. I attended a state university in Jakarta. As a female Indonesian Chinese Christian living in a predominantly Muslim context, I experienced pressures and discrimination as a minority on a daily basis, even in the academic world of a prestigious state university. For example, during a three-credit-hour class, one professor from the science department often used half of the class hour to preach Islamic teachings and would sarcastically accuse Christians of practicing

---

1. Merriam, *Qualitative Research: A Guide to Design and Implementation* (San Francisco, CA: Jossey-Bass, 2009), 219; Yvonna S. Lincoln and Egon G. Guba, "Paradigmatic Controversies, Contradictions, and Emerging Confluences," in *Handbook of Qualitative Research*, eds. N. K. Denzin and Y. S. Lincoln (Thousand Oaks, CA: Sage, 2000), 183.

2. Merriam, *Qualitative Research*, 219.

social work to gain new converts. The institution had a small number of Christian students and a handful of Christian faculty. In addition, cheating in class or laboratory assignments and exams were not uncommon. My faith and study journey during my undergraduate years was difficult, but by God's grace, I could pass and keep my faith. If it was tough for me as a minority student, it might have been challenging for the Christian faculty as well. I was intrigued to understand how Christian faculty perceived and negotiated their presence, vocation, teaching and learning in connection to their faith in a public university setting. What major challenges did they face and what kinds of support did they need?

After graduation, I worked as a lecturer at a Christian university. For the first time in my life, I was in a predominantly Christian environment and hoped for a better atmosphere. The student body consisted of young men and women from diverse religious backgrounds. The institution held weekly chapels and annual celebrations of Christmas and Easter, but I did not recall any Bible reading or prayer before class, including my classes. Although the majority of the faculty were self-professed Christians, not many of them expressed it through their work ethos. For example, many of them made jokes using filthy language in the faculty room and altered timecards by clocking in and out from 8:00 a.m. to 4:00 p.m. while their actual presence on campus was only two hours. One instructor was implicated in a bribery case after many years of asking for and receiving gifts or money from students to give them a passing grade. The institution only gave this instructor a one-year detention, after which he returned to teach as usual. As a novice faculty, I was laughed at and labeled as an "idealist" and "too young to understand the reality" of the situation. Amid this working climate, I questioned many things and tried to make sense of what it meant to be a Christian faculty.

Pertaining to teaching and learning, the dominant methods were teacher-textbook centered, one-way presentations, rote memorization, all verified by testing. Getting good scores, grades, and degrees was the main educational goal. Consequently, selfishness and a competitive spirit were high. These learning environments and teaching-learning approaches in this Christian university revealed few differences from the public university where I received my education. Further, I also practiced the teaching methods I had observed.

I resigned after five years of teaching and attended seminary in Singapore. Almost all of the professors had their advanced degrees from the United States or the United Kingdom. The academic environment was rigorous and the campus life was set by the bell. Explicitly and implicitly, the value of legalism, behaviorism, and academic performance was strongly emphasized. To a certain extent, these educational approaches had influenced my teaching at a local seminary and my role as a K-12 Christian school chaplain, and I wondered if these teaching and learning experiences might produce unintentionally oppressive environments and unjustly impact student formation.

In summary, reflections on my own teaching and learning experiences in connection to my faith have led me on this journey of seeking wisdom to better understand my vocation, teaching and learning, and practices from a Christian faith perspective. Other Christian faculty, despite their diverse backgrounds, stories, and teaching contexts, might share similar needs and desires to be equipped in integrating faith into their vocation and teaching and learning practices. This was one of the reasons that participants in this study were Christian faculty who taught in the different contexts: Christian, non-faith based, and state university. These various contexts posed different challenges in shaping the understanding and practice of faith-integrated learning. Before proposing and designing any necessary professional and faith development programs, a study to investigate how Christian faculty understand and practice the integration of faith and learning had to first be carried out. In other words, I hope that this study will act as a map for Christians working in Indonesian higher education contexts to point out *where* we are now and *where* we need to go. *How* to arrive at the destination(s) would be the professional and faith development programs designed based on *what* this study reveals.

Background of the Study

The integration of faith and learning is not merely an idea but has become "the essence of authentic Christian higher education."[3] The Council for Christian Colleges and Universities (CCCU) has faithfully advanced this essence through its core mission, which states that the CCCU exists "to advance the cause of Christ-centered higher education and to help our institutions

---

3. David S. Dockery, "Integrating Faith and Learning: An Unapologetic Case for Christian Higher Education," *Faith and Mission* 18, no. 1 (Fall 2000): 44.

transform lives by faithfully relating scholarship and service to biblical truth."[4] In fact, in just a few decades, the integration of faith and learning has become a core value of Christian higher education and has spread to other countries beyond the United States.

From the continent of Africa, James Ogunji, a Christian scholar from Babcock University, Nigeria, has introduced a conceptual model for integrated faith and learning to foster the identity and mission of Christian education in Africa. He asserts that if faith and learning were intentionally integrated into all levels of education, from administration, teaching and instruction, co-curricular programs, and community services, to spiritual development and quality assessment, it would redeem African Christian education from the invasion of secularization and a Western life style.[5]

During the last century in Asia, South Korea has experienced rapid growth of Christian higher education. Currently, South Korea has sixty-one Christian colleges and universities, or 38 percent out of 185 total colleges and universities in the country.[6] Shin Kuk-Won observes, however, that Korean Christian institutions of higher education face serious challenges including losing a distinct identity to secularization in the "process of adjusting to the changes of context, government education policy, and competition in the education market."[7] Realizing the danger of this problem, many Korean Christian colleges and universities have begun reestablishing Christian principles and values by redesigning institutional vision and mission statements, and aiming for an integrative approach to faith and learning.[8] Over the last two decades, this movement back toward the integration of faith and learning has been well-received. Further, a number of research centers have been established to advance the integration movement, including Christian Worldview Studies Association of Korea, Society for Integration Studies, and Christian Educators Association. However, Shin observes that it is rare to find Korean Christian

---

4. "Our Mission," Council for Christian Colleges and Universities, accessed November 19, 2015, http://www.cccu.org/.

5. James A. Ogunji, "Fostering the Identity and Mission of Christian Education in Africa," *Journal of Research on Christian Education* 21 (2012): 46–61.

6. Kuk-Won Shin, "Korean Christian Higher Education: History, Tasks and Vision," in *Christian Higher Education: A Global Reconnaissance*, ed. Joel Carpenter, Perry L. Glanzer, and Nicholas S. Lantinga (Grand Rapids: Eerdmans, 2014), 90–110.

7. Shin, "Korean Christian," 110.

8. Shin, 101.

scholars who truly understand faith and learning integration and exemplify how such integration can be concretized. To solve this problem, he suggests networking and collaborating with Christian scholars from North America.[9]

The international spread of the faith-integrated learning movement can be traced to Christian educational organizations originating in the United States. These organizations have large memberships and global offshore branches. One such example is the Seventh-Day Adventist Church, which runs more than 8,807 schools, colleges and universities.[10] In 1988, this organization established The Institute for Christian Teaching to help disseminate the idea of integrated faith and learning across the globe. To this end, this organization sponsored international faith and learning seminars for educators in Australia, Europe (England, Germany, France), South America (Argentina, Bolivia, Brazil, Colombia, Mexico, Peru), Central America (Jamaica), West and East Africa (Ivory Coast, Ghana, Kenya, Nigeria), South Africa, and Asia (India, Korea, Philippines, Thailand).[11] Another organization is the Association of Christian Schools International (ACSI), which has a worldwide membership of nearly 24,000 schools from K–12 to higher education, and is present in more than one hundred countries. Established in 1978, ACSI aims to integrate biblical truth into learning and professional development to enhance the excellence of Christian schools through various services.[12]

Another means for promoting the integration of faith and learning is through building global partnerships. For instance, a Michigan-based non-profit organization, the International Network for Christian Higher Education (INCHE), connects educators in Christian higher education worldwide and provides institutional and professional development programs as well as resources to advance the integration of faith and learning at a global level.[13]

---

9. Shin, 90–110.

10. "Seventh-Day Adventist Education Statistics," Seventh-Adventist Church Department of Education, last modified in 2020, accessed June 6, 2020, https://education.adventist.org/education-statistics/.

11. "About Us," The Institute for Christian Teaching, accessed June 6, 2020, http://christintheclassroom.org/about_us.html.

12. "About ACSI and Membership," The Association of Christian Schools International, accessed June 6, 2020, https://www.acsi.org/membership.

13. Perry L. Glanzer and Joel A. Carpenter, "Conclusion: Evaluating the Health of Christian Higher Education around the Globe," in *Christian Higher Education: A Global Reconnaissance*, ed. Joel Carpenter, Perry L. Glanzer, and Nicholas S. Lantinga (Grand Rapids, MI: Eerdmans, 2014), 301.

However, it is worth noting that the reasons to welcome the integration of faith and learning between Christian higher education in North America and the Majority World are slightly different. In North America, the integration of faith and learning is considered an antidote to secularized Christian higher educational systems.[14] But in addition to secularization, Christian colleges and universities in the Majority World face pervasive forces of nationalism whereby "leaders change the governance, purposes, curriculum, and culture of a university or an entire university system to uphold the interests and ideology of the state."[15] Coupled with nationalism, scarce funding faced by most Christian colleges in developing countries has forced institutions to focus only on commercial and technical-oriented education, which results in reducing "education to gaining knowledge and skills for a station in the workplace."[16] In light of these challenges, Christian scholars in the Majority World perceive that faith-integrated learning is much needed as a solution. However, given the unique socio-historical-political-cultural contexts and challenges facing Christian higher education there, to what extent can the seed of faith-integrated learning be planted in the soil of the Majority World? What contextual adaptations are needed to enable the seed to flourish? To answer these questions, further research on the understanding and practices of faith and learning integration in the Majority World is required.

In sum, the United States has continually maintained a central influence on the faith-and-learning integration movement since its inauguration in the 1950s. An expanding global influence has occurred for two reasons: serious efforts to promote the integration of faith and learning by US-based Christian education organizations, and Christian education institutions worldwide welcoming integration as a promising cure for fragmented and secularized education.

---

14. Dockery, "Integrating Faith," 53–54; Susan VanZanten, *Joining the Mission: A Guide for (Mainly) New College Faculty* (Grand Rapids: Eerdmans, 2011), 12–45.

15. Glanzer and Carpenter, "Conclusion," 279.

16. Joel Carpenter, "Introduction: Christian Universities and the Global Expansion of Higher Education," in *Christian Higher Education: A Global Reconnaissance*, ed. Joel Carpenter, Perry L. Glanzer, and Nicholas S. Lantinga (Grand Rapids, MI: Eerdmans, 2014), 23.

Problem Statement

Since its inception in the 1950s, numerous scholarly works addressing the integration of faith and learning have contributed to the development of its historical, philosophical, and theoretical concepts.[17] However, during the last two decades, limited empirical studies on how faith-integrated learning is implemented at individual and departmental levels, and how individual faculty members understand and teach integration to students, have been conducted.[18] Further, almost all of these empirical studies were conducted in the United States Christian higher education context.

In Indonesia, the idea of faith-integrated learning was only introduced by ACSI and INCHE within the last ten years. ACSI has its branch office established in Indonesia in 2005, and since then has actively sought to inculcate the idea of faith-integrated learning to Christian educators through seminars,

---

17. See e.g. David L.Wolfe, "The Line of Demarcation Between Integration and Pseudo-Integration," in *The Reality of Christian Learning Strategies for Faith-Discipline Integration*, ed. Harold Heie and David L. Wolfe (Grand Rapids: Eerdmans, 1987); John H. Coe, "An Interdependent Model of Integration and the Christian University," *Faculty Dialogue* 21 (Spring-Summer, 1994): 111–137; Lionel Matthews and Elvin Gabriel, "Dimensions of the Integration of Faith and Learning: An Interactionist Perspective," *Journal of Research on Christian Education* 10, no. 1 (Spring, 2001): 2–38; Douglas Jacobsen and Rhonda H. Jacobsen, *Scholarship and Christian Faith: Enlarging the Conversation* (New York: Oxford University Press, 2004); Jay B. Rasmussen and Roberta H. Rasmussen, "The Challenge of Integrating Faith-Learning-Living in Teacher Education," *Journal of the International Christian Community for Teacher Education* 1, no. 1 (2009): 1–10; Joshua D. Reichard, "From Indoctrination to Initiation: A Non-Coercive Approach to Faith-Learning Integration," *Journal of Education & Christian Belief* 17, no. 2 (September 2013): 285–299.

18. See e.g. Raquel B. Korniejczuk, "The Teacher as Agent in Integrating Faith and Learning: The Process of Deliberate Teacher Implementation" (paper presented at International Faith and Learning Seminar Held at Union College, Lincoln, NE, June 1993), accessed December 12, 2015, http://christintheclassroom.org/vol_10/10cc _239-255.htm; Randall L. Sorenson, "Doctoral Students' Integration of Psychology and Christianity: Perspectives via Attachment Theory and Multidimensional Scaling," *Journal for the Scientific Study of Religion* 36, no. 4 (December 1997): 530–548; Constance C. Nwosu, "Integration of Faith and Learning in Christian Higher Education: Professional Development of Teachers and Classroom Implementation," PhD diss. (Andrews University, 1999); Larry Lyon et al., "Faculty Attitudes on Integrating Faith and Learning at Religious Colleges and Universities: A Research Note," *Sociology of Religion* 66, no. 1 (Spring 2005): 61–69; Erin M. Ellis, "Faculty Interpretations of Faith-Integration in Classroom Practices," MA thesis (Baylor University, 2014); Preston B. Cosgrove, "Variations on a Theme: Convergent Thinking and the Integration of Faith and Learning," *Christian Higher Education* 14, no. 4 (August 2015): 229–243; Brian E. Eck, White Scott, and David N. Entwistle, "Teaching Integration to Postmodern and Millennial Students: Implications for the Classroom," *Journal of Psychology & Christianity* 35, no. 2 (Summer 2016): 125–136.

training, and certification programs.[19] While ACSI-Indonesia focuses mostly on K–12 Christian educators, INCHE, through Curriculum Development and Faculty Enrichment Program (FEP), equips Christian higher education faculty members for effective and integrated Christian teaching.[20]

Since the idea of faith-integrated learning is relatively new to Indonesian scholars and educators, limited research on the Indonesian context is available exploring either the conceptual or practical aspects of the integration. Michael Lessard-Clouston, a professor of applied linguistics and TESOL at Biola University, has conducted the only empirical study thus far on faith and learning integration in ESL/EFL instruction in Indonesia.[21] His research used a written questionnaire drawing from Christian faculty in two contexts – four faculty members from an American Christian university in Los Angeles, California, and four faculty members from an Indonesian Christian university in Jakarta. Lessard-Clouston noted that the study findings provide only preliminary data due to the methodological limitations and the small number of participants. Given the unique context and scarcity of resources in understanding and implementing faith-integrated learning in Indonesian Christian higher education contexts, further empirical study is urgently needed.

Purpose of the Study

The existing literature provides various definitions for the integration of faith and learning.[22] Many of these definitions focus mostly on the cognitive aspects of integration, namely ontological and epistemological issues between theology and academic discipline. This study aims to explore Indonesian Christian faculty's perceptions of the integration of faith and learning in a more holistic approach which includes the following: (1) *Being* – emphasis

---

19. "Christian Educator Certification," ACSI Indonesia, posted on March 12, 2018, accessed April 2, 2018, https://acsi.id/programs/cec?o=terbaru.

20. "What Is INCHE?," INCHE Networking Christian Scholars and Institutions Worldwide, accessed June 6, 2020, https://inche.one/what-is-inche.

21. Michael Lessard-Clouston, "Faith and Learning Integration in ESL/EFL Instruction: A Preliminary Study in America and Indonesia," in *Christian Faith and English Language Teaching and Learning: Research on the Interrelationship of Religion and ELT*, ed. Mary S. Wong, Carolyn Kristjansson, and Zoltan Dornyei (New York: Routledge, 2013), 115–135.

22. Arthur F. Holmes, *The Idea of a Christian College*, rev. ed. (Grand Rapids, MI: Eerdmans, 1987); Harold Heie, *Learning to Listen, Ready to Talk: A Pilgrimage toward Peacemaking* (New York, NY: Universe, 2007); Cosgrove, "Variations on a Theme," 229–243.

on the faculty's *self* as an integrator, whose life and vocation are infused with faith; (2) *Knowing* – faculty's understanding of the relationship between faith and their educational disciplines; and (3) *Doing* – emphasis on how faculty's faith influences their educational practices. The context in this study will be higher education in Indonesia, and the participants will be Christian faculty teaching at Christian, private non-religious, or public higher education institutions. Unique teaching contexts of Christian faculty may pose specific challenges or opportunities in efforts to integrate faith into learning. Therefore, this study will also explore Christian faculty perceptions regarding challenges, opportunities, and hopes associated with the integration of faith and learning. In sum, the purpose of this study is to investigate the perceptions of Indonesian Christian faculty about their *being, knowing, and doing* as they integrate faith and learning.

Research Questions

The following research questions will be used to guide this study:

1. How do Indonesian Christian faculty describe the value of faith in their vocation (*being*)?
2. How do Indonesian Christian faculty describe the relationship between faith and their educational discipline (*knowing*)?
3. How do Indonesian Christian faculty describe the influence of faith in their educational practices (*doing*)?

The Significance of the Study

Theoretical Significance

Indonesia, like many countries in the Majority World which experienced colonialism, has leaned heavily on Western educational systems, which includes embracing the practice of dualism and secularization.[23] Additionally, the pressure to conform to state ideology and practical-oriented education, while existing as a minority in a predominantly Muslim country, poses unique

---

23. Philip G. Altbach, "Twisted Roots: The Western Impact on Asian Higher Education," *Higher Education* 18, no. 1 (February 1989): 9–29.

challenges to Christian leaders and faculty in Indonesia.[24] In the midst of these challenges, the idea of the integration of faith and learning might seemingly present a cure for this predicament. However, as noted previously, literature documenting the nature, challenges, and implementation of faith-integrated learning outside US contexts are lacking. This qualitative study seeks to bridge the literature gap.

Practical Significance

The research resulting from this study will benefit Christian educational leaders and faculty in Indonesia in at least three ways. First, it will enrich academic inquiry in the area of teaching and learning in relation to Christian faith in Indonesia or other countries with similar contexts. Second, it will provide baseline information for further research and professional development needed by Indonesian Christian faculty. Finally, it is hoped to give encouragement for Indonesian Christian faculty as agents of transformation to envision and create a faith-shaped just and flourishing learning environment and to engage in research on integrating faith into their vocation of teaching, specific academic disciplines, and learning amidst a secularized academic and pluralistic society. As Christians, we are saved by grace through faith in Jesus Christ to love God and our neighbors, to do good works through our vocations, and to be his witness in season and out of season (Matt 5:16; Acts 1:8; Eph 2:8–10; 2 Tim 4:2).

Definition of Terms

Christian faculty. This term refers to active, self-professing, and regular church-going Christians who believe salvation comes through faith in Jesus Christ, and currently work as fulltime teaching staff at a Christian or non-Christian college or university. This study will include Christians from diverse denominational backgrounds (e.g. Reformed, Presbyterian, Baptist, Methodist, Pentecostal, or independent churches).

Integration of faith and learning. This term implies an underlying assumption that there is a separation between faith and learning that needs to be unified.

---

24. Glanzer and Carpenter, "Conclusion," 277–305.

Arthur Holmes, William Hasker, and Harold Heie approach the integration of faith and learning from a cognitive perspective and describe it as an intellectual or scholarly activity to examine subject content of an academic discipline from a biblical or a set of Christian doctrinal perspectives and to develop an integral relationship between them.[25] In contrast, Kirk Farnsworth and Steve Bourma-Prediger use the term to refer to teachers who *embody* the integration of faith and learning in their personal lives.[26] For the purpose of this study, *faith* refers to a set of Christian doctrinal beliefs, personal commitment, and a personal relationship with God; and *learning* refers to faculty's awareness of and attempts to provide good learning experiences for students which include syllabus and course design, teaching resources, assignments and evaluations, pedagogical approaches, learning climates, and interaction with students both inside and outside classrooms. Taken together, in this study the term *integration of faith and learning* is broadly defined as Christian faculty's attempts to examine, discover, develop, and live out their faith *in* and *through* their lives, vocations, teaching and learning practices, and academic disciplines.

Being-Knowing-Doing. This term is originated from the Be-Know-Do leadership development model of the US Army which aims to build a whole person, namely character (Be), competence (Know), and actions (Do).[27] In this study this term refers to the whole personhood of faculty as the integrators of faith and learning which involves: (1) *Being* Christians whose lives and vocations are shaped by their beliefs, personal commitment, and dynamic relationship with God and fellow believers (John 15:5; John 13:1–17; Heb 10:19–25); (2) *Knowing* the content (the "what") beliefs of their faith and educational discipline, and developing connections between the two; and (3) *Doing* Christians whose faith influences teaching and learning practices.

---

25. Holmes, *Christian College,* 46; William Hasker, "Faith-Learning Integration: An Overview," *Christian Scholar's Review* 21, no. 3 (March 1992): 234–248; and Heie, *Learning to Listen,* 26–27.

26. Kirk E. Farnsworth, "The Conduct of Integration," *Journal of Psychology and Theology* 10, no. 4 (December 1982): 308–319; Steve Bouma-Prediger, "The Task of Integration: A Modest Proposal," *Journal of Psychology and Theology* 18, no. 1 (March 1990): 21–31.

27. Frances Hesselbein, Erik Shinseki, and Richard E. Cavanagh, *Be-Know-Do: Leadership the Army Way* (San Francisco: Jossey Bass, 2004).

CHAPTER 2

Literature Review

The purpose of this study is to investigate Christian faculty's perceptions of being, knowing, and doing as to the integration of faith and learning in Indonesian higher education contexts. This chapter will focus on the existing literature that gives insight to the understanding of the subject and framework to this study. It is divided into five sections. The first section will briefly examine the history and development of the integration of faith and learning. Special attention will be given to contexts and factors that contributed to the secularization of the academy and various responses from evangelicals which later give birth to the faith and learning integration movement. The second section will consider various definitions of faith and learning integration as well as debates over the use of the word "integration." The third section will examine selected theoretical approaches and strategies of implementation of the integration of faith and learning. The fourth section will review empirical studies of the integration of faith and learning within the last two decades. The fifth and final section will examine research on the implementation of faith-integrated learning and associated challenges, and end with a conclusion.

Historical Background of the Integration of Faith and Learning

Tracing the conceptual genesis of the integration of faith and learning is difficult. Marie Valance, Jaliene Hollabaugh, and Thu Truong trace the concept of faith-learning integration to St. Augustine's fifth-century work.¹ Citing *De Doctrina Christiana*,² they show that St. Augustine demonstrates an understanding of the unity of faith and knowledge. In modern times, however, Kenneth Badley identifies Frank E. Gaebelein as the person who brought this idea to life in the 1950s.³ Summed up in his maxim that *all truth is God's truth*, Gaebelein contends that Christian education and its curriculum should be centered on Scripture.⁴ In fact, the term "the integration of faith and learning" was first used in his work *The Pattern of God's Truth*.⁵ However, Perry L. Glanzer refers to Arthur Holmes as the Christian scholar who promoted the idea of integrating faith and learning and defined it as an educational enterprise in the 1970s. Glanzer argues that, since then, the idea has grown into a pursuit among Christian colleges and universities in the United States.⁶

The Relationship between Faith and Learning in Different Eras

Although the origin of the integration of faith and learning concept is hard to pinpoint, Susan VanZanten argues that the emergence of faith-integrated learning in the mid-twentieth century was "a response to modernism's separation of facts and values, science and faith, the secular and the sacred."⁷ Before this, in educational systems ranging from Jewish-Hebraic schools to the medieval university, learning came from a unifying religious perspective.

---

1. Marie Valance, Jaliene Hollabaugh, and Thu Truong, "St. Augustine's Learning for the Glory of God: Adapting 'Faith-Learning Integration' Terminology for the Modern World," *Journal of the International Christian Community for Teacher Education* 4, no. 2 (2009), accessed December 10, 2015, https://digitalcommons.georgefox.edu/cgi/viewcontent.cgi?article=1053&context=icctej.

2. Augustine, *Teaching Christianity (De Doctrina Christiana)*, trans. Edmund Hill, ed. John E. Rotelle (Hyde Park, NY: New City Press, 1996).

3. Kenneth R. Badley, "The Faith/Learning Integration Movement in Christian Higher Education: Slogan or Substance?" *Journal of Research on Christian Education* 3 (Spring 1994): 13–33.

4. Frank E. Gaebelein, *The Pattern of God's Truth: Problems of Integration in Christian Education* (1954; repr. Chicago: Moody Press, 1968), 48.

5. Gaebelein, *Pattern God's Truth*, 20.

6. Perry L. Glanzer, "Why We Should Discard 'the Integration of Faith and Learning': Rearticulating the Mission of the Christian Scholar," *Journal of Education and Christian Belief* 12, no. 1 (March 2008): 42; Holmes, *Christian College*, 45–60.

7. VanZanten, *Joining the Mission*, 109.

That is, theological studies informed other disciplines.[8] Similarly, during the Reformation era, Bible-centered education was maintained and promoted by Martin Luther and other reformers – Ulrich Zwingli, Philip Melanchthon, and John Calvin.[9] It was not until the Enlightenment, with the concomitant rise of rationalism and individualism, that faith and the unified formal learning process was derailed. At this point, empirical rationality was separated from faith.[10]

George Marsden highlights the fact that the higher-educational system in the United States prior to the nineteenth century was "built on a foundation of evangelical Protestant colleges."[11] In fact, the first few generations of college leaders in the United States were ardent believers and based their leadership on a Protestant ethos. Although the United States was a pluralistic society, Protestantism had a dominant influence in its cultural centers. The pursuit of scholarship was an "integral part of a religious-cultural vision," and it was common for almost all state universities to hold chapel services and revival meetings and encourage their students to attend Sunday church worship.[12] Sadly, within a mere half-century, most of these evangelical colleges underwent a metamorphosis and "by the 1920s the evangelical Protestantism of the old-time colleges had been effectively excluded from leading university classrooms."[13] All these changes started as colleges embraced specialization and secularization which "created dualisms of every kind – a separation of head knowledge from heart knowledge, faith from learning, revealed truth from observed truth, and careers from vocation."[14]

David Dockery explains that a further diminution of religious influence in scholarship occurred during the early twentieth century when colleges in the United States were influenced by the controversy over the modernist-fundamentalist approach.[15] During this time, although a belief in objective

---

8. Korniejzcuk and Kijai, "Integrating Faith," 79; Holmes, *Christian College*, 9.

9. Riemer Faber, "Martin Luther on Reformed Education," *Clarion* 47, no. 16 (August 1998): 376–379.

10. Matthews and Gabriel, "Dimensions of the Integration," 24.

11. George Marsden, *The Soul of the American University: From Protestant Establishment to Established Nonbelief* (New York: Oxford University Press, 1996), 4.

12. Marsden, *Soul of the American University*, 3.

13. Marsden, 4.

14. Dockery, "Integrating Faith," 44.

15. Dockery, 45.

truth was still maintained, faith and scholarship were totally separated as two distinct realities. The pursuit of scholarship was no longer informed by faith, and religious life was pushed to the periphery. However, the worst was yet to come, Dockery observes. The relation between faith and scholarship changed drastically with the rise of postmodernism at the dawn of the twentieth century "which includes the loss of a belief in normative truth and the influence of relativism in almost all spheres of knowledge."[16] In short, the Protestantism that had founded and structured the establishment of higher education in the United States was incrementally ignored and rejected. It is a case similar to Max Weber's position that Protestantism was the underlying force behind the development of the capitalistic economy but after the system of capitalism was established, the ascetic values of Protestantism were abandoned and replaced by secularization;[17] much like children who forget about and then abandon their parents who have given them birth.

The Disestablishment of Protestantism in the United States Educational System

The question still remains: Why did Protestantism's disestablishment from the main currents of academia in the United States take place so quickly? Analyzing from a macrosocial level, Christian Smith asserts that the accelerated secularization of American society, including higher education, was an outcome of the intentional efforts by discontented insurgents to overthrow Protestant's dominance, exclusivity, and old-fashioned nature.[18] These insurgents were mostly scholars or leaders from theologically liberal Protestant, atheistic, and agnostic backgrounds. They were fervently promoting the ideas of privatization of religion, naturalism, and materialism as superior ideological alternatives to achieve a secular, prosperous, and more developed society in the United States. Their revolutionary attempts were aided by other excluded religious groups as well as favorable historical moments of growing capitalism and territory.[19] In contrast to Smith's perspective,

---

16. Dockery, 46.

17. Max Weber, *The Protestant Ethic and the Spirit of Capitalism*, trans. Talcott Parsons (New York: Charles Scribner's Sons, 1930).

18. Christian Smith, *The Secular Revolution: Power, Interests, and conflict in the Secularization of American Public Life* (Berkeley: University of California Press, 2003).

19. Smith, *The Secular Revolution*, 1–2.

Marsden argues that the most compelling reason for Protestant's fast-paced disestablishment is a result of Christian colleges and universities *voluntarily* abandoning their religious heritage to adopt secularism.[20] In *The Soul of the American University*, Marsden identifies three major factors contributing to this phenomenon. First, there was pressure for colleges and universities to serve the technological needs of society. This pressure resulted in two significant developments. First, there was an increased need for more practical and scientific subjects in the curriculum. Notably, state schools were encouraged to orient toward agricultural and technical education as alternatives to liberal arts colleges. Second, decades after the Civil War, the United States was trying to claim its place in the modern world. To achieve this, one strategy was to produce scholars who were technologically skillful and innovative. The old-style American colleges could not meet this demand because they were based on a cleric-controlled classism educational system meant to produce experts in classics and mostly taught by clergymen. This system was opposed to scholarly specialization and scientific progress because it provided amateur science and little space for scholarship. It was believed that in order to achieve professionalism and specialization, a higher education institution had to be free of Christian dogmatism and clerical control. Correspondingly, it was thought that the role of clergy needed to be separated from the teaching profession. Universities now required a PhD as a qualification for teaching.[21]

Liberal Protestants who dominated the universities strongly supported these principles because they believed that academic freedom, professionalization, and technological methodology would foster the best hope for the advancement of civilization in the United States. At the same time, they thought that universities would be enabled to meet the demands of the growing technology industry and in turn, gain financial support for further technical research and university development.[22] Marsden concluded that this led to a phenomenon that was somewhat ironic: "while twentieth-century universities have prided themselves on becoming free of outside religious control, they have often replaced it with outside financial control from business

---

20. George M. Marsden, "The Soul of the American University," *First Things* 9 (January 1991): 35.

21. Marsden, "Soul of the American University," 36–37.

22. Marsden, 36–38.

and government, which buy technical benefits from universities and hence shape their agendas."[23]

The second contributing factor to the speedy disestablishment of Protestantism in American academia was the benefits offered by secularization. Christian scholars and educational leaders saw the *methodological approach* of secularization to science and everyday life as apparently posing no harm to Christianity. Instead of conflict, they saw it as complementary. Thus, they endorsed methodological secularization as a means to gain greater scientific objectivity and better results in their professions (including in courts of law or medical offices). According to this view, embracing methodological secularization meant helping Christians better fulfill their service to humanity and God. However, methodological secularization was soon followed by embracing *ideological secularization* which brought fundamental changes to higher education.[24]

By the 1920s, the progressive education movement pioneered by John Dewey joined with liberal Protestants who embraced a Comtean positivist view. Both parties wanted to use science to liberate people of the United States from superstitious and religious beliefs. As a result, they allied to demean Biblicism by using the theory of evolution and aggressively promoting a scientific worldview. Both groups agreed that technical science was best pursued without reference to religious faith and they further maintained that objective scientific inquiry would yield universal moral principles. These movements were remarkably successful in marginalizing the traditional Christian view in the academic world. Consequently, following World War II, and the fight against moral crisis brought about by Nazism and Marxism, higher education in the United States found itself with no alternative but to make secular humanism the source for a coherent curriculum and instruction. As a result, religious ideology loosened and was replaced by secularism, and students drifted even further in moral orientation. For example, sexual virtues among students changed drastically as they eschewed the "repression" of previously-held Christian standards.[25]

---

23. Marsden, 38.
24. Marsden, 39.
25. Marsden, 39–40.

The third significant factor contributing to the disestablishment of Protestantism in colleges and universities in the United States was cultural change and pluralism. Before the nineteenth century, Protestantism had played a major role in US national culture. At the dawn of the nineteenth century, however, Protestantism was considered too exclusive as American society became increasingly ethnically and religiously diverse. Integrative ideals were needed to create a common culture and principles. To fill this void, the scientific method and democratic principles came into play. Some believed that the scientific method could provide universal objective moral principles for America's pluralistic society. Liberal Protestants affirmed and supported this project, assuming it was their cultural responsibility to unite the nation. At the same time, democratic values provided public consensus and principles of equity to unite the nation, and soon these democratic values became common objectives in education.[26] Dewey, the most prominent figure in the progressive education movement, was a champion for imparting democratic values in education. In *Democracy and Education*, Dewey asserts that the central aim of education is growth. By growth, he means students increase in their capacity to learn from experience and direct future experience in a meaningful way. For this kind of growth to take place, Dewey argues that schools must be democratic.[27]

State schools, aiming to serve the whole society, were the first to distance themselves from their religious heritage. Institutions of Christian higher learning, on the other hand, were caught in between opinions. As church institutions, they aimed to serve Christians, but leaders realized they were also public institutions that had an obligation to serve the whole society. If they hoped to serve a pluralistic society, Christian colleges and universities needed to embrace democratic values and give space for other voices. However, these institutions attempted to maintain their religious heritage. They adopted a broad nonsectarian definition of religion in order to suit liberal opinions and a "two-level approach" to truth in which science and professionals determined curricula at colleges, and religious truth became

---

26. Marsden, 40.

27. See especially chapter 4 and 7 in John Dewey, *Democracy and Education: An Introduction to the Philosophy of Education* (New York: Macmillan, 1916).

only an added value.[28] Slowly, these institutions also distanced themselves from churches and removed explicitly religious courses that represented religious creeds. Compulsory chapel ended, although the formerly Ivy League universities such as Yale and Princeton still maintained beautiful chapels to preserve their historical religious heritage. However, Christianity had all but disappeared from the core of education, and was instead redefined as "promoting good character and democratic principles."[29] The eroded bonds between Christian higher education and its ecclesial origins were also followed by "replacement of the church-related faculty," a change of financial resources from the church to "alumni, foundations, philanthropists, and the government," and a shift of "accounting of its stewardship" from the church to government and accrediting agencies.[30]

Secularized liberal post-Protestant education, believed to be the best means to advance American civilization, unfortunately, had come to an end by the mid-sixties.[31] The combination of mass education and a culture that questioned objective universal principles succeeded in derailing it.[32] John Thelin considers mass education from 1945 to 1970 as the golden era of American higher education. He observes that the availability of federal funding combined with the increasing birth rate and migration of post-World War II have led to this dramatic growth of college admissions.[33] Marsden adds that mass education was widely supported because of its ideal practicality which produced graduates equipped with technical skill and professionalism able to meet the demands of the emerging technology industry and services. Consequently, this trend gave birth to diverse sub-disciplines which further broke apart the already fragmented educational system and encouraged faculty members to prioritize research over teaching. Second, to maintain objectivity, secularized scientific education depersonalized learners and knowledge, and detached faculty from their work and relationships

---

28. Marsden, "Soul of the American University," 41.

29. Marsden, 41.

30. James T. Burtchaell, *The Dying of the Light: The Disengagement of Colleges and Universities from Their Christian Churches* (Grand Rapids, MI: Eerdmans, 1998), 837.

31. Marsden, "Soul of the American University," 43.

32. Marsden, 43.

33. John R. Thelin, *A History of American Higher Education* (Baltimore: Johns Hopkins University Press, 2004), 260–316.

with students. This gave rise to a postmodern generation that questioned "the myth of objective consciousness."[34] In the midst of these changes, how did Christian scholars respond?

The Response of Christian Scholars to the Secularization of the Academy

Mark Noll, a Christian historian, summarizes succinctly various responses of Christian scholars toward faith and learning over the last century:

> Traditional Bible-believers first competing in the intellectual marketplace as full partners in the academic discussion of Scripture (roughly 1880 to 1900); then retreating from that world to the fortress of faith (roughly 1900 to 1935); then slowly realizing the value of some participation in that wider world (1935 to 1950), finding the strategies to put themselves back in the professional picture once again (1940 to 1975), and finally confronting new spiritual and intellectual dilemmas because of success in those ventures (1960 to the present).[35]

As the culture changed, Christian scholars found themselves situated between two communities. As members of the Christian community they embraced and practiced their faith, while as members of a professional community they needed to maintain intellectual neutrality. Indeed, the two communities have often had hostile interactions.[36] At the start of the twentieth century, evangelical scholars experienced challenges when professionalization was adopted as a norm in scholarship. Professionalization demanded that scholars be committed to: "(1) rigorous inquiry; (2) specialized study; (3) an orientation to academic peers instead of the general community; (4) a German model of scholarship stressing scrupulous objectivity; (5) a commitment to science in organic, evolutionary terms instead of mechanical, static ones; and (6) an iconoclastic, progressive spirit."[37]

---

34. Marsden, "Soul of the American University," 43.
35. Mark A. Noll, *Between Faith and Criticism: Evangelicals, Scholarship, and the Bible in America* (Vancouver, BC: Regent College Publishing, 2004), 7.
36. Noll, *Between Faith and Criticism*, 7.
37. Noll, 33.

Not all of these commitments were difficult. Evangelical scholars possessed a strong commitment to rigorous inquiry, some had a specialized discipline, and many dealt well with Darwin's theory of evolution. Most troubling to them was a commitment to a progressive spirit "that later was always better, earlier always more primitive," a thought promoted by Hegel.[38] Given this widespread assumption, it is understandable why progressive education, fueled by Dewey, was well accepted by most educators and overtook the traditional teacher-textbook centered education.[39] As for evangelical scholars overall, Noll notes that they did not adjust well to these professional commitments which had taken hold of academia in the United States.[40]

Responding to the secularized academic culture, some Christian scholars began to question values held by the community of believers and even strayed from their faith. Others, holding firmly to traditional Christian beliefs, strongly resisted modern scientific criticism, and as a result, began to retreat from the academy. In between these two groups, some scholars found that professional and scientific inquiry enriched their understanding of the Christian faith, and sought to represent a middle party. Members of this middle-party, including Charles A. Briggs and Henry P. Smith, attempted to unite evangelical scholars and secularized Christian scholars. However, instead of uniting the parties, the gaps between them widened, and the middle party's efforts ended. As a result, conservative scholars further isolated themselves from the academic world while continuing to militantly defend traditional Protestant beliefs against anti-supernatural teachings from liberals, and fuel a nationwide anti-evolution movement.[41] These conservative Christians united with popular revivalists, to form a fundamentalist movement in the 1900s. Although the two groups were unlikely allies, they had no choice but to combine forces to oppose "the expanding terrain of modernism in the churches and naturalistic scholarship in the academy."[42] The fundamentalist movement marked the decline of evangelical involvement in academia.

---

38. Noll, 34.

39. William F. Reese, "The Origins of Progressive Education" *History of Education Quarterly* 41, no. 1 (Spring 2001): 1–24.

40. Noll, *Between Faith and Criticism*, 33.

41. Noll, *Between Faith and Criticism*, 36–38; George Marsden, *Fundamentalism and American Culture* (New York: Oxford University Press, 2006), 164–170.

42. Noll, 38.

The Reawakening of Christian Scholarship and the Beginning of the Integration of Faith and Learning Movement

It was not until the mid-1930s that fundamentalists "reawakened to the value of scholarship."[43] Scholars including Harold J. Ockenga, Bernard Ramm, and Carl F.H. Henry, believed that instead of isolation, Christians should engage scholarship and the wider culture constructively. Ockenga was the first to coin the term "neo-evangelical" to describe "someone who, while believing in traditional Protestant orthodoxy, also valued scholarship and took an active concern for society."[44] Carl F. H. Henry, in his seminal work *The Uneasy Conscience of Modern Fundamentalism,* called for evangelicals to renew their intellectual and cultural responsibility through reestablishing Christian schools and developing literature in all disciplines from K-12 schools through university, all written from a Christian perspective.[45] In the area of science, Bernard Ramm, in his controversial book *The Christian View of Science and Scripture,* argued for a favorable relationship between evangelical theology and scientific enterprise.[46] Through his writings and involvement in the American Scientific Affiliation, Ramm significantly changed evangelical views about the relationship between science and Scripture.[47]

It was during this reawakening that evangelical scholars worked "consciously to recoup the losses of their forebears"[48] and tried to reverse "multiversity to university" with a unifying educational goal.[49] These evangelical scholars were Christians who had "a high view of the Bible, stress on the need for experiencing God's grace, and a commitment to the divine nature of Christ's saving work."[50] The reawakening gave birth to the integration of

---

43. Noll, 93.

44. Noll, 94.

45. Carl F. H. Henry, *The Uneasy Conscience of Modern Fundamentalism* (1947; repr. Grand Rapids, MI: Eerdmans, 2003), 68–69.

46. Bernard Ramm, *The Christian View of Science and Scripture* (Grand Rapids, MI: Eerdmans, 1954).

47. Joseph L. Spradley, "Changing Views of Science and Scripture: Bernard Ramm and the ASA," *Perspective on Science and Christian Faith* 44, no. 1 (March 1992): 2–9, accessed on October 28, 2019, https://www.asa3.org/ASA/PSCF/1992/PSCF3-92Complete.pdf.

48. Badley, "Faith/Learning," 16.

49. Holmes, *Christian College*, 9.

50. Mark A. Noll, "Common Sense Traditions and American Evangelical Thought," *American Quarterly* 37, no. 2 (Summer 1985), 216.

faith and learning movement. For example, Frank Gaebelein, an evangelical educator and author, was the first to use the phrase "the integration of faith and learning" in 1952 when he delivered the W. H. Griffith Thomas Memorial Lectures at Dallas Theological Seminary.[51] His series of lectures was then published in 1954 by Oxford University Press as *The Pattern of God's Truth: the Integration of Faith and Learning*, in which Gaebelein asserts that Scripture should be integral in Christian curriculum and teachers must embody the integration of faith and learning.[52] Within a few years, the idea of the integration of faith and learning flourished and became an ideal for evangelical Christian education. However, it was Arthur Holmes, in his classic *The Idea of a Christian College*, who further defined the concept and theoretical approach for integrating faith and learning.[53] Since that time, the phrase has grown into a common core value for Christian schools as well as institutions of Christian higher education.[54]

Another major intellectual who influenced the integration of faith and learning was Abraham Kuyper, a Dutch Reformed theologian and politician. His teachings on the nature of Christian scholarship, made known to scholars in the United States through his famous Stone Lectures at Princeton Theological Seminary in 1898,[55] were further developed and spread by Dutch Reformed scholars in the United States, among them Nicholas Wolterstorff and Alvin Plantinga.[56] Evangelicals had come into close contact with Dutch Reformed theology in the 1920s and its theology had influenced some key evangelicals including Gordon Clark, Carl F. H. Henry, and Arthur Holmes.[57] That said, still other Christian scholars who contributed to the development of the integration of faith and learning came from various denominational

---

51. Albert R. Beck, "All Truth Is God's Truth: The Life and Ideas of Frank E. Gaebelein," PhD diss. (Baylor University, 2008); D. Bruce Lockerbie, *The Way They Should Go* (New York: Oxford University Press, 1972), 243.

52. Gaebelein, *Pattern of God's Truth*, 48.

53. Holmes, *Christian College*, 45–60.

54. Glanzer, "Why We Should," 42.

55. Abraham Kuyper, *Lectures on Calvinism* (Grand Rapids, MI: Eerdmans, 1931).

56. Beck, "All Truth," 161–170; Dariusz M. Brycko, "Steering a Course between Fundamentalism and Transformationalism: J. Gresham Machen's View of Christian Scholarship," in *Christian Scholarship in the Twenty-First Century: Prospects and Perils*, eds. Thomas M. Crisp, Steve L. Porter, and Gregg A. Ten Elshof (Grand Rapids, MI: Eerdmans, 2014), 80–96.

57. Noll, *Between Faith and Criticism*, 100.

backgrounds such as Roman Catholic, Lutheran, Mennonite, Wesleyan, and Restorationist.[58]

Biblical and Theological Foundations for the Integration of Faith and Learning

A common assumption behind the separation of faith and learning is that faith is irrational, a belief based on unevidenced proof, whereas learning is a rational activity supported by evidence.[59] Are faith and learning different entities? If so, how do they relate to each other and why do they need to be united? Does sin affect human thinking? Are there any differences between Christian and non-Christian thinking? If yes, in what ways? Can Christians incorporate non-Christian findings into their learning? What does the Bible say about faith and learning? To answer these questions, we need enlightenment from biblical and theological perspectives.

The integration of faith and learning involves teachers and learners, thinking faculties, and interaction with non-Christian scholars and research findings. Thus, for the biblical and theological foundations for the integration of faith and learning, I will employ a Creation-Fall-Redemption-Restoration framework, with special attention given to the nature of human beings, human reason, and general and special grace.

Creation

The creation account of human beings in Genesis 1:26–28 reads:

> Then God said, "Let us make mankind in our image, in our likeness, so that they may rule over the fish in the sea and the birds in the sky, over the livestock and all the wild animals, and over all the creatures that move along the ground." So God created mankind in his own image, in the image of God he created them; male and female he created them. God blessed them and said to them, "Be fruitful and increase in number; fill the earth

---

58. See, e.g. Richard T. Hughes and William B. Adrian, eds., *Models for Christian Higher Education: Strategies for Survival and Success in the Twenty-First Century* (Grand Rapids, MI: Eerdmans, 1997).

59. John Hick, *Faith and Knowledge: A Modern Introduction to the Problem of Religious Knowledge* (1957; repr. Eugene, OR: Wipf & Stock, 2009), 11.

and subdue it. Rule over the fish in the sea and the birds in the sky and over every living creature that moves on the ground."

Theologians have different interpretations of the image of God. Generally, their views can be grouped into three categories, namely substantive, relational, and vocational.[60]

The substantialists view the *imago Dei* as an innate ability given by God at the creation which differentiates humans from animals and the rest of creation. These endowments of gifts and capacities include human reasoning faculties, moral and aesthetic awareness, and free will.[61] Among the proponents of the substantive view are Thomas Aquinas and John Calvin. For Aquinas, intellect is a person's most God-like quality, whilst for Calvin, the image of God is primarily found in human souls and includes true knowledge, righteousness, and holiness.[62] Calvin asserts that "God has provided the soul of man with intellect, by which he might discern good from evil, just from unjust, and might know what to follow or to shun."[63] In line with Augustine, Calvin believes that prior to the fall, human reason can gain "a simple knowledge of God."[64]

The relationalists understand human beings created in the image of God as relational and communal beings who are able to have relationships with God, fellow human beings, and other creatures (Gen 1:27; Gen 2:18).[65] This interpretation is based on two key statements. The plural pronouns in Genesis 1:26, "Let us make humankind in our image, according to our likeness," identify the Triune God as essentially relational; and followed by Genesis 1:27, "So God created humankind in his image . . . male and female," shows sexual differentiation as a relational component. The key proponents of the

---

60. Paul Sands, "The *Imago Dei* as Vocation," *Evangelical Quarterly* 82, no. 1 (January 2010), 29.

61. Anthony Hoekema, *Created in God's Image* (Grand Rapids: Eerdmans, 1986), 68–73; Sands, "*Imago Dei*," 31–34.

62. Hoekema, *Created in God's Image*, 36–43.

63. John Calvin, *Institutes of the Christian Religion*, ed. John T. McNeill, trans. Ford Lewis Battles (Louisville: Westminster John Knox Press, 1960), I.xv.8.

64. Stephen K. Moroney, *The Noetic Effects of Sin: A Historical and Contemporary Exploration of How Sin Affects Our Thinking* (Lanham, MD: Lexington Books, 2000), 3.

65. Robert L. Saucy, "Theology of Human Nature," in *Christian Perspective on Being Human: A Multidisciplinary Approach to Integration*, eds. J. P. Moreland and David M. Ciocchi (Grand Rapids, MI: Baker, 1993), 17–53; Sands, "*Imago Dei*," 34–36.

relational view are Karl Barth and Emil Brunner. Barth asserts that God bestows humans being with the possibility of confrontational I-thou relationship between men and women, and between humans and God. This confrontational I-thou relationship is the image of God. Thus, for Barth, between God and man is not an analogy of being (*analogia entis*), but the analogy of relation (*analogia relationis*).[66] The image of God, for Brunner, is man's relationship to God, his responsibility to God, and the possibility of fellowship with God.[67]

The vocationalists or functionalists assert that "Genesis 1:26–28 says less about the nature of the *imago* than about the task assigned to humankind," hence, *imago Dei* is best interpreted as a God-given vocation.[68] Sands contends that the syntax of Genesis 1:26 and Psalm 8:5–6 suggest human beings have been created to exert dominion, thus humans image God "when whole persons mediate the divine presence, power, and rule."[69] He adds, "The vocational view provides theological grounding for an actively engaged, missional approach to the world. If the *imago Dei* is constitutive of the human and entails the fulfillment of a God-given vocation, then the fulfillment of this vocation is the actualization of the human."[70] In other words, work is God's design for human beings. It is "a core element of the personal dignity of every individual; it is one of the central purposes God originally created humanity to fulfill (Gen 2:15)."[71] Taken together, "created in the image of God" means human beings are finite creatures bestowed with the whole essence of personhood – being, knowing, and doing – that enables us to think, choose, relate, and carry out God-given tasks.

Fall

Genesis 3:1–11:32 recounts that human beings deliberately choose to rebel against the Creator and consequently, all good things that God created are marred by sin. In Genesis, sin is associated with humans' desire to attain the

---

66. Hoekema, *Created in God's Image*, 50.
67. Hoekema, 53.
68. Sands, "*Imago Dei*," 38.
69. Sands, 39.
70. Sands, 39.
71. Lester DeKoster, *Work: The Meaning of Your Life* (Grand Rapids: Christian's Library Press, 2010), 65.

"knowledge of good and evil" (Gen 2:5; 3:22), a "moral autonomy" which is the prerogative of God. Sin, in essence, is "assuming the position of godhood over one's life and living independently from the true God" and from this, all sinful behaviors spring up.[72] The image was not lost after the fall. Psalm 8 describes man an image-bearer of God, the highest creature who is a little lower than God, and under whose feet is dominion over the rest of creation. This description of human beings is after the fall, yet it echoes Genesis 1:27–28. The image of God in fallen mankind is also affirmed by God's prohibition of killing human beings (Gen 9:6) and cursing others (Jas 3:9).[73] That said, sin affects the whole being of a person.

Sin alienates human beings from God, the source of life, truth, and love (Gen 3). Sin had a proliferative effect on Adam's descendants by treating others with hate and violence (Gen 4). Like yeast permeates the whole batch of dough, sin soon fills the earth with violence (Gen 6). Christopher J. H. Wright describes succinctly the pervasiveness of sin:

> *Physically*, we are subject to decay and death, living within a physical environment that is itself under the curse of God. *Intellectually*, we use our incredible powers of rationality to explain, excuse and "normalize" our own evil. *Socially*, every human relationship is fractured and disrupted – sexual, parental, familial, societal, ethnic, international – and the effect is consolidated horizontally through the permeation of all human cultures, and vertically by accumulation through the generations of history. And *spiritually*, we are alienated from God, rejecting his goodness and authority. Romans 1:18–32 outlines all of these dimensions in its analysis of the fruit of Genesis 3.[74]

Vocationally, sin turns our "loyalty, energy, and desire away from God and God's project for this world" to serve an entirely wrong end.[75]

---

72. Saucy, "Human Nature," 45.

73. Hoekema, *Created in God's Image*, 16–19; Saucy, "Human Nature," 29–30.

74. Christopher J. H. Wright, *The Mission of God's People* (Grand Rapids, MI: Zondervan, 2010), 40.

75. Cornelius Plantinga, Jr. *Not the Way It's Supposed to Be: A Breviary of Sin* (Grand Rapids: Eerdmans, 1995), 40.

Pertaining to human reason, Calvin opposed the Roman Catholic's view at his time that "man was corrupted only in the sensual part of his nature, that reason remained entire, and will was scarcely impaired."[76] According to Calvin, sin leads to "total depravity" that describes the "pervasive inward distortion of character tainting all human acts and rendering the person utterly unworthy before God."[77] Fallen human beings can only know earthly things, not heavenly things pertaining to "true knowledge of God, the method of righteousness and the mysteries of the kingdom."[78] Yet, common grace continues to exist and fallen human beings still have a sense of moral virtues.[79]

Abraham Kuyper and Herman Bavinck are in line with Calvin pertaining to common grace. Kuyper asserts that God's common grace is obvious in the Noahic covenant, and the presence of common grace is to restrain "operations of Satan, death, and sin" and preserve goodness that makes human life bearable and the development of civilization possible.[80] Building on Calvin, Bavinck maintains that after the fall, all creation was sustained because of God's grace; but now grace is divided into common and special grace. Through common grace, God's providence is given and the task to steward the earth continued.[81] In contrast, Barth, Brunner, Cornelius Van Til, and Herman Dooyeweerd argue that there is no room for the doctrine of common grace. For them, there is only one grace; that is, saving grace.[82] Consequently, non-Christians corrupted by sin are unable to understand truth, both spiritual and scientific truth.[83]

In sum, sin has corrupted the whole person – being, knowing, and doing. Romans 1:28–32 tells us that we reject "the *knowledge* of God," and *become* wicked, evil, greedy, depraved, deceitful, arrogant, slanderers, and God-haters;

---

76. Calvin, *Institutes*, II.ii.4.

77. Richard A. Muller, *Calvin and the Reformed Tradition* (Grand Rapids, MI: Baker Academic, 2012), 48.

78. Calvin, *Institutes*, II.ii.13.

79. Calvin, *Institutes*, II.ii.22.

80. Abraham Kuyper, *Encyclopaedia of Sacred Theology: Its Principles*, trans. J. H. de Vries (New York: Charles Scribner's Sons, 1898), 279.

81. Herman Bavinck, "Herman Bavinck's 'Common Grace,'" *Calvin Theological Journal* 24, no. 1 (1989): 35–65.

82. William Masselink, *Common Grace and Christian Education or a Calvinistic Philosophy of Science* (Grand Rapids: Heritage Hall, 1951), 56.

83. Cornelius Van Til, *Junior Systematics* (Glenside: Westminster Theological Seminary, 1940), 22.

thus we "invent ways of *doing* evil." However, God did not abandon fallen human beings, but actively sought them out and gave his common grace by curbing sin and preserving the good, as well as his special grace through the promised Messiah, Jesus Christ.

Redemption

Sin caused Adam and Eve to live in nakedness and fear that their "threadbare self, with all its deficiencies and deformities, will be undraped before other's eyes, before God's eyes, before our own eyes, and that we will then want the mountains to fall on us and the hills to cover us."[84] Humans' attempt to cover themselves with leaves was not sufficient. God made garments of skin to clothe Adam and Eve; this first animal sacrifice pointed to Christ's sacrifice in years to come. The redemption process began as God promised a redeemer through the woman's seed (Gen 3:15). God proceeded by electing Abraham, through whom the long-promised Messiah, Jesus Christ came (Gen 22:18; Isa 7:14; 53:1–12; Matt 1:1; Luke 1:26–31; Mark 15:1–47; Rom 5:6–8). On the cross, Jesus paid once and for all for our transgressions (Heb 7:27; 9:12; 10:2–10). His death and resurrection are the answers to "every dimension of sin and evil in the cosmos and all their destructive effects."[85] "For since by a man came death, by a man also came the resurrection of the dead. For as in Adam all die, so also in Christ all will be made alive" (1 Cor 15:21–22).

Our nakedness can only be clothed in Christ (John 3:16; 14:6; Rom 5:1–2; Gal 3:26). It begins when a person comes into the saving grace of Jesus Christ through the work of the Holy Spirit. This regenerative process is a transformative experience so that the person is "once again enabled to live in love, in three directions: toward God, toward the neighbor, and toward nature."[86] Believers continue to grow in sanctification, a restorative process of the image of God to become more like Jesus in our being, knowing, and doing. Christ is the image of God (2 Cor 4:4; Col 1:15; Heb 1:3). Jesus Christ is the real image of God, for he is the Son of God; whereas we are created in the image of God and become God's children by adoption in Christ (John 1:12; 1:18;

---

84. Cornelius Plantinga Jr., *Engaging God's World: A Christian Vision of Faith, Learning, and Living* (Grand Rapids: Eerdmans, 2002), 73.

85. Wright, *Mission of God's People*, 43.

86. Hoekema, *Created in God's Image*, 86.

1 John 5:20). Thus, Anthony Hoekema says that "there is no better way of seeing the image of God than to look at Jesus Christ."[87]

The regeneration provided by Jesus Christ also includes the redemption of human reason. Kuyper asserts that regeneration "breaks humanity in two, and repeals the unity of the human consciousness," which implies that Christians are less influenced by sin than non-Christians in their thinking.[88] A much stronger antithesis of human reason is held by the writers who reject common grace, Barth, Van Til, and Dooweyeerd. For them, there is no compatibility between Christian and non-Christian thinking. Thus all sciences discovered by non-Christians need to be totally reconstructed.[89] Bavinck, Wolterstorff, and Brunner, disagree with this antithesis. They argue that it ignores the objective side of human reason, and that there is "much agreement between Christians and non-Christian science, scholarship, and learning."[90] Stephen Moroney also warns that by holding to this antithesis, Christians would think of themselves as superior to non-Christians.[91]

Brunner asserts that sin affects all spheres of knowledge but in different degrees, yet similar to Kuyper, he exempts mathematics and natural science from the effects of sin.[92] He proposes a principle of "closeness of relation," that "The more closely a subject is related to man's inward life, the more natural human knowledge is 'infected' by sin; while the further away it is, the less will be its effect."[93] Contrary to Kuyper and Brunner, Moroney asserts that all spheres of knowledge are affected by sin and none is exempted.[94] Building on Calvin, Kuyper, and Brunner, Moroney proposes a six-level model to describe the variability of the noetic effects of sin both in the spheres of knowledge and the learners or "knowing subjects." The first category is the object of knowledge which is divided into impersonal creation, human beings, and God. The second category is the knowing subject which is divided

---

87. Hoekema, 22.
88. Kuyper, *Sacred Theology*, 152.
89. Masselink, *Common Grace*, 56–66.
90. Dewey Hoitenga, "The Noetic Effects of Sin: A Review Article," *Calvin Theological Journal* 38 (2003): 71.
91. Moroney, *Noetic Effects*, 35.
92. Hoitenga, "Noetic Effects," 72.
93. Emil Brunner, *Christian Doctrine of Creation and Redemption*, trans. Olive Wyon (Philadelphia: Westminster Press, 1952), 27.
94. Moroney, *Noetic Effects*, 37.

into individual differences, the influence of communities, and regeneration and sanctification.[95]

In sum, the regeneration of Jesus Christ makes us new persons (Rom 6:1–23; 2 Cor 5:17; Gal 2:20; Col 3:9–10). Because of God's love, we are dead but made alive (1 Cor 15:22; Eph 2:4–5). However, sin still affects the lives of Christians, including our thinking faculties, the process of thinking or ways of knowing, and the products of thinking. Thus, through the indwelling of Christ and Holy Spirit, we are called into a continuing sanctification process of renewing our being-knowing-doing: hearts (Rom 8:26–27; 2 Tim 3:2–5; Heb 8:10), minds (Rom 8:5–7; Rom 12:2; 1 Cor 2:16), and works (Matt 5:16; Matt 25:31–46; Eph 2:8–9; Jas 2:1–26).

Restoration

This world belongs to God our Father. Though it was fallen, God decisively chose to redeem it. N.T. Wright explains that "God's plan is not to abandon the world, the world which he said was 'very good.' Rather, he intends to remake it. And when he does, he will raise all his people to new and bodily life to live in it."[96] At the final return of Christ, God will make everything new. Our renewed image of God will be perfected so that we shall become like Christ (1 John 3:2), there will be no more sin and death (Isa 25:8; 1 Cor 15:42; Rev 21:4), our mortal bodies will be transformed into glorious bodies (Phil 3:21), and our threefold relationship with God, others, and nature will be consummated.[97] At the *parousia* of Christ will come the day of judgment (Matt 16:24–27; 1 Pet 4:1–6; Rev 20:11–5). Christopher Wright contends that the judgment is "good news that evil will not have the last word but will ultimately be destroyed by God," yet he adds, "it is the bad news about the wrath of God that makes the gospel such good news for our fallen world."[98] Hence, while we are here, we have many good works to do in God's redemptive projects (Eph 2:9–10).

---

95. Moroney, 36.

96. N. T. Wright, *Simply Christian: Why Christianity Makes Sense* (New York, NY: Harper One, 2010), 219.

97. Hoekema, *Created in God's Image*, 92–94.

98. Wright, *Mission of God's People*, 44.

What are "good works?" In Cornelius Plantinga's view, "an ordinary occupation done conscientiously builds the kingdom of God."[99] In the light of sanctification, Martin Luther views work as putting one's old self to death daily and raising the new self out of sin; there is a cross in our work, where we put ourselves to death for the benefit of our neighbors.[100] In academia, Christians are called to participate in "good works" through scholarship, teaching, and learning. Wolterstorff asserts that scholarship is an obedient act of Christians to fulfill God's command of the cultural mandates, and this is essential in cultural formation and transformation that contribute to the common good of all people.[101] Kuyper also strongly encourages Christians that instead of retreating from the secularized academic world, we should pursue all kinds of disciplines.[102] The implication for education is well stated by H. Henry Meeter of Calvin College that "Science and art were the gifts of God's common grace, and were to be used and developed as such. Nature was looked upon as God's handiwork, the embodiment of His ideas, in its pure form the reflection of His virtues. God was the unifying thought of all science since all was the unfolding of His plan."[103]

Although corrupted by sin and a distorted, fragmented understanding of truth, Kuyper encourages regenerated Christians to examine fragmented science under the principles derived from the Scripture. In doing this, faith restores science or learning.[104] In line with Kuyper, Wolterstorff asserts that both Christian and non-Christian scholars have control beliefs which can be explicit or implicit; thus it is important to weigh whether the control beliefs conflict with Christian faith at a fundamental level. He contends that "the religious beliefs of the Christian scholar ought to function as control beliefs within his devising and weighing of theories."[105] By acting as control beliefs, religious beliefs entail a superior standard against other sciences. As such,

---

99. Plantinga, *Engaging God's World*, 123.

100. Gustaf Wingren, *Luther on Vocation*, trans. Carl C. Rasmussen (Eugene, OR: Wipf & Stock Publishers, 2004), 28–29.

101. Nicholas Wolterstorff, *Reason within the Boundary of Religion* (Grand Rapids, MI: Eerdmans, 1984), 140–150.

102. Kuyper, *Lectures on Calvinism*, 124.

103. H. Henry Meeter, *The Fundamental Principle of Calvinism* (Grand Rapids: Eerdmans, 1930), 92.

104. Kuyper, *Lectures on Calvinism*, 110–141.

105. Wolterstorff, *Reason within the Boundary*, 70.

when there is a conflict, these other sciences may have to be rejected or modified to fit into the theological belief framework.[106] However, Moroney maintains that theological beliefs are interpretations and systematized studies made by theologians who cannot escape from the noetic effects of sin. Thus, he proposes a reciprocal criticism that instead of using theological beliefs as one-way integration, Christian scholars can humbly be corrected or benefited from science. An example of this two-way integration is between social psychology and Christian theology.[107]

In sum, we are saved *so that* we may do good works (Eph 2: 9–10; Titus 2:14; Col 1:10). Our daily work is an act of gratitude to God and a service to others, including the vocation of a scholar-educator. Christian educators are called to partake in God's redemptive mission through teaching, research, and service – to be a *tsaddiq* (righteous) to the world (Prov 11:10), a channel of peace and blessings to bring people back to God and to equip them to take their roles in God's Story. At Christ's return, we will be perfected and the whole creation will be renewed. Our work will be rewarded according to what we have done (Rev 22:12; Matt 25:14–30; 1 Cor 3:10–15).

Theological and Educational Necessity for the Integration of Faith and Learning

Over time, secularization effectively separated learning from faith and promoted scientific inquiry as the only means to truth.[108] From a theological perspective, the integration of faith and learning underlies the unity of truth. That is, Christians believe that God is the author of all truth, and therefore that all truth is God's truth – be it learned through nature or Scripture.[109] Holmes argues that the necessity of integrating faith and learning is based on the "basic conviction that Christian perspectives can generate a worldview large enough to give meaning to all the disciplines and delights of life and to the whole of a liberal education."[110] Similarly, William Hasker asserts that

---

106. Wolterstorff, 76.

107. Moroney, *Noetic Effects*, chap. 5.

108. Marsden, *Soul of the American University*, 37.

109. Gaebelein, *Pattern of God's Truth*, 22–23; Arthur F. Holmes, *All Truth Is God's Truth* (Grand Rapids: Eerdmans, 1977), 111.

110. Holmes, *Christian College*, 10.

there is unity of truth, thereby "no separation between what is known and experienced" and "to love God with all our minds requires that we try to think in a single, unified pattern all the truth he has enabled us to grasp."[111] Hasker further explains that although there is unity of truth, there are various means of knowing. It is because we are confronted by these diverse ways of knowing that we need an integration in which "the vision of a unity of truth is gained."[112]

From an educational perspective, the integration of faith and learning is needed since teaching and learning does not happen in a philosophical vacuum.[113] The worldview of a teacher plays an important role in informing and forming the worldview of the student. Thus, Hasker maintains that in order to carry out effective Christian education, a teacher's thinking should be "*already* permeated by Christian attitudes and beliefs, by Christian ways of seeing God's world."[114] Unfortunately, many Christian faculty who receive graduate training from prestigious secular universities have little or no experience in integrating their faith with knowledge. Unable to teach from a Christian perspective of integrated learning, these faculty might pass on and even reinforce secular perspectives in students.[115]

In essence, a distinctive of Christian education is providing not merely a connection but a thorough integration of faith and learning to encompass the "development of Christian perspectives in all areas of life and thought" beyond practical knowledge and skills to prepare students for a particular vocation.[116] It is precisely for this purpose that the integration of faith and learning is necessary.

---

111. Hasker, "Faith-Learning Integration," 238.
112. Hasker, 158.
113. Gaebelein, *Pattern of God's Truth*, 37.
114. Hasker, "Faith-Learning Integration," 236.
115. Hasker, "Faith-Learning Integration," 237; Terry Anne Lawrence, Larry D. Burton, and Constance C. Nwosu, "Refocusing on the Learning in Integration of Faith and Learning," *Journal of Research on Christian Education* 14, no. 1 (Spring 2005): 17–50.
116. Holmes, *Christian College*, 8.

The Multifaceted Definition of the Integration of Faith and Learning

While most evangelical scholars agree on the necessity of faith-integrated learning, they differ regarding its definition. In Hasker's seminal work, *Faith-Learning Integration: An Overview*, he describes the integration of faith and learning as "a scholarly project whose goal is to ascertain and to develop integral relationships which exist between the Christian faith and human knowledge, particularly as expressed in the various academic disciplines."[117] In his definition, Hasker focuses on the "cognitive content of faith."[118] He views faith and the subject matter of a discipline as related to one another, such that their relationship is inherently integral; thus the task of integration is to "ascertain and develop" this relationship. In line with Hasker, John H. Coe proposes that the integration of faith and learning seeks to maximize a dialogue between theology and natural disciplines with respect to the task of "exploring God and His world in order to provide the fullest possible picture of them."[119] Similarly, Harold Heie views integration as the task of asking integrative questions to which both student and teacher seek answers by drawing references to Christian faith and the discipline itself.[120]

From the aspect of worldview, another definition for the integration of faith and learning is offered by Robert Harris. He argues that Scripture offers both knowledge and worldview to understand the world, and "an objective measure" to evaluate the underlying assumptions of all disciplinary knowledge.[121] For him, all truth is God's truth and the relationship between faith and learning is compatible. Hence, Harris contends that "integration seeks to unify faith with every other aspect of learning . . . It's a two-way process, with faith informing learning and learning informing faith."[122]

The aforementioned definitions of the integration of faith and learning primarily focus on the cognitive concept. These definitions seem reductionistic

---

117. Hasker, "Faith-Learning Integration," 234.
118. Hasker, 235.
119. Coe, "Interdependent Model of Integration," 111.
120. Harold Heie, "Mathematics: Freedom within Bounds," in *The Reality of Christian Learning*, eds. Harold Heie and David L. Wolfe (Grand Rapids: Eerdmans, 2007), 170.
121. Robert Harris, *The Integration of Faith and Learning: A Worldview Approach* (Eugene, OR: Wipf & Stock, 2004), 4.
122. Harris, *Integration of Faith*, 224.

to some scholars, yet they are still favored among many within Christian higher education. For example, Gaylen J. Byker, former president of Calvin College, launched the branding slogan "Minds in the Making" to promote the college as a distinctively Christian, yet academically excellent institution.[123] Wolterstorff, an influential scholar, believes education is for life and explains that "one shapes life by shaping thought."[124] However, some scholars criticize this view. Based on his works, Jeffrey J. Arnett points out that current college students are emergent adults marked by feelings of lost identity, intensely searching for meaning in life, seeking to belong, spending most of their time alone in a virtual world, and reflecting detachment from religious institutions.[125] In addition, Christian Smith and others identify five major problems faced by emerging adults today: moral confusion, consumerism, fake feelings of happiness, sexual promiscuity, and disengagement from social and political life.[126] Consequently, there are those who believe Christian colleges and universities need to adopt an operative definition of the integration of faith and learning extending beyond the cognitive domain in order to shape the lives and thoughts of this distinct generation.

In recent years, James K. Smith has objected to both the cognitive and worldview approaches to define the integration of faith and learning.[127] He argues that the cognitive approach bases its philosophical anthropology on the Enlightenment and modernity's picture of human beings as "primarily thinking things." Consequently, Christian education has been reduced to "information rather than formation" and "the dissemination and communication

---

123. Gaylen J. Byker, "Calvin College: Institutional Positioning and Marketing Summary," accessed October 3, 2016, https://www.calvin.edu/admin/public_relations/minds /pdf/ipms_pages_1to20.pdf.

124. Nicholas Wolterstorff, *Educating for Shalom: Essays on Christian Higher Education*, eds. Clarence W. Joldersma and Gloria G. Stronks (Grand Rapids: Eerdmans, 2004), 98.

125. See, e.g. J. J. Arnett, "Emerging Adulthood: A Theory of Development from the Late Teens through the Twenties," *American Psychologist* 55, no. 5 (May 2000): 469–480; idem., "A Congregation of One: Individualized Religious Beliefs among Emerging Adults," *Journal of Adolescent Research* 17, no. 5 (September 2002): 451–467.

126. Christian K. Smith et al., *Lost in Transition: The Dark Side of Emerging Adulthood* (New York: Oxford University Press, 2011).

127. James K. Smith, "Beyond Integration: Re-Narrating Christian Scholarship in Postmodernity," in *Beyond Integration: Interdisciplinary Possibilities for the Future of Christian Higher Education*, eds. Todd C. Ream, J. Pattengale, and David L. Riggs (Abilene, TX: Abilene Christian University Press, 2012), 19–48.

of Christian *ideas* rather than the formation of a peculiar people."[128] Smith also criticizes the worldview approach to the integration of faith and learning since the discourse focuses on "a set of doctrines or a system of beliefs" from a "Christian point of view."[129] Instead of integrating faith into the whole aspect of learning, this worldview approach perpetuates the practice of dualism by focusing primarily on the cognitive aspects of individuals. For Smith, Reformed theology is meant to counter dualistic rationalism, and he refers to worldview as "pre-cognitive lived-commitments that were more 'existential' than cognitive."[130] Objecting to dualism, Smith contends that human beings' intellectual endeavors are embedded in the affective domain. Given this, Christian teaching and learning "are not *primarily* about *ideas*; they are concerned with the formation of the *imagination* that happens largely (but not only) through affective means . . . of symbols, sign, and story – just the sort of world one finds in the practices of liturgy and worship."[131]

In an attempt to create a more holistic definition for the integration of faith and learning, David N. Entwistle offers a multidimensional scholarly definition that includes a "multifaceted attempt" by educators to discern and explicate the underlying truths between faith and one's discipline, integrate the findings, apply or live out these findings, and seek for wholeness as an individual and as a community in relationship with God.[132] However, this definition does not explain how the cognitive, affective, and volitional domains are incorporated.

In sum, human beings are more than just thinking or believing creatures. Rather, humans possess non-cognitive aspects of both faith and learning that enable them to love, desire, and feel.[133] Therefore, the integration of faith and learning should move beyond attempts to unite compartmentalized theoretical realities at a cognitive level and seek to incorporate the whole human being into its definition. Putting all these together, the integration of faith

---

128. Smith, "Beyond Integration," 20.

129. Smith, 21.

130. Smith, 22.

131. Smith, 42.

132. David N. Entwistle, *Integrative Approach to Psychology and Christianity: An Introduction to Worldview Issues, Philosophical Foundations, and Models of Integration* (Eugene, OR: Wipf & Stock, 2004), 242–243.

133. Smith, "Beyond Integration," 23.

and learning can be redefined as Christian scholars' attempts involving all aspects of their humanity – emotional, volitional, and intellectual domains – to examine, interpret, discover, and develop the intrinsic connections between Christian faith and their disciplines, teaching and learning practices, and personal lives.

The Debate over the Semantic Use of "Integration"

The phrase "integration of faith and learning" bears various interpretations and has become an issue of debate over the last five decades. David Wolfe indicates that some Christian scholars object to the term "integration" because it is ambiguous and "presuppose(s) a denial that truth is already one."[134] Hasker acknowledges this semantic problem, yet favors the term because he believes there is a unity of truth. Since all creation is created by God and is under his sovereignty, it is the responsibility of human beings as his image-bearers to seek understanding and discover the already existing connections.[135] From a practical perspective, Wolfe and Heie contend that integration is a convenient and appealing phrase for Christian liberal arts education.[136]

Douglas Jacobsen and Rhonda Jacobsen critique the phrase "integration of faith and learning," holding it as too philosophical and too Reformed. That is, integration language may not communicate well across non-Reformed traditions such as Lutheran, Wesleyan, Pentecostal, Anabaptist, and so on.[137] On the other hand, Glanzer, a Reformed thinker, asserts that although the phrase is highly philosophical it is not Reformed enough. His concern is with the "habits of thinking" that promote the semantic use of "integration."[138] In light of the biblical drama of creation, fall, redemption, and restoration, he urges scholars to discard the phrase "integration of faith and learning," and adopt "creation and redemption of scholarship" which better "captures the theological mission of Christian scholars."[139] The latter terminology, which entails

---

134. Wolfe, "Line of Demarcation," 4.
135. Hasker, "Faith-Learning Integration," 238.
136. David L Wolfe and Harold Heie, *Slogans or Distinctives: Reforming Christian Higher Education* (Lanham, MD: University Press of America, 1993), 1.
137. Jacobsen and Jacobsen, *Scholarship and Christian Faith*, 22–29.
138. Glanzer, "Why We Should," 41.
139. Glanzer, 42.

core Reformed theological concerns, is even more exclusively Reformed than the former phrase. Thus, in order to be accessible to non-Reformed scholars, further discussion of Glanzer's terminology is needed.[140]

Kevin D. Miller also critiques the phrase "integration of faith and learning" because it harbors a superiority or imperialistic impulse to other theistic and atheistic scholarship.[141] Drawing on an analogy from Dietrich Bonhoeffer's idea of "religionless Christianity," he proposes an "incarnational scholarship" that is grounded in incarnational humility, meekness, and solidarity with all scholars in seeking and understanding truth.[142] Still another opponent, Crystal L. Downing, objects to the word "integration" because she believes it carries modernistic dualism and proposes the architectural term "imbrications."[143] This term refers to a postmodern approach in which scholars see the overlapped discourses as an interconnected wholeness and intelligently piece them together for the service of humanity.[144] Other terms frequently used interchangeably with the integration of faith and learning are "thinking Christianly" and "Christian worldview."[145]

It seems that scholastic debate over the phrase "integration of faith and learning" will continue. Hopefully, the ongoing debate will lead to a new direction by which better terminology will be offered and adopted. A language that speaks humbly and inclusively to all educators, from a variety of Christian traditions and walks of life, is needed. Searching for a phrase with the clarity of meaning that the phrase intends to convey is certainly important. Some scholars, however, assert that there is something more important than this quest, namely the actual implementation of integrating faith and learning. Instead of spending energy on finding a better phrase, Wolfe and Heie urge educators toward the goal of integration, that is, helping students build Scripture-informed frameworks for thinking across disciplines, critically

---

140. Valance, Hollabaugh, and Truong, "St. Augustine," 1.

141. Kevin D. Miller, "Reframing the Faith-Learning Relationship: Bonhoeffer and an Incarnational Alternative to the Integration Model," *Christian Scholar's Review* 43, no. 2 (January 2014): 131–138.

142. Miller, "Reframing," 133.

143. Crystal L. Downing, "Imbricating Faith and Learning: The Architectonics of Christian Scholarship," in *Scholarship and Christian Faith: Enlarging the Conversation*, eds. Douglas Jacobsen and Rhonda H. Jacobsen (New York: Oxford University Press, 2004), 33–44.

144. Downing, "Imbricating Faith and Learning," 40–44.

145. Lawrence and Burton, "Refocusing on the Learning," 18.

analyzing the world and its culture, and then using these frameworks and analyses to engage in meaningful actions.[146] Similarly, Dockery asserts that faith-integrated learning aims to prepare students for academic excellence as well as their chosen vocation through which they become salt and light in the world.[147]

Theoretical Approaches to the Integration of Faith and Learning

An early theoretical framework for the integration of faith and learning was developed by Holmes. In this framework, he incorporates four approaches to integration, namely: (1) the attitudinal approach – a positive attitude toward learning informed by one's faith commitment and theology; (2) the ethical approach – ethical guidance of one's scholarly works that is grounded in biblical teaching and theological reflection; (3) the foundational approach – examining the philosophical foundations of a discipline; and (4) the worldview approach – a worldview formed by Christian faith that provides a framework to see all learning and its relationship with God, the Creator.[148] Holmes' framework of integration was further developed by Akers into four teaching models: (1) complete disjunction, (2) injunction, (3) conjunction, and (4) integration or fusion.[149] A teaching model of complete disjunction occurs when a teacher presents faith and learning as two separate worlds that are totally unrelated. An injunction model is when a teacher emphasizes the dichotomy of faith and learning and suggests only hypothetical possibilities that might bridge the difference. Conjunction is partial integration where a teacher occasionally uses themes of the Bible to relate faith to a discipline. Integration or fusion occurs when a teacher presents the subject content as a unified truth from a Christian worldview that can be logically understood by students. However, the bipolar continuum from complete disjunction to

---

146. Wolfe and Heie, *Slogans or Distinctives*, 5.
147. Dockery, "Integrating Faith," 54.
148. Holmes, *Christian College*, 47–60.
149. George H. Akers, "The Measure of a School," *Journal of Adventist Education* 40, no. 2 (December 1977): 7–9; 43–45.

complete integration is theoretical in nature, and impossible for human beings to fully comprehend the wholeness of truth.[150]

Another theoretical approach, proposed by Ronald L. Nelson, identifies three strategies for integration: the compatibilist, the transformationalist, and the reconstructionist.[151] The compatibilists perceive no tension between their disciplines and faith. They view inherent commonalities between faith and learning and believe their task is to show the unity of truth that already exists. The transformationalists, unlike the compatibilists, see some tensions between discipline and faith. They find some commonalities as well as contradictions between the two, and view their task as identifying areas of difference that need to be corrected and transformed from a Christian worldview. The reconstructionists perceive fundamental tensions between faith and their discipline. They find that the underlying assumptions of the existing disciplines have been secularized and are anti-Christian. Thus, they totally reject these assumptions and reconstruct the discipline on a biblical foundation. These three strategies are distinct yet inseparable, and therefore Hasker suggests it is best to view them as a continuum.[152] He also finds parallels between these strategies and H. Richard Niebuhr's typology of a Christian's response to culture.[153] That is, the strategy of the transformationalist corresponds to "Christ the transformer of culture," the reconstructionist strategy to "Christ against culture," and the compatibilist to "Christ above culture" and "the Christ of culture." Hasker pairs the last stance, "Christ and culture in paradox" to an unresolved tension between faith and a discipline in which the two conflict but each retains its own validity. In this last stance, Hasker suggests that through in-depth study, Christian scholars might discover whether to embrace, transform, or reject the differences.[154]

---

150. Warren A. Shipton, Elainie Coetzee, and Rajdeep Takeuchi, *Worldviews and Christian Education: Appreciating the Cultural Outlook of Asia-Pacific People* (Singapore: Trafford, 2013), 469.

151. Ronald L. Nelson, "Faith-Discipline Integration: Compatibilist, Reconstructionist, and Transformationalist Strategies," in *The Reality of Christian Learning Strategies for Faith-Discipline Integration*, eds. Harold Heie and David L. Wolfe (Grand Rapids, MI: Eerdmans, 1987), 317–339.

152. Hasker, "Faith-Learning Integration," 242.

153. H. Richard Niebuhr, *Christ and Culture* (San Francisco: Harper Collins, 1951).

154. Hasker, "Faith-Learning Integration," 240.

Harris develops Nelson's strategies of integration into a broader theoretical approach taking worldview into account. Harris defines worldview as "a comprehensive and unifying way of looking at all life, a means of bringing coherent meaning to one's experiences, thoughts, feelings, and so on."[155] This worldview-centered approach provides broad and general guidance to the integration of faith and learning through five categories. Three of these categories are similar to those of Nelson: the compatibilist, the transformationalist, and the reconstructionist. However, Harris adds two more: the two realms approach and the false distinction approach. The former claims that "disciplinary knowledge and Christian faith exist in separate realms that are essentially mutually exclusive," whereas the latter argues that "all knowledge is one" and therefore, no conflict exists.[156] Since both approaches express total exclusion or inclusion, consequently they deem the integration between faith and learning as unnecessary. Integration occurs only when secular truth and sacred truth is intentionally brought together into a unified reality. In the process of integration, educators find that the Christian worldview and academic disciplines might reciprocally affirm, supplement, or challenge each other.[157]

Contrary to Harris's broad approach to the integration of faith and learning, Sidney Greidanus narrows down the integration approach to the use of the Bible in scholarship.[158] He contends that "Christian scholars can make more specific use of the Bible than the general (often rather vague) notions of 'my faith' and 'the biblical framework.'"[159] He then proposes four levels at which the Bible is used for the purpose of integration: (1) the call of faith primarily focusing on the redemptive purpose of Scripture, (2) the biblical worldview based on the grand biblical narrative – creation, fall, redemption, and restoration, (3) biblical norms to guide Christian scholars in particular disciplines, and (4) biblical virtues or particular biblical teachings that shape the Christian scholar's habits of mind to carry out their teaching and scholarship.

---

155. Harris, *Integration of Faith*, 77.
156. Harris, 223.
157. Harris, 236.
158. Sidney Greidanus, "The Use of the Bible in Christian Scholarship," *Christian Scholars Review* 11, no. 2 (1982): 138–147.
159. Greidanus, "Use of the Bible," 22.

Another theoretical approach to integrating faith and learning is suggested by Raquel Korniejczuk and Jimmy Kijai. Combining Hall and Loucks' Concerns-Based Adoption Model (CBAM)[160] and Holmes's model of the integration of faith and learning,[161] Korniejczuk and Kijai propose a hypothetical model. This model consists of seven levels of deliberate integration to assist teachers in identifying where they operate on the continuum of integrating faith and learning in their classrooms. The seven levels are described as follows:[162]

> *Level 0: Non-Use* – No integration occurs. Teachers believe that faith and learning are two separate fields, and/or they do not know that faith and their discipline might have different sets of underlying values that need to be integrated from a biblical perspective.
>
> *Level 1: Orientation* – Teachers have some basic ideas about the integration of faith and learning and show interest in doing so, but there is no actual implementation.
>
> *Level 2: Preparation* – Teachers understand the importance of integrating faith into learning and plan to do it in their classroom. However, they lack knowledge about how to incorporate it into classroom curriculum and instructions, hence they relate faith to the subject they teach in an unsystematic way.
>
> *Level 3: Irregular or Superficial* – Teachers understand the importance of teaching their discipline from a Christian worldview, but due to various dynamics and limitations of their time and resources, they inconsistently implement the integration or only touch upon it at a superficial level by taking a portion of the Bible to fit into the subject content.

---

160. Gene E. Hall and Susan F. Loucks, "A Developmental Model for Determining Whether the Treatment is Actually Implemented," *American Educational Research Journal* 14, no. 3 (May 1977): 263–276.

161. Holmes, *Christian College*, 47–60.

162. Raquel I. Korniejczuk and Jimmy Kijai, "Integrating Faith and Learning: Development of a Stage Model of Teacher Implementation," *Journal of Research on Christian Education* 3, no. 1 (Spring 1994): 79–102.

Level 4: Routine – Teachers begin consistently integrating faith into curriculum, subject content, and teaching approaches. However, they only focus on their own perspective and do not invite students to give feedback to improve their faith-integrated learning approaches.

Level 5: Refinement – Teachers consistently practice the integration of faith and learning and begin to involve students in the integration process. They are also open to students' suggestions and evaluations in order to achieve better faith-integrated learning.

Level 6: Dynamic Integration – This highest level of integration involves both teachers and students in the consistent and systematic practice of faith-integrated learning. At this level, teachers reach out beyond their own classroom by making efforts to build collaborative and communal teaching and learning within their institution to exchange ideas and improve ways of doing the integration.

All the aforementioned theoretical frameworks for the integration of faith and learning suggested by Christian scholars can be summed up as follows. First, they follow a similar pattern that describes the integration of faith and learning as a continuum of levels which fall between two extremes: total exclusion (no integration) and total inclusion (high level of engagement to seek a unifying truth). The level which the educators identify with most strongly depends on their understanding of the relationship between the Christian faith and the foundational assumptions of their disciplines. Second, all these theoretical frameworks focus on seeking the relationship between cognitive contents of faith and an academic discipline without involving affective and volitional aspects of a person as the integrator.

Integrative Strategies and Methodologies

Scholars have developed various concepts and theoretical frameworks for the integration of faith and learning. The next question is, what does the integration of faith and learning look like in practice? There are a variety of approaches. Hasker differentiates theoretical disciplines from applied disciplines on the basis that theoretical disciplines are more concerned with epistemological and metaphysical questions than applied disciplines.[163] For theoretical disciplines, Hasker incorporates four dimensions of integration: (1) worldview foundations; (2) disciplinary foundations; (3) disciplinary practice; and (4) worldview contribution.[164]

The first dimension, namely, worldview foundations, seeks to discover in what ways a Christian worldview provides fundamental insights and convictions for a particular discipline. For example, the theological anthropology of man as imago Dei is relevant to the study of human sciences. The next dimension, disciplinary foundations, looks into the foundational assumptions of a discipline such as its ontological and epistemological foundations, and examine them under the scrutiny of Scripture. One example of this dimension is analyzing the underlying assumptions of psychological behavioral theories and examining them from biblical and theological perspectives to discover whether they are in harmony or dissonance with each other. The third dimension, disciplinary practice, is concerned with issues of how Christian scholars from particular disciplines do their job on a daily basis. Christian scholars continue to grow in areas of their expertise and gain insights that might inform their disciplines as well as their faith. The last dimension, worldview contribution, focuses on the scholars' endeavors to make the findings of their own disciplines available to the public, after a process of refining them from the other three dimensions. In this way, scholars contribute to the overall vision of the integration of faith and learning that is integral within one's own discipline as well as across all disciplines. These contributions add to the overall Christian worldview and enable faculty to share responsibility in communicating this Christian worldview to students.

Concerning applied disciplines, Hasker incorporates four dimensions of integration: (1) theory applied to practice, which concerns the implications of a specific theory into practice; (2) ethics and values, which deals with ethics and principles guiding a scholar in practicing the applied disciplines; (3) attitudes, which concerns the practitioner's attitude in carrying out his or her service, and (4) contribution to the kingdom of God, which leads scholars to

---

163. Hasker, "Faith-Learning Integration," 244.
164. Hasker, 244–246.

ponder the ways in which their practices or particular activities contribute to the flourishing of others, both human beings and other creatures.[165]

Another integrative strategy is proposed by Wolfe. He focuses on substantive (ontological) and methodological (epistemological) presuppositions, tensions on value commitments, and "relating the results of the disciplinary study to Christian beliefs within a broader framework that embraces both."[166] Based on this strategy, Wolfe asserts that some disciplines may lean on one of these approaches more than another.[167] For example, in mathematics, a philosophical rather than applicational approach would better suit the integration.

In contrast to Hasker's and Wolfe's approaches to the integration of faith and learning which primarily emphasize the scholarly or cognitive task, Kirk Farnsworth focuses on the integrative task from an *intrapersonal* aspect. He proposes a concept of "embodied integration" which stresses the intrapersonal integration of orthodoxy and orthopraxy.[168] Here, teachers as integrators manifest the integrative activities between their scholarly endeavors and personal lives as interconnected entities.[169] In other words, teachers live out what they teach.

Daniel Helminiak disagrees with Farnsworth's idea of embodied integration. He argues that embodied integration is a personal and existential experience which does not guarantee the truth of one's belief. He maintains that "like it or not, the project of integration is a conceptual or intellectual affair, and such a pursuit must not be denigrated."[170]

Opposite to Farnsworth's *intrapersonal* integration, Jerry H. Gill introduces *interpersonal* integration which applies incarnational theology to the integration of faith and learning.[171] He emphasizes "the human context" of learning in which teachers adopt an incarnational posture as that of Christ,

---

165. Hasker, "Faith-Learning Integration," 246–267.
166. Wolfe, "Line of Demarcation," 9.
167. Wolfe, 10.
168. Farnsworth, "Conduct of Integration," 310.
169. Farnsworth, 310.
170. Daniel A. Helminiak, *Religion and the Human Sciences: An Approach via Spirituality* (Albany, NY: State University of New York Press, 1998), 35.
171. Jerry H. Gill, "Faith in Learning: Integrative Education and Incarnational Theology," *The Christian Century* 96, no. 33 (October 1979): 1009–1013.

to know their students personally and to assist them to be their best – not merely helping them with content, but also the process of learning.[172]

Steven Bouma-Prediger attempts to include both intrapersonal and interpersonal aspects in his integration model. He incorporates four types of integration: (1) interdisciplinary, (2) intradisciplinary, (3) faith-praxis, and (4) experiential integration.[173] *Interdisciplinary* describes integration between two disciplines, for example, theology and biology. *Intradisciplinary* attempts to harmonize theory and practice within a discipline. *Faith-praxis* is practical in nature and focuses on the integration of one's faith commitment and way of life. Finally, *experiential integration* is concerned with both practical and praxical integration in a person's life which aims to lead a divided self toward becoming a whole and authentic being.

To be sure, there is no single approach to how the integration of faith and learning should be practiced. Emphasizing one aspect alone might create a dichotomy about human beings and dualism of thinking. An integrative pluralism approach or a combination of various models is needed in order to yield a well-rounded result.[174] On the individual faculty level, this combination might include intrapersonal, interpersonal, intradisciplinary, and interdisciplinary approaches. However, to make this integrative pluralism approach possible, the institutional or departmental leaders need to support faculty through professional development, a workload policy based on teaching hours and the number of students, and a career and reward system that incorporates faculty's work on integrating faith into their teaching, research, and service.

Loci of Integration

The integration of faith and learning cannot happen in vacuum; it requires a locus. Potential loci where integration take place include the following: teachers, students, curriculum, pedagogy, and institutions.[175] To achieve maximum

---

172. Gill, "Faith in Learning," 1010.
173. Bouma-Prediger, "Task of Integration," 23–29.
174. Hasker, "Faith-Learning Integration," 243.
175. Gaebelein, *Pattern of God's Truth*, chs. 1, 2, 3; Badley, "The Faith/Learning," 26–27; Larry Burton and Constance C. Nwosu, "Student Perceptions of the Integration of Faith,

results, all of these elements need to work collaboratively to facilitate meaningful faith-integrated learning experiences.

Teachers

The first locus for the integration of faith and learning is teachers, who are central to integrating faith and learning. First, it should be noted that teachers should be Christians through regeneration since, as Gaebelein contends, there can be "no Christian education without Christian teachers."[176] In order to carry out the task of integration, teachers need to continue to grow in their worldview. And their worldview ought to be founded on general and special revelation through personal study of the Scripture, works of Christian thinkers, and discussions with like-minded faculty.[177] In all of these, Scripture is central in forming a teacher's mind. Gaebelein writes, "No teacher or minister who does not have the Bible at the center of his life and thought to the extent of living daily in this book can hope to develop a Christian frame of reference."[178]

Teachers are not just integrators, or persons who do integration; integration itself should be embodied in their lives. Farnsworth asserts that "substantial integration" or interdisciplinary integration alone is not enough. Instead, he proposes that "embodied integration" is needed, in which integration is "based in *living* truth, not just *knowing* about truth."[179] Parker Palmer agrees that good teaching arises from teachers who live authentic lives, because "we teach who we are."[180] To accomplish the task of integration, Korniejczuk suggests that teachers need to humble themselves under the guidance of the Holy Spirit, which enables them to teach from a Christian perspective as well as to serve as living models for students to imitate as they try to integrate faith and learning.[181] In addition, teachers must have some training about the

---

Learning, and Practice in an Educational Methods Course," *Journal of Research on Christian Education* 12, no. 2 (Fall 2003): 101–135.

176. Gaebelein, *Pattern of God's Truth*, 37.
177. Gaebelein, 43–44.
178. Gaebelein, 45.
179. Farnsworth, "Conduct of Integration," 308.
180. Parker J. Palmer, *The Courage to Teach: Exploring the Inner Landscape of a Teacher's Life* (San Francisco: Jossey-Bass, 2007), 2.
181. Korniejczuk, "The Teacher as Agent," 250.

integration of faith and learning and the philosophical issues that underlie certain subjects in the curriculum.[182] It is not an exaggeration when Larry Lyon et al. maintain that the future of Christian higher education depends on the faculty's commitment and preparedness to integrate faith and learning in their classrooms, and to enable their students to do the same.[183]

Curriculum

The second locus for integration is curriculum. Gaebelein explains that some subjects are more difficult to integrate than others. For instance, mathematics is the hardest, whereas history, literature, and science are most easily integrated.[184] In addition to some subjects not lending themselves to integration, not all educators support a systematic integration of faith and learning into their curricula. A study conducted by Lyon et al. found there are Christian teachers who regard the inclusion of faith in core curricula as inappropriate.[185] Another study by Todd Ream, Michael Beaty, and Larry Lyon reveals that many faculty members at Christian research universities appreciate the purpose of faith-integrated learning but believe it is best to keep faith independent from the curriculum.[186] However, these researchers maintain the optimistic view that faith and learning still can co-exist and conclude that "while faith's place in the religious research university is far from secure, the complete separation of faith and learning has not yet occurred among its faculty."[187]

Glanzer and Ream concur that including faith in the co-curriculum is a solution for some Christian colleges and universities that want to maintain their espoused mission of integrating faith and learning.[188] In fact, they observed that it was this motivation that may have contributed to the professionalizing of co-curricular activities and the rise of the profession of student development. Consequently, the spiritual formation of the students is no

---

182. Korniejczuk, 250.
183. Lyon et al., "Faculty Attitudes," 63.
184. Gaebelein, *Pattern of God's Truth*, 57.
185. Lyon et al., "Faculty Attitudes," 64.
186. Todd Ream, Michael Beaty, and Larry Lyon, "Faith and Learning: Toward a Typology of Faculty Views at Religious Research Universities," *Christian Higher Education* 3, no. 4 (Oct-Dec 2004): 349–372.
187. Ream, Beaty, and Lyon, "Faith and Learning," 367.
188. Perry L. Glanzer and Todd C. Ream, *Christianity and Moral Identity in Higher Education* (New York: Palgrave Macmillan, 2009), 52.

longer addressed in the curriculum or by the faculty.[189] Having said that, for the sake of students' whole being formation, Glanzer and Ream still maintain that curriculum is a necessary locus for the integration of faith and learning to take place.[190]

Pedagogy

Pedagogy is another significant locus where integration occurs. However, only a small amount of scholarly work and research is available in this area. David I. Smith and James K. Smith point out several interesting facts about the lack of scholarly works on pedagogy.[191] For example, a survey conducted by the Kuyers Institute for Christian Teaching and Learning revealed a phenomenon in which philosophy and history, disciplines central to the debate about the integration of faith and learning, produced no scholarly writing on pedagogy.[192] Ernest Boyer also lamented the lack of scholarship on teaching and learning in many liberal arts disciplines.[193]

The selection of a pedagogical approach is not merely about choosing a technique to teach a class, but reflects the influence of faith on a faculty's underlying beliefs about the nature of knowledge, knowing, and learners. In other words, the use of a particular teaching method will influence both the content and outcomes of learning. For example, an educator might teach foundational concepts of faith-integrated learning but use a banking approach resulting in students having an oppressive pedagogical experience.[194] You Jung Jang conducted a research among teachers in ACSI-affiliated elementary schools in the United States and found that most teachers had a high level of faith and learning integration.[195] However, their pedagogical approaches

---

189. Glanzer and Ream, *Christianity and Moral Identity*, 54.

190. Glanzer and Ream, 194–196.

191. David I. Smith and James K. A. Smith, *Teaching and Christian Practices: Reshaping Faith and Learning* (Grand Rapids: Eerdmans, 2011).

192. Smith and Smith, *Teaching and Christian Practices*, 3.

193. See especially the preface and chapter 1 in Ernest L. Boyer, *Scholarship Reconsidered: Priorities of the Professoriate* (Princeton, NJ: The Carnegie Foundation for the Advancement of Teaching, 1990).

194. Paolo Freire, *Pedagogy of the Oppressed* (New York: Continuum, 1970).

195. You Jung Jang, "An Analysis of the Integration of Faith and Learning Implemented by Christian Elementary School Teachers," PhD diss. (Southern Baptist Theological Seminary, 2011), accessed December 5, 2015, http://hdl.handle.net/10392/3735.

were teacher-centered and unwilling to involve students' opinions. The teachers thought that they had successfully practiced integration, but this view was a one-sided perception. Students treated as passive learners might not understand the message of integrating faith and learning in a meaningful way.[196]

Arguing that "we are formed by the practices in which we participate, and not merely by the ideas we exchange," Smith and Smith published a compilation of essays that offer pedagogical wisdom from various disciplines drawn from historical Christian practices.[197] These selected Christian practices include prayer, meditation, hospitality, testimony, fellowship, charity, and Sabbath-keeping, to name a few. The pedagogy of hospitality, for example, regards teachers as hosts who "recognize both the need and full humanity" of the students as "guests" and fellowship and testimony are practiced under the umbrella of this virtue.[198] Similar to this idea is Palmer's concept of learning space that requires openness, boundaries, and hospitality.[199] Openness gives students the freedom to share their thoughts, beliefs, and experiences without fear and to explore ideas and creativity. Boundaries allow for discipline and focus. Hospitality counters fear and allows for warmth, sensitivity, and respect for each other.

Another aspect of pedagogy is the assignment of reading. David Smith asserts that educators are responsible for the process of shaping students to become "the kinds of readers that we [as students] have become or are becoming."[200] In contemporary pedagogical practice, Smith observes an undesirable reading practice among students that promotes reading texts merely to withdraw information for practical application.[201] This "consumerist reading" attitude values speed and using texts as a source of information and citation that can be immediately discarded once exams or assignments are

---

196. Jang, "Analysis of the Integration of Faith," 145, 157.

197. Smith and Smith, *Teaching and Christian Practices*, 6.

198. Carolyn Call, "The Rough Trail to Authentic Pedagogy: Incorporating Hospitality, Fellowship, and Testimony into the Classroom," in *Teaching and Christian Practices: Reshaping Faith and Learning*, eds. David I. Smith and James K. A. Smith (Grand Rapids, MI: Eerdmans, 2011), 67.

199. Parker J. Palmer, *To Know as We Are Known: Education as a Spiritual Journey* (San Francisco: HarperOne, 1993), 71–75.

200. David I. Smith, "Reading Practices and Christian Pedagogy: Enacting Charity with Texts," in *Teaching and Christian Practices: Reshaping Faith and Learning*, eds. David I. Smith and James K. A. Smith (Grand Rapids: Eerdmans, 2011), 44.

201. Smith, "Reading Practices," 43–60.

done.[202] In contrast to this consumerist approach to reading, Paul Griffiths proposes "religious reading," a pedagogy and habit of reading that resemble the practice and attitude of reading sacred texts with reflective, humble, and vulnerable hearts in order to be transformed.[203] Similar to religious reading, Smith introduces "charitable" or "spiritual" reading in which texts are handled with "disciplined attentiveness, reading slowly, repeatedly, contextually, and with humble care."[204] Integration is not merely a philosophical or ethical matter but is also about attitudes, including a learner's posture of humility toward a text and its author.

Beyond the Classroom

Gaebelein also calls for integration to move from the individual and classroom level to an institutional level. He proposes integration in areas such as extra-curricular programs, including art, music, and athletic activities; disciplinary administration that integrates biblical principles to restore and heal a person; chapels that aim both for spiritual conversion and formation of students; and institutional policy where faith influences the university's promotional practices and relationship with stakeholders.[205] Humberto Rasi adds that support staff members and educational administrators play significant roles in how the integration of faith and learning takes place on campus.[206] Educational leaders on the board, council, and administration play a role in setting the direction of the institution through formulating vision and mission statements, making policies, and endorsing campus-wide plans. Staff in student support services (such as library, facility and maintenance, financial services, sport fields, counseling center, dining service, etc.) disseminate institutional values and beliefs about the integration of faith and learning as they serve the students on a routine basis.[207]

---

202. Paul J. Griffiths, *Religious Reading: The Place of Reading in the Practice of Religion* (New York, NY: Oxford University Press, 1999), 42.

203. Griffiths, *Religious Reading*, ix–x.

204. Smith, "Reading Practices," 47.

205. Gaebelein, *Pattern of God's Truth*, 84–104.

206. Humberto M. Rasi, "The Integration of Faith and Values with Teaching and Learning: A Definition and Applications," The Institute for Christian Teaching, 2006, accessed December 15, 2015. http://ict.aiias.edu/ifl_definition.html.

207. Rasi, "Integration of Faith."

To conclude, the integration of faith and learning plays out in various loci. Teachers are the agents of integration as well as a locus where integration occurs. In order to carry out the task of integration responsibly, teachers need to continue to grow in their knowledge of their disciplines and the Bible, and live out the truths they have learned. Besides teachers, for systematic integration to happen, the integration of faith and learning must be incorporated into the explicit and implicit curriculum, guided by the selection of teaching practices, and fully supported by institutions through their policies, equal recognition of the scholarly work of research and teaching, and faculty development. To achieve this high level of integration is a challenge and hard work for all Christian administrators and educators. Yet, as Gaebelein affirms, "it is a glorious work" because Christian education is helping form "growing human souls."[208]

Empirical Studies on the Integration of Faith and Learning

Numerous works on the integration of faith and learning, focusing especially on historical, philosophical, and theological perspectives, are available, but research on the actual implementation of this concept is limited.[209] Within the last two decades, empirical studies on the integration of faith and learning have been growing slowly. Various aspects addressed by these studies included but were not limited to the following: the understanding and practices of the integration of faith and learning from the perspectives of faculty, students, alumni, and administrators; and how the integration of faith and learning was implemented at individual and institutional levels.[210] The following are reviews on selected empirical studies that cover the issues of the integration of faith and learning over the last twenty years (1996–2016).

---

208. Gaebelein, *Pattern of God's Truth*, 108.

209. Matthews and Gabriel, "Dimensions of the Integration," 2–38; Rasmussen and Rasmussen, "Challenge of Integrating," 1–10; Elizabeth C. Sites et al., "A Phenomenology of the Integration of Faith and Learning," *Journal of Psychology and Theology* 37, no. 1 (Spring 2009): 28–38.

210. See e.g. Korniejczuk, "The Teacher as Agent"; Sorenson, "Doctoral Students,'" 530–548; Nwosu, "Integration of Faith"; Lyon et al., "Faculty Attitudes," 61–69; Ellis, "Faculty Interpretations"; Cosgrove, "Variations on a Theme," 229–243; Eck, Scott, and Entwistle, "Teaching Integration," 125–136.

Joyce Hardin, John Sweeney, and Jerry Whitworth conducted a quantitative study using survey questions designed on a Likert-type scale to examine the perception of the integration of faith and learning integration among faculty members in a teacher education department of institutions affiliated with the Churches of Christ.[211] Seventy surveys were returned with 91 percent agreeing that faith should play a major role in faith-based teacher education, and 81 percent disagreeing that faith and learning should be separated. Most teachers held that faith must permeate every aspect of a teacher's life. Many of the faculty understood the integration of faith and learning as expressing their faith in their teaching – not as a specific doctrine, but as positive values and principles of faith.[212]

A similar study about faculty attitudes toward integrating faith and learning was conducted by Lyon et al. at six faith-based universities.[213] From a survey of 1,902 faculty respondents, they found the surprising result that most faculty belonged to one of these two camps: the separatist camp (36%) or the integrationist camp (48.5%). Only a minority (15%) of the faculty respondents were somewhere in between. In the words of these researchers, faculty are "integrationist in their view of the curriculum, supporting Christian interpretations throughout the core curriculum, or they are separatist, viewing the systematic inclusion of Christian perspectives as inappropriate anywhere in the core curricula."[214] Using logistic regression, they found that a faculty's position toward the integration of faith and learning was mostly influenced by the type of institution previously attended – liberal arts college or research university – and the faculty's denominational background.

In a qualitative study conducted by Harrison C. Morton, he sought to understand how the faculty's faith impacted their academic responsibilities.[215]

---

211. Joyce Hardin, John Sweeney, and Jerry Whitworth, "Integrating Faith and Learning in Teacher Education" (paper presented at the Extended Annual Meeting of the Association of Independent Liberal Arts Colleges for Teacher Education, Abilene, TX, February 24, 1999), accessed December 7, 2015, http://files.eric.ed.gov/fulltext/ED429044.pdf.

212. Hardin, Sweeney, and Whitworth, "Integrating Faith," 7.

213. Lyon et al., "Faculty Attitudes," 63.

214. Lyon et al., 64.

215. C. Harrison Morton, "A Description of Deliberate Attempts of the Integration of Faith and Learning by Faculty Members at Colleges Affiliated with the Southern Baptist Denomination," PhD diss. (University of South Carolina, 2004), retrieved from ProQuest Dissertations and Theses database (UMI No. 3157171).

Thirty faculty members at three Southern Baptist-affiliated colleges were selected for interviews by their academic deans. These faculty members were identified for their deliberate integration of faith and learning. The findings showed that the faculty practiced faith and learning integration in multiple academic areas that included teaching, research, and service. Morton further identified that love for God and humanity was the internal motivation that drove these faculty members to value their students and colleagues as well as the community outside the college.

Erin M. Ellis used both qualitative and quantitative methods to investigate factors that contributed to faculty understanding of faith and learning integration in tertiary education classrooms at a Christian research university.[216] She identified three major elements that contributed to the faculty participants' overall conception of faith and learning integration: (1) theological convictions and beliefs that guide their virtues and attitudes in teaching; (2) academic passions that help shape their curriculum approach; and (3) faculty variables that arise from their personal life experiences, faith traditions, and educational backgrounds.

Frederick A. Milacci employed phenomenological inquiry to study how eight adult education teachers teaching in non-religious settings understood spirituality and how that understanding impacted their educational practice.[217] Participants were selected for their reputation and work, which were grounded on some form of the Christian faith. He found the faculty participants acknowledged that faith helped them understand that teaching was their calling or mission and informed their practices, including community building with students as well as with colleagues. They sought to engage students at a deeper level of learning and equip and assist students to grow.

Other scholars have approached the integration of faith and learning from student perspectives. In a qualitative study, Michael Sherr, George Huff, and Mary Curran presented their findings collected from 120 undergraduate

---

216. Ellis, "Faculty Interpretations," 26.

217. Frederick A. Milacci, "A Step towards Faith: The Limitations of Spirituality in Adult Education Practice," PhD diss. (Liberty University, 2003), accessed December 10, 2015, http://digitalcommons.liberty.edu/fac_dis/2; Frederick A. Milacci, "Moving Towards Faith: An Inquiry into Spirituality in Adult Education," *Christian Higher Education* 5, no. 3 (2006): 211–233.

students at seven CCCU-affiliated colleges.[218] They explored the participants' perception of salient indicators of the integration of faith and learning in the classroom and found two main indicators. First, students observed the faculty member's relationship with God and other students, and second, students noted faculty member's competence in integrating faith into curriculum and providing an academically-safe learning climate.

A similar study was carried out by Elizabeth Sites et al. The researchers used phenomenological inquiry to study eight faculty members who taught at an evangelical Christian liberal arts university in the Southeastern United States. These faculty members were asked to describe their understanding and practice of the integration of faith and learning. All faculty participants were nominated based on the students' perceptions that the faculty had effectively integrated faith and learning. Findings showed that these faculty members perceived faith and learning as two inseparable entities. Their understanding of their faith informed their educational practices. The inseparability of faith and practice was described by the faculty as "faith in ontological terms such as the essence of their being, inseparable in every way from every aspect of their life and work, the center of everything they do."[219] The manifestation of faith in practice was shown through pedagogical incorporation of Scripture into a curriculum, teaching from a Christian worldview, and building genuine interpersonal relationships with students and colleagues.[220]

A recent study was completed by Brian E. Eck, Scott A. White, and David N. Entwistle focusing on teaching the integration of faith and learning to millennial learners.[221] Fifty faculty members who taught explicit integration courses from CCCU-affiliated psychology departments participated in the survey. Findings revealed that faculty perceptions over the last twenty years suggesting there were changes in the nature of the courses and the learners. Based on these findings, the researchers suggested that faculty needed to think and teach differently by incorporating more relevant content and structure

---

218. Michael Sherr, George Huff, and Mary Curran, "Student Perceptions of Salient Indicators of Integration of Faith and Learning (IFL): The Christian Vocation Model," *Journal of Research on Christian Education* 16, no. 1 (March 2007): 15–33.

219. Sites et al., "Phenomenology of the Integration of Faith," 32.

220. Sites et al., 33–35.

221. Eck, Scott, and Entwistle, "Teaching Integration," 113.

to the courses, and engaging millennial students in "active, experiential, in-service, and collaborative learning."[222]

There is only a handful of studies on the integration of faith and learning from the perspective of alumni and administrators. In a quantitative study, Claude O. Pressnell assessed 960 alumni from Taylor University on their ability to integrate faith into their current occupation.[223] The findings of the study suggested that generally, the participants perceived themselves as seeing the world and their vocation through a Christian worldview perspective and frequently integrating faith in their works. These alumni gave credit for their successful integration of faith and vocation to faculty, family members, and peers. Another study of faith-integrated learning from the alumni perspective was recently conducted by Kwany H. Bunduki.[224] Using a phenomenological approach, Bunduki focused his study on the pedagogical aspect of the integration of faith and learning by investigating the lived experiences of alumni in integrating their faith into community learning service. The findings revealed that this active service-learning approach had helped the alumni experience faith-integrated learning through engaging their mind, heart, soul, and body, and as a result, they learned what it means to be a servant-leader and dependent on God.

From the perspective of educational leaders, Jang focused on the role of the academic dean in the integration of faith and learning.[225] The findings of this investigation demonstrated that the academic deans could perform these three roles in facilitating a successful integration of faith and learning at their institutions: "(1) achieving a consensus on the understanding of faith-learning integration, (2) designing a curriculum that intentionally guides the integration process, and (3) developing the faculty so that they effectively bring faith and learning together in their classrooms and in their research."[226]

---

222. Eck, Scott, and Entwistle, 134.

223. Claude O. Pressnell Jr., "Assessing Faith/Learning Integration Among Alumni at Taylor University," *Research on Christian Higher Education* 3 (January 1996): 1–32.

224. Kwany Honore Bunduki, "A Phenomenological Reflection on Integrated Learning at a Christian University for Community Transformation in the Democratic Republic of the Congo," PhD diss. (University of South Africa, 2016).

225. Kyumin Jang, "The Administrative Role of the Academic Dean in the Integration of Faith and Learning in Christian Higher Education," PhD diss. (Southwestern Baptist Theological Seminary, 2016).

226. Jang, "Administrative Role," 1.

Nathan Alleman, Perry Glanzer, and David Guthrie recently carried out the largest scale empirical research on the integration of faith and learning by drawing upon multiple sets of data from an online survey of 2,309 faculty members employed at forty-eight Council for Christian Colleges and Universities (CCCU) member institutions.[227] The findings indicated that overall the Christian faculty integrated their particular faith tradition into the courses they taught in eight distinctive ways. The first four activities were taken by the faculty, including the following: the integration of Bible references into courses; a faith-tradition interpretive approach to teaching and learning objectives; curriculum design; and pedagogical selection. The remaining four activities focused on the students to help them to grow in spiritual disciplines, Christian worldview, theological traditions, and ethical thinking and action.

Overall, attention given by Christian scholars to the empirical study of the integration of faith and learning has slowly increased over the last twenty years. It is important to note that almost all of these empirical researches were conducted in the United States Christian higher education context. In a global survey, Perry Glanzer, Joel Carpenter, and Nick Lantinga reported there was a significant growth of Christian higher education outside North America.[228] They identified at least 579 institutions spread across Africa, Asia, Europe, Latin America, and Oceania. Asia in particular has what Toru Umakoshi asserts is "the largest and most diverse private higher education sectors in the world," including Christian colleges and universities.[229] However, many of these global Christian higher education institutions are struggling with the issues of secularization and pressures to conform to state ideology and policies.[230] Amidst these struggles, the integration of faith and learning is considered to be one way to reverse the effects of secularization and maintain

---

227. Nathan F. Alleman, Perry L. Glanzer, and David S. Guthrie, "The Integration of Christian Theological Traditions into the Classroom: A Survey of CCCU Faculty," *Christian Scholar's Review* 45, no. 2 (Winter 2016): 103–124.

228. Perry L. Glanzer, Joel A. Carpenter, and Nick Lantinga, "Looking for God in the University: Examining Trends in Christian Higher Education," *Higher Education* 61, no. 6 (June 2011): 721–755.

229. Toru Umakoshi, "Private Higher Education in Asia," in *Asian Universities: Historical Perspectives and Contemporary Challenges*, eds. P. G. Altbach and T. Umakoshi (Baltimore: Johns Hopkins University Press, 2004), 34.

230. Glanzer and Carpenter, "Conclusion," 279.

their distinct Christian identity. However, both conceptual and empirical studies on the integration of faith and learning outside the North American context are scarce. There is a wide gap in the literature that needs to be filled.

Challenges in Implementing Faith-Integrated Learning

Understanding the concept of the integration of faith and learning does not automatically result in good implementation. Several challenges facing Christian leaders and educators in practicing integration can be identified as follows.

Gaps between Belief and Practice

The gap between understanding the integration of faith and learning and actual practices might exist. Chris Argyris and Donald A. Schön refer to this phenomenon as *espoused theories* and *theories-in-use*.[231] *Espoused theories* are what people believe or think about their practice while *theories in-use* are what they actually do in practice. They explain, "When someone is asked how he would behave under certain circumstances, the answer he usually gives is his espoused theory of action for that situation… however, the theory that actually governs his actions is his theory-in-use."[232] A study conducted by Korniejzcuk and Kijai revealed that a majority of teachers (80%, N=104) recognized the benefits of the integration of faith and learning and expressed an interest in implementing it.[233] In interviews, these participants said they knew how to implement the integration, shared ideas on how the school could implement the integration, and said they believed that they had been practicing integration to some degree. Interviews with students and analysis of their course plans, however, reflected no integration in practice by these teachers.[234] Overall, Korniejzcuk and Kijai concluded that teachers had little knowledge about how integration should be carried out in their curriculum and pedagogical approaches.

---

231. Chris Argyris and Donald A. Schön, *Theory in Practice: Increasing Professional Effectiveness* (San Francisco: Jossey-Bass, 1974).
232. Argyris and Schön, *Theory in Practice*, 6–7.
233. Korniejzcuk and Kijai, "Integrating Faith," 90.
234. Korniejzcuk and Kijai, 88.

Another possible contributing factor to the gap between what Christian leaders and educators believe about the integration of faith and learning and their actual implementation is *pseudo-integration*. Wolfe defines pseudo-integration as a superficial form of integration which could be manifested as substituting knowledge from an academic discipline as "illustrative, devotional, or apologetic purposes" for spiritual truths.[235] For example, a mathematics teacher explains that "two plus two is always four . . . and God is always the same."[236] In contrast to genuine integration, Wolfe explains that in pseudo-integration the educator does not examine the ontological and epistemological foundations of an academic discipline; thus, no integral relationship between the disciplines and Christian faith is shown.[237] Pseudo-integration could also take the form of equating the integration of faith and learning to "the cultivation of personal Christian living on the part of the faculty member" and "a public relations program designed to convince constituents of the Christian character of an institution."[238]

Insufficient Practical Knowledge and Experience

The lack of implementation of the integration of faith and learning is also due to insufficient knowledge on the part of educators about how to practice it, a lack of institutional endorsement, inadequate time to prepare for courses and instruction, and a scarcity of reliable literature. Hasker observes that Christian college faculty members who received graduate education from prestigious secular universities had "little or no guidance in relating their graduate training to their Christian faith."[239] Jacobsen and Jacobsen also recognize that this insufficient ability to integrate faith into classroom practice leads to a "cognitive imbalance in the lives of many scholars who also happen to be Christians: while they have developed detailed and nuanced understandings of their academic disciplines, many have allowed reflection on faith to languish at a Sunday school level of insight."[240] Nwosu argues that while many faculty members have received some practical training about the

---

235. Wolfe, "Line of Demarcation," 4.
236. Wolfe, 4.
237. Wolfe, 4.
238. Hasker, "Faith-Learning Integration," 235–236.
239. Hasker, 237.
240. Jacobsen and Jacobsen, *Scholarship and Christian Faith*, 18–19.

integration of faith and learning, they did not have an intentional follow-up to put this training into practice.[241] Without practice, the internalization of the knowledge and skills of integration never takes place. She concludes that "to learn about something is different from learning to do something."[242]

Lack of Institutional Support and Resources

Christian colleges embracing the integration of faith and learning as one of their educational core values have different perspectives on how it might be implemented. In *The Making of the Modern University*, Julie Reuben explains that some Christian research universities view faith as a restriction to the progress of scholarship and research, yet they do not wish to fully abandon the idea of the integration faith and learning. Therefore, they see the best way to integrate faith and learning is through co-curricular venues such as chapel services, and religion and theology courses. To oversee these activities, Christian colleges hire chaplains. This means that faculty members do not share the responsibility of informing and forming their students' spiritual lives. Reuben asserts that "in a modern research university, religion would simply coexist along with many other university-sanctioned activities."[243] Consequently, some faculty members might be interested in integrating faith into their disciplines, but lack institutional support to receive relevant training or professional development.

Parents are other stakeholders who affect the institutional implementation of faith-integrated learning. Practically-minded parents want every dollar spent to help their children gain socioeconomic advantages from higher education.[244] For this transactional purpose, professional and technical education is more favorable than that provided by a liberal arts college. Holmes asserts that "the integration of faith and learning remains the distinctive task of the Christian liberal arts college."[245] Yet, many Christian liberal arts institutions

---

241. Constance C. Nwosu, "Professional Development of Teachers: A Process for Integrating Faith and Learning in Christian Schools" (paper presented at the Annual Meeting of the Michigan Academy of Arts, Science, and Letters, Alma, MI, February 27, 1998), 7–8, accessed December 10, 2015, http://files.eric.ed.gov/fulltext/ED422326.pdf.

242. Nwosu, "Professional Development," 9.

243. Julie A. Reuben, *The Making of the Modern University: Intellectual Transformation and the Marginalization of Morality* (Chicago: University of Chicago Press, 1996), 132.

244. Marsden, "Soul of the American University," 43.

245. Holmes, *Christian College*, 8.

in the United States are facing crises, struggling to adjust to market demands or having their institutions fail.[246] With this parental mindset and pressure for market value education, Christian liberal arts institutions face the daunting task of implementing the integration of faith and learning.

Pertaining to the lack of resources to support teachers who practice faith integration in the classroom, Smith and Smith observe a tendency from both Christian faculty and colleges to place a greater emphasis on research and scholarship rather than on teaching practices. They assert that "our commitment to Christian scholarship has been significantly more articulate that our commitment to Christian pedagogy."[247] This is not surprising because faculty development and sabbatical leaves are meant to encourage faculty members to advance their academic knowledge and position as well as to make scholarly contributions to their disciplines.[248] Huber and Hutchings concur that the current culture of higher education emphasizes reward and career systems on disciplinary research, thereby cultivating a perception that faculty whose energies are spent in teaching have lower status and are mediocre in their intellectual ability.[249] Recently, David I. Smith, Joonyong Um, and Claudia Beversluis examined a sample of 9,028 articles from twenty-six Christian journals published between 1970 and 2009 and found that not more than 10 percent of all these articles addressed pedagogical concerns, and that engagement was spread unevenly across disciplines.[250]

Contemporary Western Culture of Mind

Another challenge to faith-integrated learning is the current Western culture of mind dominated by naturalism and autonomism.[251] In fact, these

---

246. Jerry Logan and Janel Curry, "A Liberal Arts Education: Global Trends and Challenges," *Christian Higher Education* 14, nos.1–2 (2015): 66–79.

247. Smith and Smith, *Teaching and Christian Practices*, 3.

248. Jerry G. Gaff and Ronald D. Simpson, "Faculty Development in the United States," *Innovative Higher Education* 18, no. 3 (March 1994): 167–176.

249. See especially chapters 4 and 5 in Mary T. Huber and Pat Hutchings, *The Advancement of Learning: Building the Teaching Commons* (San Francisco: Jossey-Bass, 2005).

250. David I. Smith, Joonyong Um, and Claudia D. Beversluis, "The Scholarship of Teaching and Learning in a Christian Context," *Christian Higher Education* 13, no. 1 (February 2014): 74–87.

251. Alvin Plantinga, "On Christian Scholarship," in *Christian Scholarship in the Twenty-First Century: Prospects and Perils*, eds. Thomas M. Crisp, Steve L. Porter, and Gregg A. Ten Elshof (Grand Rapids: Eerdmans, 2014), 18–33.

two habits of mind might be the strongest challenge facing Christian scholars and educators seeking to integrate faith into their disciplines. Citing philosopher John R. Lucas, Alvin Plantinga asserts that naturalism "is at present the orthodoxy of the academy," and it is stronger than atheism because naturalists reject God or anything like God.[252] Contemporary naturalism, rooted in Darwinian evolutionary theory, understands the existence and development of human beings and their behavior as distinctly contributing to survival and reproduction. In other words, the environment takes control of a human's life.[253] On the one hand, autonomism, which bloomed in the eighteenth-century Enlightenment and was further shaped by Immanuel Kant, teaches that human beings hold ultimate control over the universe. For an autonomist, the world would not exist unless human beings "conferred" and "constituted" it through mental activities.[254] It is humankind who perceives and interprets things around them, and then names and categorizes them, which gives both meaning and the structure by which they come to exist. In short, human beings "create" the world. Further, because every person has the ability to construct his or her own "universe," autonomism leads to subjective truth. In addition to academia, these two schools of thought have dominant influence over elite culture in the United States and are reflected in the media, medicine, law, and politics.[255] Christian scholars and educators face at least two challenges as a result of these two dominant habits of mind. First, Christian scholars belong to two communities: the community of faith and the community defined by their professional discipline. To play it safe, scholars might adopt two realms of truth that effectively separate their faith from scholarly work. However, scholars who wish to integrate faith into scholarly work could possibly face exclusion from mainstream academia, which is unfriendly not only to Christianity but also to pluralism in general.[256] Will Christian scholars choose their faith over academic careers and prestige? Second, the streams of thought in which Christian scholars and educators received their previous education, by and large, will form their habits of mind. Although attempting

---

252. Plantinga, "On Christian Scholarship," 20.
253. Plantinga, 21.
254. Plantinga, 22.
255. Plantinga, 24.
256. Plantinga, 32.

to practice faith-integrated learning, they might still operate under their previously trained epistemological frameworks. For example, Gaebelein, the champion for the integration of faith and learning, was a rationalist and held to Common Sense Realist epistemology as a primary means in understanding truth, which was popular among American evangelicals in the nineteenth and twentieth centuries.[257]

In summary, while scholarship on the integration of faith and learning has spanned several decades, the idea has not been followed by many implementations. Insufficient knowledge by practitioners, lack of support from institutions, limited availability of scholarly research on pedagogy, and pressure from mainstream academic culture have collectively impeded the implementation of faith-integrated learning.

Summary

In Christian higher education, the integration of faith and learning is a vital movement in the United States and beyond. Historically, the educational system of higher education in the United States, built on a Protestant ethos and value system, derailed from that path as the academy adopted secularism. Sadly, Christian colleges and universities followed the same path because they mistakenly believed that secularization posed no threat to Christianity. As a result, faith was separated from learning and pushed to the periphery. Responding to this condition, the integration of faith and learning movement was born as a theological and educational necessity to combat the dualism introduced by secularization and to bring faith back into learning.

Believing in the unity of truth, Christian scholars from diverse theological backgrounds, including Kuyper, Gaebelein, Holmes, Akers, Hasker, and Jacobsen and Jacobsen, agreed that faith and learning should and may be united. Many Christian educational leaders welcomed this movement, and within a short time, the integration of faith and learning became a core value guiding institutional vision and incorporated into mission statements, policies, and practices as well as faculty members' endeavors in scholarship and teaching.

---

257. Beck, "All Truth," 81–99; Noll, "Common Sense," 216–238.

Two important points are worth noting as Christian scholars have endeavored to advance the integration of faith and learning in Christian higher education. First, Christian scholars have developed various definitions, concepts, theoretical approaches, and implementation strategies for the integration of faith and learning, but these attempts have been heavily focused on the cognitive-abstract-rational aspect. It appears that Christian scholars have focused on integrating faith and learning as two realms which become one (a single reality), but have not been followed through by resolving dualistic thinking. Consequently, instead of overcoming the dualism of faith and learning, head and heart, and spiritual and secular, this over-emphasis on the cognitive aspect of the integration of faith and learning has perpetuated and further strengthened the existing dualist-rationalism. It is necessary to develop concepts, frameworks, and implementations of the integration of faith and learning that include holistic ways of thinking, being, and doing. This reflects the Christian belief that humans are God's image-bearers and thus spiritual, relational, emotional, and intellectual beings.

Second, most Christian scholars agree that a fundamental way to integrate faith into learning is by examining the ontological and epistemological foundations of an academic discipline under the scrutiny of the Scripture. However, this is not enough. Christian scholars and educators are in one way or another informed and formed by their previous educational training. They carry this influence into their scholarship and teaching. Therefore, in relating to the first point, it is important for Christian scholars and educators to examine their own underlying assumptions of beliefs and ways of thinking. Here, critical reflection is informed by the word of God. "For the word of God is alive and active. Sharper than any double-edged sword, it penetrates even to dividing soul and spirit, joints and marrow; it judges the thoughts and attitudes of the heart" (Heb 4:12).

Finally, a literature review of more than five decades of the integration of faith and learning movement reflects that Christian scholars have invested considerable efforts to develop theoretical concepts of the integration of faith into learning. Empirical studies on the integration of faith and learning during the last two decades have been growing, albeit at a slow pace. The scope and context of empirical studies are narrowed and limited, primarily focusing on perceptions and practices of US-based faculty and students regarding faith-integrated learning within Christian higher education contexts. Discrepancies also occur between understanding the theory and actually implementing faith-integrated learning both at the classroom and institutional levels. These two gaps, literature and field research, and theory and practice, signal that the integration of faith and learning movement is still in its early stages of development and Christian scholars and educators have a great opportunity as well as the responsibility to help fill in the gaps.

CHAPTER 3

Methodology

Research Design

This study was a basic qualitative research study investigating Christian faculty's perceptions of being, knowing, and doing on the integration of faith and learning in Indonesian higher education contexts. The focus of qualitative research was on "process, understanding, and meaning."[1] For this purpose, interviews were the best research method to investigate the participants' understanding of their teaching and learning experiences in connection with their faith.[2] In-depth interviews allowed participants to provide *emic* perspectives about their opinions, feelings, knowledge, experiences, and understanding of their experiences.[3] In addition, interviews allowed participants to express their phenomenological teaching and learning experiences which involved their reactions and emotions.[4] Interviews also offered flexibility and adaptability where the interviewer could follow up the participants' responses to gain more information and to make necessary clarifications.[5] The researcher

---

1. Sharan B. Merriam, *Qualitative Research: A Guide to Design and Implementation* (San Francisco, CA: Jossey-Bass, 2009), 14.

2. Anna D. Bremborg, "Interviewing," in *The Routledge Handbook of Research Methods in the Study of Religion*, eds. M. Stausberg and S. Engler (Abingdon, UK: Routledge, 2011), 310.

3. Meredith Gall, Joyce Gall, and Walter Borg, *Educational Research: An Introduction*, 7th ed. (New York: Longman, 1996), 287–289; Michael Q. Patton, *Qualitative Research and Evaluation Methods* (Thousand Oaks: Sage, 2002), 340–341; Merriam, *Qualitative Research*, 88.

4. Irving Seidman, *Interviewing as Qualitative Research*, 4th ed. (New York: Teacher College Press, 2013), 18.

5. Gall, Gall, and Borg, *Educational Research*, 289.

collected the data by using semi-structured interviews following a series of open-ended interview questions contained in appendix 1. The study produced richly descriptive data through which the researcher generated possible themes for an in-depth analysis.[6]

Purpose Statement

The purpose of this qualitative study was to investigate the perceptions of faith-integrated being, knowing, and doing among Christian faculty in Indonesian higher education contexts.

Research Questions

The following research questions guided this study:
1. How do Indonesian Christian faculty describe the value of faith in their vocation (*being*)?
2. How do Indonesian Christian faculty describe the relationship between faith and their educational discipline (*knowing*)?
3. How do Indonesian Christian faculty describe the influence of faith in their educational practices (*doing*)?

Population and Sample Selection

The population for this study was Christian faculty who were active teaching staff at a college or university, either a Christian, private non-religious, or state higher education institution in Indonesia. The population included faculty with various terms of employment contracts: *dosen tetap* and *dosen tidak tetap* (equivalent to the United States: adjunct and tenured professors); and academic ranks: *asisten ahli, lektor, lektor kepala*, and *professor* (equivalent to the United States: assistant professor, associate professor, and [full] professor).[7]

---

6. Merriam, *Qualitative Research*, 14.

7. Susilo B. Yudhoyono, Undang-Undang Republik Indonesia Nomor 14 Tahun 2005, "Tentang Guru dan Dosen," *Lembaran Negara Republik Indonesia Tahun 2005 Nomor 157* [Law of the Republic Indonesia No 14 Year 2005, "About Teachers and Lecturers," *State Document of the Republic of Indonesia Year 2005 No 157*] (December 30, 2005), accessed February 6, 2017, http://luk.staff.ugm.ac.id/atur/UU14-2005GuruDosen.pdf.

Qualitative interviews need to ensure that the empirical data is rich enough to make analyses and develop data into a theory. Therefore, research participant sampling and selection assumed that the individual would provide a broad entrance into the data collection and contribute to the relevant knowledge.[8] The research sample for this study was based on purposeful sampling.[9] Snowball or referral sampling was used to locate potential participants. To increase the possibility for the transferability of this study, a strategy for maximum variation which sought diversity in the sample selection included faculty with a variety of types of institution, academic discipline, and gender.[10] Participants were Christian faculty who had five or more years of teaching experience with the assumptions that they had adjusted to their teaching environment and had sufficient teaching experience for them to reflect upon. A total of thirty-six participants were interviewed.

Description of Participants

Thirty-six faculty were interviewed, nineteen women and seventeen men. Twelve were teaching at Christian universities, eleven were at private non-faith based universities, and thirteen were at state universities (table 1). All participants were Christians, active members of a local church, and attended Sunday service regularly. The geographic area of the higher education institutions where the participants worked was spread across three different provinces but all located in Java Island. Seven institutions were located in the greater Jakarta area, three in West Java, and another three in East Java. Years spent in teaching ranged from 6 to 37 years, with an average of 19.7 years. In terms of employment contracts, all participants were full-time faculty members or *dosen tetap* (tenured). In terms of academic ranks, nine were *asisten ahli* (associate lecturers) twenty-one were *lektor* (lecturers), and six were *lektor kepala* (senior lecturers).

Of the thirty-six participants, twenty-seven hold doctoral degrees or are currently enrolled in doctoral degree programs and nine hold master's degrees. Almost all participants (35) received their undergraduate education in

---

8. Bremborg, "Interviewing," 313–314.
9. Merriam, *Qualitative Research*, 76–80.
10. Merriam, 227–228.

Indonesia; one graduated from a college in Germany. A majority (25) continued their master's and doctoral studies in Indonesia and the remaining eleven faculty had their advanced academic degrees from abroad (Thailand, Japan, Australia, and the USA). Academic disciplines of the participants included teacher education (3), economics (4), accounting (2), engineering (4), medical sciences (5), dentistry (1), agriculture and fisheries (4), mathematics (3), physics (1), psychology (3), linguistics (1), hospitality and tourism (1), philosophy (1), communication (1), arts and design (1), and anthropology (1).

Table 1. Participants and Types of Institution

Types of Institution	Gender		Total Participants
	Male	Female	
Private Christian university	2	10	12
Private non-faith based university	7	4	11
State university	8	5	13
Total	17	19	36

In the area of professional development, almost all participants reported that they did not receive any training that focused on the integration of faith and learning. Only three participants mentioned training or seminars they attended in the last five years that related to the topic of faith and learning. One participant who recently graduated from a Christian university in the USA considered her two-year graduate program as her professional development related to faith-integrated learning. Another two participants recalled a seminar of "faith and knowledge" they received from a national retreat for Christian faculty organized by a parachurch organization in 2016.

Higher Education in the Indonesia Context

Indonesia is the world's most populated Muslim country. According to the 2010 census, Indonesia has 237 million people, of which 60 percent reside in Java Island.[11] The country has the fourth-largest population in the world.

---

11. Badan Pusat Statistik, "Penduduk Indonesia menurut Provinsi" [Indonesian Population by Provinces], accessed September 13, 2017, https://www.bps.go.id/linkTabelStatis/view/ id/1267.

Indonesia is an archipelago country which has more than 13,000 islands and consists of more than 1,000 ethnic groups of which Javanese, Sundanese, Malay, Madurese, Batak, and Balinese are among the main groups.[12] Officially, only six religions are recognized by the government. The followers of Islam are about 87.18 percent, Protestantism 6.96 percent, Catholicism 2.9 percent, Hinduism 1.69 percent, Buddhism 0.72 percent, and Confucianism 0.05 Percent.[13] Due to its socio-cultural makeup, ethno-religion tensions and conflicts are rampant.[14] To unite the vastly diverse ethnic groups, the nation has *Bahasa Indonesia* as its national official language, *Pancasila* (The Five Principles) as the national ideology, and *Bhinneka Tunggal Ika* which means unity in diversity as its national motto.

The Indonesian education system is based on a 9-year basic compulsory education and 3-year secondary education, followed by a 4-year undergraduate education or 1-to-3-year diploma of higher professional education. There are three types of secondary school: senior secondary education, Islamic senior secondary education, and senior vocational education. All graduates from these schools are eligible to apply for higher education through entrance examinations to state institutions or private institutions. Currently, there are about 3,350 colleges and universities in Indonesia which consist of 92 public institutions and one Open University, 3,200 private institutions, and 52 Islamic institutions.[15] Private higher-education institutions can be divided into two categories: faith-based and non-faith based institutions. All institutions are under the Ministry of National Education, except for

---

12. Leo Suryadinata, Evi N. Arifin, and Aris Ananta, *Indonesia's Population: Ethnicity and Religion in a Changing Political Landscape* (Singapore: Institute of Southeast Asian Studies, 2003), 104.

13. Badan Pusat Statistik, "Jumlah Penduduk Menurut Wilayah dan Agama yang Dianut" [Population by Regions and Religions], Sensus Penduduk 2010 [2010 Census], accessed October 3, 2017, http://sp2010.bps.go.id/index.php/site/tabel?tid=321&wid=0.

14. See e.g. Eliza Griswold, *The Tenth Parallel: Dispatches from the Fault Line between Christianity and Islam* (New York: Farrar, Strauss, & Giroux, 2010); John T. Sidel, *Riots, Pogroms, Jihad: Religious Violence in Indonesia* (Ithaca: Cornell University Press, 2006).

15. Bagyo Y. Moeliodihardjo et al., "University, Industry, and Government Partnership: Its Present and Future Challenges in Indonesia," *Social and Behavioral Sciences* 52 (December 2012): 307–316.

Islamic education institutions (public and private) which are regulated by the Ministry of Religious Affairs.[16]

Private institutions are self-funded; until recently they received a portion of their financial support from the government through the provision of a teacher certification program and a competitive research grant. The major financial source is students' tuition and fees. Mohamad Fahmi observes that students who graduate from Christian schools have more opportunities to attend higher education than public schools and other types of private schools due to their academic achievement and financial ability.[17] However, the overall accessibility and affordability of higher education are still limited to a small population in Indonesia. UNESCO reported that the total tertiary enrollment was 24.3 percent of the college-age population.[18] By Gross National Income (GNI) per capita, Indonesia is classified as a lower middle income ($1,026–$4,035) country of which more than 28 million people are living with $3.10 income a day.[19]

Besides poverty, unequal and limited access to higher education is also caused by a lack of strategic planning and funding mechanisms, inefficient centralized educational bureaucracy, and poor accountability.[20] Consequently, the quality and relevance of higher education in Indonesia were poor as described by Wicaksono and Friawan:

> [T]he low levels of the teaching staff qualification, inadequate laboratory facilities (especially in the private HEIs) and limited library holdings. Meanwhile, low efficiency is best demonstrated

---

16. Teguh Y. Wicaksono and Deni Friawan, "Recent Developments in Higher Education in Indonesia: Issues and Challenges" (paper prepared for discussion at the DPU/EABER Conference on Financing Higher Education and Economic Development in East Asia, Bangkok, July 16–17, 2008), 1–37, accessed February 15, 2018, http://aber.eaber.org/system/tdf/documents/WPS_DPU_2008_45.pdf?file=1&type=node&id=21949&force=.

17. Mohamad Fahmi, "Indonesian Higher Education: Gaps in Access and School Choice," Working Papers in Economics and Development Studies (WoPEDS) 201414, Department of Economics, Padjadjaran University, revised Oct 2014, accessed February 15, 2015, https://ideas.repec.org/p/unp/wpaper/201414.html.

18. UNESCO, "Gross Enrolment Ratio, Tertiary, Both Sexes (%)," accessed February 15, 2018, https://data.worldbank.org/indator/SE.TER.ENRR?locations=ID.

19. World Bank, "2017 World Development Indicators," accessed February 15, 2018, https://openknowledge.worldbank.org/bitstream/handle/10986/26447/WDI-2017-web.pdf?.

20. Moeliodiharjdo et al., "University, Industry, and Government Partnership," 307–336.

by the extended enrolment period in which a typical undergraduate – in both public and private HEIs – spends about five to six years completing their studies instead of the four years required. Low internal efficiency can also be seen from the low student-teacher ratios of about 12:1, limited utilization of physical space, and the low number of student/staff contact hours.[21]

To improve the quality, efficiency, and relevance of higher education, the government has taken several steps which focused on policy and structure reforms, teacher professionalism, and educational budget upgrades. As a result, the national expenditure on education has increased over the years from 2.9 percent of GDP in 2005 to 3.6 percent in 2015.[22] The number shows a strong commitment of the current government to fulfill the constitutional mandate to allocate at least 20 percent of the total national budget to education. For example, in 2007 the national expenditure on education was only 16.9 percent, which was lower as compared to neighboring countries such as Malaysia (27 percent), or Thailand (27 percent).[23] However, in the years 2010–2017 the Indonesia government spent 20 percent of its total national budget for education.[24] Asian Development Bank reported that in 2010, only 10 percent of the educational expenditure was allocated to higher education, and only about 7 percent from this amount went to private higher education institutions which had about two-thirds of total student enrolment.[25] Current data show that expenditure in tertiary education has increased to 15.1 percent

---

21. Wicaksono and Friawan, "Recent Developments," 2–3.

22. Knoema, "Indonesia: Public Spending on Education as a Share of Gross Domestic Product," accessed February 15, 2018, https://knoema.com/atlas/Indonesia/topics/Education/ Expenditures-on-Education/Public-spending-on-education-as-a-share-of-GDP.

23. Arze del Granado et al., "Investing in Indonesia's Education: Allocation, Equity, and Efficiency of Public Expenditures," The World Bank, Policy Research Working Paper, No. 4329 (Washington, DC: World Bank, 2007), accessed February 15, 2018, http://hdl.handle.net/10986/7280.

24. Kementerian Keuangan Indonesia (Ministry of Finance Indonesia), "Anggaran Pendidikan 2010–2017," Direktorat Penyusunan APBN – Direktorat Jenderal Anggaran, accessed May 17, 2018, http://www.data-apbn.kemenkeu.go.id/Dataset/Details/1007.

25. Asian Development Bank, "Sector Assessment (Summary): Education. Country Partnership Strategy: Indonesia, 2012–2014," accessed February 15, 2018, https://www.adb.org/sites/default/files/linked-documents/cps-ino-2012-2014-ssa-02.pdf.

in 2015, but there was no figure available on how this number is split between state and private higher education institutions.[26]

In 2000, educational reforms of policy and structures started to decentralize the education system. The reforms introduced a corporate-like structure and management that allowed more flexibility for higher education institutions to regulate their bodies, seek external funding, and promote quality and accountability to the public.[27] The reforms also focused on improving teacher professionalism. In 2005, the government passed the Law of Teacher and Lecturer (No. 14/2005) to guide teacher management and development which included: "pre-and in-service education; induction; certification; performance appraisal; and career development."[28] Curriculum, pedagogy, and assessment training were provided to give teachers new paradigms and skills that would shift them from teacher-centered to student active learning, from outcome-focused to process approach, and from text-book oriented to more contextual and experiential learning. Teachers and lecturers who passed certification programs were considered certified educators and would receive a professional allowance from the central government that was double their existing salary.[29]

Despite the above innovative and strategic moves by the government, change for a better quality of education in Indonesia still has a long way to go. Studies showed no difference between certified and uncertified teachers in the quality of their teaching performance and student learning outcomes.[30] The reforms that gave autonomy to higher education institutions also led to privatization, massification, and commercialization of education that shifted the purpose of education from public good to private good.[31] Welch asserts

---

26. Knoema, "Indonesia."
27. Wicaksono and Friawan, "Recent Developments," 27–34.
28. Tatang Suratno, "The Education System in Indonesia at a Time of Significant Changes," *Revue internationale d'éducation de Sèvres [Online], Education in Asia in 2014: What Global Issues?* (12–14 June 2014): 4.
29. Suratno, "Education System," 4.
30. Mae Chu Chang et al., *Teacher Reform in Indonesia: The Role of Politics and Evidence in Policy Making* (Washington, DC: World Bank, 2014), 149–151; Prita N. Kusumawardhani, "Does Teacher Certification Program Lead to Better Quality Teachers? Evidence from Indonesia," *Education Economics* 25, no. 6 (July 2017): 590–618.
31. A. R. Welch, "Blurred Vision?: Public and Private Higher Education in Indonesia," *Higher Education* 54, no. 5 (October 2007): 665–687; Azyumardi Azra, "Indonesian Higher Education: From Public Good to Privatization," *Journal of Asian Public Policy* 1, no. 2 (June

that "this is only likely to sharpen existing difficulties around longstanding issues of quality, equality, and regulatory capacity."[32]

Data Collection

The main means for data collection was a face-to-face interview. Data collection was conducted within a span of two months from July to August 2017 in five different cities. About one-third of the participants were colleagues and acquaintances I knew from my previous teaching institution. The rest of the participants were referred by colleagues or friends from churches and para churches. Potential participants were contacted by email and/or phone and asked for their willingness to participate in this study. An electronic invitation letter was sent to each participant to briefly introduce the context, significance, and purpose of the study (see appendix 1). A consent letter was sent to candidates who agreed to participate seeking their voluntary agreement to share their personal life experience, feelings, and perceptions in relation to the research topic (see appendix 2). After receiving consent, a schedule for the interview was arranged according to the participant's convenience. Some participants preferred to sign the consent letter on the day of the interview. Most interviews were conducted at the location where the participants worked: Jakarta (14), Depok (6), Bogor (3), Bandung (5), and Surabaya (6). Two interviews were conducted via Skype. One participant canceled the interview on the day of the appointment due to filling in for her Muslim colleague who could not lead a field trip during Ramadan. The other participant was not able to meet in person due to her tight schedule between working at the university, running her own dental clinic, and taking modular-doctoral classes abroad.

All interviews were conducted in *Bahasa Indonesia* following a protocol of semi-structured interview questions (see appendix 2). All interviews were recorded using a portable MP3 recording device. Prior to the interview, all participants were notified that the interview would be recorded and transcribed

---

2008): 139–147; Dewi Susanti, "Privatisation and Marketisation of Higher Education in Indonesia: The Challenge for Equal Access and Academic Values," *Higher Education* 61, no. 2 (February 2011): 209–218.

    32. Welch, "Blurred Vision?," 665.

for purposes of analysis. One participant used phrases in her local dialect to answer the interview questions. I took notes and asked the participant to explain and/or to find other terms that were equivalent to *Bahasa Indonesia*. Each interview lasted forty-five to sixty minutes.

At the end of each interview, I gave the participants a thank you card and a keychain representing US cities or a classic Christian book for those I knew personally. This modest gift was a token of thank you for their participation in the research.

Data Analysis

All interviews were transcribed from audio to a Word document by the researcher herself. The analysis and coding were done in the original language (*Bahasa Indonesia*). Translation of the data from Indonesian into English was done in presenting the themes, quotes, and supporting evidence. The main reason for this procedure was that the researcher was more skilled in reading data and identifying emergent themes in her native language (Indonesian) than in English. To ensure the accuracy of the translation, the researcher asked a bilingual person to translate a sample of the English data back into the Indonesian language. The primary mode of analysis was inductive which involved a process finding "recurring regularities in the data" to establish emerging themes.[33] The naming of the themes and subthemes are taken from the literature, a summary of the participants' narratives, in-vivo quotes, and the researcher's ideas. The presentation of the findings included the participants' voices and the researcher reflexivity.[34]

Translation-Related Issues

Interviews and data analysis were carried out in *Bahasa Indonesia* (hereafter *Bahasa*), the national language of Indonesia. The researcher also translated the interview protocol, letter of invitation, letter of consent, and some key terms from English to *Bahasa*. Translation between languages involves

---

33. Merriam, *Qualitative Research*, 18, 177.

34. John W. Creswell, *Qualitative Inquiry and Research Design: Choosing among Five Approaches* (Thousand Oaks, CA: Sage, 2012), 44.

interpretation; thus the meaning might be diluted in the process of translation.³⁵ To ensure the translation was as close as possible to its original meaning, the researcher carefully considered both the literal and conceptual meaning of the word or term. However, when the two languages did not have lexical equivalence, conceptual equivalence was employed to ensure the comparability of the meaning of the word.³⁶ In this study, special attention in translation was given to the following terms:

Integration of faith and learning. The lexical equivalence to this term in Bahasa was "integrasi iman dan pembelajaran." This translation was highly abstract and needed an explanation. Also, the word "learning" was commonly associated with student learning; thus to maintaining the conceptual meaning it was translated as "teaching and learning" (belajar dan mengajar) to point to faculty who engaged students in learning through their teaching activities. The literal translation of this term was still maintained in written *Bahasa* so that when the readers want to check for the term in English, it would be easier for them to locate. However, to make it understandable to the participants without diluting its conceptual meaning, during the interview the "integration of faith and learning" was translated as "integrasi iman dalam belajar dan mengajar" or "pengaruh iman dalam belajar dan mengajar." The word "influence" *(pengaruh)* was also used interchangeably with "reflect" *(mencerminkan)*, "manifest" *(menyatakan)*, or "color" *(mewarnai)* as they are commonly used in Indonesian educational discourse.

Being-Knowing-Doing. This term could be translated literally as "Menjadi-Mengetahui-Melakukan," but it needed further explanation to capture its conceptual meaning. "Being" was translated as *keberadaan diri* that pointed to the personal being of a faculty member. "Knowing" referred to cognitive understanding and was translated as *pengetahuan* or *pemahaman*, and "doing" that emphasized teaching and learning activities provided by the faculty was translated as *aktifitas belajar mengajar*.

To ensure the accuracy of the translation, the researcher also did the following: (1) conducted a *pilot interview* with three Indonesian colleagues

---

35. Fenna Van Nes et al., "Language Differences in Qualitative Research: Is Meaning Lost in Translation?" *European Journal of Ageing* 7, no. 4 (December 2010), 313.

36. Fred E. Jandt, *An Introduction to Intercultural Communication: Identities in a Global Community,* 5th ed. (Thousand Oaks, CA: Sage, 2007), 130–135.

who had some teaching experiences in higher education. Necessary changes were then made following the results from these pilot interviews; (2) asked a bilingual person to do *back translation* by translating a sample of data from English to *Bahasa*; (3) consulted and discussed the use and meaning of particular words or terms with other bilingual colleagues.[37]

Transferability

According to Merriam, transferability is "the possibility of the results of a qualitative study 'transferring' to another setting."[38] The focus of this research was the participants' understanding of their vocation, disciplines, and teaching experiences in relation to their Christian faith. Maximum variation was purposely included in this research, but the research participants were limited to Indonesian Christian faculty who were teaching in higher education. The results of this descriptive study might be transferred to Christian faculty in other countries who share similarities in their faith, teaching experiences, and socio-cultural contexts. In addition to descriptive characteristics, Merriam asserts that qualitative study is particularistic and heuristic.[39] This means that though the descriptive study was conducted in particular contexts or at particular events, it might still provide insights to readers enabling them to bridge learning to their own contexts, discover new meaning, and expand or affirm their own experiences.

---

37. Maria Birbili, "Translating from One Language to Another," *Social Research Update* 31 (Winter 2000), accessed April 6, 2017, http://sru.soc.surrey.ac.uk/SRU31.html.

38. Merriam, *Qualitative Research*, 227.

39. Merriam, 43–44.

CHAPTER 4

Findings

The purpose of this qualitative study was to investigate the perceptions of faith-integrated being, knowing, and doing among Christian faculty in Indonesian higher education contexts. The following research questions guided this study:

1. How do Indonesian Christian faculty describe the value of faith in their vocation (*being*)?
2. How do Indonesian Christian faculty describe the relationship between faith and their educational discipline (*knowing*)?
3. How do Indonesian Christian faculty describe the influence of faith in their educational practices (*doing*)?

This chapter focuses on key findings from thirty-six interview participants' descriptions of their perceptions and experiences in faith-integrated being, knowing, and doing in their respective contexts. The findings are organized according to themes and subthemes that emerged from the data analysis. Reporting includes descriptive summaries and direct quotations from the participant responses. The chapter begins with descriptions of professoriate roles among Christian faculties in Indonesia. Then the three main sections focus on the findings that follow the order of the research questions used in the study.

Descriptions of Professoriate Roles in Indonesian Higher Education Contexts
Tridharma: Trilogy of Higher Education
The initial interview question asked participants to describe their job as a

faculty member. Common responses included teaching, research, and service, which they refer to as *Tridharma Perguruan Tinggi* (trilogy or three principles of higher education). The first role, teaching, was described by most participants as teaching activities in the classroom and/or laboratory, student academic advising, and supervising students' final projects (e.g. BS1, DS1, ET2, EW2, WU3). Variations in teaching tasks depend on the faculty's department or field of academic discipline. For example, EW2, a faculty member teaching in a psychology department explained, "Because I have a psychology clinical background, I teach mostly clinical classes. I am also an advisor for student theses, internships . . ., making test questions, [attending] many faculty meetings, such as the preparatory meeting, mid-semester meeting, end of semester meeting, peer review meeting for clinical courses and still many others." In a similar fashion, BS1 described his teaching tasks in the engineering department as "classroom-teaching, academic advising, and supervising senior projects." Another faculty, CS1, who taught fisheries science, explained, "Besides teaching in the classroom and laboratory, most of my time is spent in the field with students."

The second role is research, which includes literature, field, and experimental research and publishing the research results in either national or international journals but most preferably in peer-reviewed or Scopus indexed journals (e.g. CH1, DA1, JS2, SW3, ES3). Some participants view research as a mandatory task to fulfill their obligation as government-certified educators and to upgrade their academic ranks. For example, ES3 stated, "I need to write at least one article per semester because I have gotten my lecturer certification. So I have to fulfill the demands as a certified-lecturer recipient." Another faculty member, EP1 explained, "Research is required as one of the qualifications for upgrading academic ranks. Every year the government provides a competitive research grant, so we must compete to write proposals to get the grant." For JS2, who worked for a private non-faith based university, research was one of the key measurements of faculty productivity. He stated, "Our institution uses the Key Performance Indicator (KPI), so all faculty members are obliged to do research: minimum one paper per semester, published in the international journal or accredited and indexed Scorpus journal, otherwise the KPI value will be zero. Any faculty from assistant to full professor, without exception, must write and publish."

Other participants view research in a broader sense and are concerned about how their research will benefit the students and society (e.g. BS1, RS1, CH3, DY3). CH3 said that not all his writings receive positive reviews from the journal editors or get published but he aims to use his writings to enrich his teaching content. He explained further, "I have to make sure what I research or what I teach is applicable to society. So, I have to keep communicating with particular people in society to make my research relevant." Similarly, DY3 asserted, "If I do a research project I want it to be useful for my students, not just to add points." In the engineering field, BS1 explains that research is "aimed to contribute to society, namely applicative research projects or research partnerships with industry."

The third mandatory role for a faculty is community service. The frequency of community service varies among the participants. ET2 does her community service twice each semester, YP2 once a year, and for faculty who teach in pure science "community service is not popular" (DS1) and is only conducted occasionally (HT1). The services include a wide range of activities from providing seminars and workshops based on the community needs to conducting research to give input to the local government. For example, JS2 described his community service as follows:

> In addition to being a speaker of seminars or workshops, I also teach English in locations that have been adopted by my institution, for example, R-Petra and orphanages. Faculty members are sent to teach according to their fields. Children do not go home directly after school but stop by R-Petra, located in the neighborhood, nearby the county offices. Children gather and study. Most students are from middle-lower socio-economic backgrounds, but some are from the "haves." It's free. Besides English, there are many other subjects as well.

As a trained psychologist and a full-time faculty, EW2 has a tight schedule but for her, "community service is a must." Finding her way to give to the community, she said, "I provide counseling services for those who pay as well as pro-bono counseling services. I give training to companies if they invite me. I am so busy that I could not open my own practice, so I do my practice here [on campus]." RS1, a statistician, contributes her services by providing research training for companies and theological schools and assisting government agencies such as the Department of Labor and the Department of Food and Drug to design questionnaires and surveys.

Another faculty member, LT2, who teaches urban planning and design, reports that his department recently had a partnership with the local government as one of the community service programs. He explained, "We are conducting a study on Panggang Island to give input to the local government about the possibility to readjust its urban planning because the island has a high population density. We are not paid, it is a community service. It takes many years and we are just starting." Another interesting community service is shared by EP1, who teaches in the agribusiness and horticulture department:

> I have to travel to other provinces to conduct field workshops for farmers as a part of my community service. I must finish the program before the *Eid al Fitr* celebration. My field is in the seed technology lab. The Ministry of Agriculture has a program to provide paddy seeds throughout Indonesia. We are working with the local government from 16 provinces. These farmers need to be taught how to produce certified seeds, not just any seeds. So we teach them how to produce certified seeds. We have to come to them because now is the planting season. One month later we need to go back to teach them what to do next when the plants are two months old, and then harvesting, and so on. So it is kind of a mentoring program.

It is noteworthy that a group of participants who work at the same institution add one more role to their professoriate tasks, namely self-development. Instead of *Tridharma*, these participants are proud of their *Caturdharma*, or four principles of higher education. JA2 states, "Our rector explains that *caturdharma* implies interrelated roles. What we do in research can become teaching materials; what we do in community service can be documented to enrich teaching contents. So self-development means that we cannot keep teaching old materials, out-dated materials. Thus, we need to attend seminars or workshops that are related to our field."

Similarly, JA2 and EW2 explain that for self-development they need to attend seminars or workshops, provided either by their institutions or other institutions. As a senior faculty, EW2 says that instead of *tetralogy* she practices *pentalogy*, because "sometimes I am asked to give training for faculty members here. So, I have five roles."

Struggles to Keep the Trilogy in Harmony

Although the trilogy of higher education is mandatory, in practice many participants find its demands are unrealistic. Participants in this study are often caught between competing obligations, especially those who assume administrative roles in addition to their teaching tasks (e.g. LT2, RT1, HS1, EP1, DY3). For example, HS1 expressed that writing a proposal and getting a research grant is not difficult but finding time to conduct the research is a real challenge. HS1 added, "Research should be done outside of teaching and student advising time. So I have to manage my time wisely in order to find spare time for research. In addition, right now I am a program director. All the administrative work consumes my time." Likewise, LT2, a faculty member and administrator at a private non-faith based university, asserted: "We are still a teaching university. Becoming a research university is a long way off. Here, I have to teach a minimum of 12 credit hours. That said, it still includes other responsibilities, such as I am now a secretary for the master's program. Other faculty members sometimes teach 16 to 18 credit hours. Are we not dying?"

A similar tension is also expressed by RT, who teaches at a state university. In addition to teaching undergraduate and master's students, he said, "I am also a Head of Internal Audit for the university. Besides, I also do my community service by giving training to companies. Research is a must but with all the workload . . . I cannot find spare time, maybe next year I will do it."

However, there are some participants who do not give up on the situation but strive their best to keep the trilogy in harmony (e.g. DS1, CS1, BS1). DS1, who was currently doing her doctoral program, argued, "Teaching is a scheduled and assigned task, but research is different, it is not assigned or demanded by my superiors. We must take our own initiative to do research."

One way to fulfill the trilogy was by combining the tasks. CS1, a fresh PhD holder in ichthyology from Japan, expressed enthusiastically how he ran the tasks consecutively:

> Last week I went to Papua to conduct my research. As an output of the research, I can publish a book or a journal article. My

daily activities are mostly filled with teaching. Thus, I must make time to do research, either in the laboratory or in the field. I try to combine my research and community service. For example, while I was in Papua doing my research, I also gave a seminar to faculty members and a general lecture to the students at the local university.

Another way to fulfill the trilogy, especially the challenge of doing research, is through "co-publishing" with students as expressed by several faculty (e.g. BS1, MC2, EP1, RT1, DS1). Faculty members who supervised the student research were allowed to be co-authors. BS1 explained, "Every week I go the lab, and this is mutualism. I supervise the students and we co-publish together." Besides publishing jointly, EP1 explained, "I also share my research grants with my students, especially graduate students who have limited research funds, so we can do the research together." MC2 expressed it more explicitly, "I have one big topic and divided it into several subtopics. Students who want to do research under my supervision will choose among those subtopics."

Section 1: The Integration of Faith and Teaching Vocation

The first research question was to seek the participants' responses to: "How do Indonesian Christian faculty describe the value of faith in their vocation (*being*)?" All participants placed a high value on faith in shaping their calling and living out their vocation as Christian faculty. To the participants, faith gave: (1) a strong sense of calling; (2) purpose and meaning in their work; (3) moral and ethical guidance; (4) a strong work ethos; (5) strength and hope in the face of adversity; and (6) desire for personal growth.

Faith Gives a Strong Sense of Calling

This first theme echoed strongly among the participants that going through a series of the experiential and discerning process have led them to a conviction of calling to their current vocation as faculty. This theme is divided into two subthemes: the conviction of calling and the discerning process of finding God's calling.

Figure 1. Six Aspects of Faith-Integrated Being

The Conviction of Calling

A majority of participants in the research believed that God has led them into teaching ministry in higher education. For some faculty members, the conviction of calling occurred before or soon after they enter the teaching career (e.g. CS1, BS1, DS1, YP2, JS2, JS3). CS1 confidently said, "I believe that God's calling for me is to be a faculty member. I must be faithful to live out my calling. God has called so I had to follow the calling." Likewise, AS1 expressed joyfully, "It is not just about calling but I also enjoy my work." For JS2, teaching in higher education had been a dream job since she was a college student. Reflecting on her teaching journey, she said, "I see the process that God has been leading me through . . . that I am here now, not because of my will alone, but it is God's calling that I can serve here as God's fellow worker." A similar experience was also shared by YP2, saying, "My calling is to be a lecturer. After I graduated from my undergraduate and graduate studies, I could work at the banks, companies, or government institutions, but no . . . a picture of me as a lecturer was always in my mind."

Other participants come to the conviction of calling after a few years or even almost at the end of their teaching career (e.g. WU3, HS1, JS3, DT3).

WU3, a medical doctor, received an offer to teach at her alma mater upon her graduation but she refused the opportunity because she wanted to be a pediatric specialist. Due to many unexpected challenges, she could not achieve her dream and turn her direction to become a lecturer. Reflecting on her seventeen years of a teaching career, she said, "Teaching is not my original choice, but now I learn to love it. To love what the Lord has given me. I see if the Lord has said come back, then yes, I must come back [to my alma mater]." Both JS3 and HS1 expressed that the beginning of their teaching career was difficult but as they kept progressing, the sense of God's calling became stronger and stronger and they learned to love their jobs. For example, JS3 said, "I see God's guidance along the way. During the early years of my teaching career, I felt I could not do anything. But then, God gave me an opportunity to go for graduate education. Also, here I am given the opportunity to engage in spiritual activities and discussions with colleagues that hone my understanding of God's calling. My existence here is not because of my will but there is a call for what I can give to this institution as a coworker of God."

For DT3, the conviction of vocational calling came much later, after more than thirty years in her teaching career. Growing up as a "static Christian" in a church that did not care much about doctrinal teaching and discipleship, DT3 expressed, "I did not understand what calling was all about at that time . . . only recently, because I faced many struggles that forced me to get to know more deeply about my faith. I moved to another church and joined their faith formation classes. Only recently, I came to realize and understand [my calling]."

The conviction of calling was also shared by the participants who formerly worked as professionals but then decided to enter a teaching career in higher education (JH2, KC2, LS3).

JH2 spent more than a decade working at an IT company before joining a newly founded private non-faith based university as a faculty member. Pondering his career change to education, JH2 asserted, "From the perspective of Christian faith, I see my calling as a faculty is to make an impact. So I do not judge something from financial gain. If so, I might not be interested [in teaching]." KC2 was an executive for a large firm for many years, but he was fond of teaching and decided to move to a teaching career in 2012. Reflecting on his major change of vocation, he said, "I felt I was called to be an educator... I was offered an opportunity to teach and I said yes, although the salary compared to my previous job as an executive was far different. Teaching takes devotion, giving our best for others. For me, it is also a ministry." A similar experience was also shared by LS3 who had stayed and worked in Germany for about fifteen years. Moving back to Indonesia was a big shift in her life and she wondered what she could do with her arts and design background. Almost at the same time, the local Christian university that planned to start a department of art and design offered her a teaching position as well as membership in a leadership team. Convinced that she was called to share her gifts and years of experience in art and design, LS3 said, "God has given me this gift of design; by becoming a lecturer I can teach, do research and community service . . . I can give to others."

The Discerning Process of Finding God's Calling

Almost all participants mentioned that becoming a faculty member was not their original dream job. Only three participants planned to be a faculty since they were college students (MP1, YP2, AS1). How did the majority of the participants change from their original desirable job to become teaching faculty in higher education? To most participants, arriving at a conviction of calling and a decision to become a faculty was not an instant moment but involved a series of experiences, which included among others: insights and encouragement from influential people, identifying one's gift and passion, seeing the need, and experiencing God's intervention. There was no clear-cut pattern among these elements but often interrelated with each other as the participants shared their stories. Here, a series of participants' experiences in finding God's calling is divided into three categories: (1) formative experience; (2) directive experience; and (3) affirmative experience. Some participants had all these three experiences (CS1, BS1, DS1, EW2, ES3, EP1) but many mentioned only one or two of those experiences.

Formative Experience

The formative experience that directed many participants to their calling of teaching includes time spent in youth or student ministry either in church or parachurch and early socialization to the teaching vocation modeled by their teachers and/or parents.

Many participants found that spiritual formation during their high school and college years played an important role in their formative stage of discerning the calling to be educators in tertiary education (e.g. EW2, CS1, BS1, DS1, HS1, ET2, ES3). Planning to work as a researcher at a government agency, CS1 explained that his plan was changed, "Because over the time, I saw my alma mater was an incredible place, students came from all over Indonesia. I used to be trained and involved in campus ministry. I saw this institution was a mission field." During college years, BS1 attended a three-year program of evening Bible school that gave him a strong foundation of biblical understanding, prayer life, and evangelism. He was also active in student fellowship and Bible study on campus. In addition, as a fresh college graduate, he joined a four-month alumni retreat organized by a missionary couple from OMF (Overseas Missionary Fellowship) which BS1 described as a "turning point" life experience:

> For me, this program was not just helpful but it was an important milestone. This program was not aimed at theological or pastor training. We were trained to integrate faith into our work, so we learned about work ethics, church ministry, community service, law, social issues. I learned to examine the Bible systematically because, for OMF, Bible exposition was very important. So I felt that this was a very important milestone for me.

EW2 had been active in student ministry since she was in high school and throughout her college years. These formative years had inspired her to study psychology and later to become an educator at a non-faith-based university where she could interact with students from all religious backgrounds. Being a shy person, ET2 never thought that she would become a faculty member but then she explained, "God had molded me through my involvement in the student ministry organizations . . . that I liked to serve, meet people, chat, and the like."

Some participants related their formative experiences to their involvement in church ministry during college years (SW3, MP1, RT1). For example, SW3 expressed:

> I like to teach. Since I was in college, I have been a private academic tutor and teaching a study club organized by my church for children from lower-income families, opened for Muslims or Christians. I also taught the children's choir. I like to transfer my knowledge. I have been serving in youth and young adult

ministry for a long time. I am hanging out with young people a lot and I feel that God has called me and used me to change the lives of these young people, likewise the campus students.

RT1 said that his passion for teaching started as a Sunday school teacher. MP1 also expressed a similar experience: "I love to teach because I used to be a Sunday school teacher."

To other participants, early socialization to the teaching vocation was through their teachers and parents. JA2 explained, "Personally, I was quite close to my teachers when I was a teenager. They were my role models. I communicated well with them and also had a lot of discussions when I was in middle and high school. Both my father and mother were also teachers, private tutors. From there, my calling to be an educator has been socialized." A similar formative experience that led to a teaching vocation was also expressed by RM2, "I think it's like the bloodline. My father is also a faculty member teaching at the Art Institute of Indonesia. My mother too is a piano teacher." In contrast to JA2 and RM2, DY3 said, "I did not want to be an educator because my father and mother had more time for other children than their own children." But later when she was introduced to higher education by becoming a substitute lecturer for a friend who took a one-year leave, she began to appreciate her parents' teaching vocation. Thinking to share her life in a meaningful way, she decided to enter a teaching career but it took years to be convinced that it was her life calling. She said, "Students need friends to talk to, guidance for their life issues, such as dating, relationship with parents, etc. Finally, I understand that my calling is not just to teach in class, sharing knowledge, but it's more than that, sharing my life."

Directive Experience

Many participants described the following experiences that have directed them to consider the vocation of teaching: passion and talent, a desirable job, seeing the need, and opportunity. To these participants, the directive experiences were one of the ways that helped them understand God's calling for their lives.

Passion and talent. Some participants expressed that teaching experiences during the college period, such as being a teaching or laboratory assistant for their professors, had helped them to identify their passion and talent in education (e.g. CS1, BS1, ES3, HS1, AS1). BS1 was a teaching assistant in an engineering department and did not realize that his professor had been observing his potential. He said, "I did not know that I could teach but my professor who had monitored me for a year said that I had natural talent. I also asked God if I really had a gift of teaching. I was not sure about myself but my professor assured me for he has observed me for a year. Also, from the end-of-semester evaluations, students gave me a good score, 3.5 out of 4."

HS1, a faculty member in a mathematics department, expressed that being a lecturer was not his original plan, but when he was a junior in college, he said, "I was recruited as an assistant to give and help students working on math problems. And from there, I saw that I had talent."

In addition to working experience as a laboratory teaching assistant, some participants discovered their calling by taking a spiritual gifts test. For example, CS1 explained, "In my small group, there was a session for us to find out our gifts and where God wants to send us. From there, I began to think to be a lecturer." Likewise, AS1 found his gift of teaching through a series of spiritual gifts tests. The test results confirmed what he liked to do as a youth when he said, "I started teaching as an academic tutor when I was in high school. I taught physics, chemistry, and especially mathematics. When I was a junior at college I was a teaching assistant in the mathematics department. I enjoy teaching . . . so teaching is not just my calling but I also like it." Similarly, YP2 demonstrated her passion and talent for teaching by saying: "I loved to picture myself standing and speaking in front of many people . . When I was a student, I enjoyed class presentations. I did not know any other job besides to be a lecturer. So, upon graduation, I knew this was a suitable job for me."

Desirable job. Some participants considered teaching as a desirable job for various reasons. Some thought that the teaching job was enjoyable and less stressful compared to other jobs. DC2 who worked several years for a consulting company prior to his teaching job explained, "I was working under stressful conditions to meet the project deadline. Then I thought it's better for me to move to a teaching career. Here, sometimes I feel stress but I still enjoy my work. I love knowledge and learning."

For other participants, LI1 and DY3, teaching was more desirable than other jobs because they saw more possibilities to balance work and personal life. LI1 who has been teaching agriculture for eighteen years told her story:

> To be a lecturer was not my first choice but I like agriculture. Upon graduation, I was offered a teaching position by my professor. I thought to myself that being a woman if I worked at a company I would go in the morning and come home late at night. If I had children who would take care of them? What if I had a good position and salary and my husband said I had to quit my job? Rather than becoming a problem later, it's better for me to make a decision now. I thought being a lecturer was a better choice because I could manage my time.

A similar story was also shared by DY3 who dreamt of working in media. Knowing that the job would demand long working hours and an irregular schedule, she then opted to teach. She explained, "These would disrupt my worship and ministry at church. If I insisted on working in media, I would have to work on Sundays. Then, I started to apply for a teaching position at a Christian university and I was accepted."

Seeing the need. For many participants, seeing the need was one of the major experiences that directed them to the teaching vocation. For example, EP1, CS1, DS1, MC2, CH2, and EW2 saw the need to reach out to students and campuses were a strategic place to begin. EP1, a faculty member at a state university, explained, "Here, Christian faculty can be counted on our fingers, especially in my department, only three of us . . . So this is a good opportunity to show how we actually live out our Christian faith . . . This is a strategic ministry because students come from all over Indonesia." CS1 also saw a similar need when he was thinking about a teaching job. "These students will go back to their own towns and become leaders. I cannot travel all over Indonesia but if I become a lecturer I could reach them all." For EW2, a three-year experience working for a student ministry organization led her to pursue graduate study and consider the teaching vocation. She explained, "I was asked to be a fulltime minister, but I saw many cases of troubled youths. If they did not get help they would carry the problems throughout their adult lives even until after they got married. So I thought to myself, I wanted to be a psychologist." Upon graduation EW2 decided to be bi-vocational, a clinical psychologist and a teaching faculty member, which suited her passion to serve the younger generation.

Graduated from a prestigious state university, MC2's original plan was to be a faculty member at her alma mater, but she was led to consider a teaching job at a private non-faith based university for two reasons. First, the institution needed her skills in research, and second, MC2 explained, "I saw the student ministry on this campus was weak and I wanted to help. By being a lecturer I had the authority to get involved." Another directive experience story was also shared by CH2, a seminary graduate.

> After I was sure that God gave me the gift of teaching, I applied to two churches and one university . . . This university started a new program, teacher education with 26-credit hour of theology classes. I learned to see their vision that to train teachers who would go back to their own cities, mostly small and underdeveloped cities, to teach. The aim was to give them a good education and a solid faith foundation. I began to see the need and felt that this was in line with what I believe. I prayed and finally, the institution responded very well."

Affirmative Experience

Toward the end of the decision-making process, many participants described that they had positive experiences that affirmed their calling of teaching. Included in these affirmative experiences were: the open door to opportunity, spiritual experiences, support from family members, and affirmation from mentors.

The open door of opportunity. Some participants perceived that the open door of opportunity was one of the God-given affirmative signs for their teaching vocation (e.g. BS1, CS1, LS3, EW2, DA1). DA1 spent six years working in the industry before he took graduate courses without knowing that he would be offered a teaching job by his professor. He took the opportunity gladly, saying, "I felt bored with my previous job and I needed something for a change. I went to graduate school with a scholarship from an NGO foundation. My supervisor was the secretary of the program. Approaching my graduation, he offered me a teaching position and I said yes." For another participant, BS1, the opportunity to teach also came through his academic supervisor. He explained:

> I did not apply but I was offered the job right after my thesis defense. He said to me, "[BS1], you can choose your profession, but we would like to offer you a teaching profession." I just finished my undergraduate degree but right away they did the civil servant hiring process and I was sent for graduate study. I never dreamt to be a faculty member because my grades were good but not cum laude. I thought I would work in the private sector upon graduation but suddenly, again I said suddenly because I never dreamt [to be a faculty member] but God opens the opportunity in such a way.

LS3, a seasoned interior designer, was working on a project for a Christian university when she was offered a teaching position. She explained:

> "While working on the project I got to know the leaders, including the president. I met one of the leaders at the church and he shared about the plan to open the arts and design department. I jokingly asked, "Do you think the institution would accept a person like me to teach?" He followed up our conversation seriously, I was surprised. He said, "OK. We are going to have a professor from America and he will give a presentation about what arts and design look like, and I want you to become part of our team."

The opportunity to be a teaching faculty member at a state university with a predominantly Muslim environment was rare, so CS1 planned to work as a researcher for a government agency upon graduation. However, the door was opened in an unexpected way when he explained,

> While doing my senior research project, one microscope in the lab was missing and I was accused of stealing the microscope. As a consequence, I had to work as a teaching assistant for a year to pay for the microscope. Actually, the microscope was stolen by a faculty member. The salary was small but I kept being faithful. I got to know the climate, the people here, and the job of a faculty because I followed and worked with them in the field and lab. This was the process God used to open doors for me to work here as a faculty member."

For EW2, the teaching opportunity also came from a place that was least expected. Approaching the end of her graduate school, she sent applications to several places. She put her hope on one institution whose dean was a good friend of her husband. To her disappointment, she received no reply. Surprisingly, she got an interview from a private non-faith based institution, which she found through ads in the newspaper. She said, "Actually they were looking for a career consultant but I just applied; who knew they might need a lecturer too. Soon after that, I got a call. I was surprised. I have finished my study but have not received the diploma nor attended the graduation ceremony yet."

Spiritual experiences. In the process of discernment and decision-making, some participants experienced spiritual experiences such as answered prayers, visions, and God's intervention in unique ways. These experiences were considered as means God used to affirm their calling of becoming faculty members. For example, LI1 shared that her journey from application to hiring process was impossible if God had not intervened. She explained:

> When I applied here it was not easy. The process of civil servant hiring was difficult, especially since I was a Christian, but thanks to God nobody strongly opposed me in my department. There were several candidates. I was called by the program secretary and asked if I still wanted to continue the process. He said, "I want to tell you, here it is not easy, we only receive one person each year. If you were fifth in the order it meant that your turn would come in the next five years." I remained firm, O God help me not to cry. I said, "It's OK, I will wait." At home, I *prayed* [emphasis], "Lord Jesus, please help me. Nothing is impossible for you!" Praise the Lord, one year later I was accepted… I feel my journey to this job is full of God's intervention, including the whole process of applying scholarship and graduate school… I knelt down, prayed, fully surrendered to God.

During college, DS1 felt that she was called to be a faculty member, but she was not sure until she went through a series of experiences, including the following affirmative experience when she took a step to apply for a teaching position at her alma mater, a reputable state university. She described:

The first job that I applied for was teaching. I was accepted. I was surprised because there were several applicants, including a senior who supposed to be the most probable candidate because she was a recipient of the bond scholarship from the higher education department. My concentration was research operation (RO) and there was only one expert in RO and she was my supervisor. During the hiring process, the program director asked the professor and she said," OK, no problem." I was accepted because my professor said OK. But I didn't know about it before that she was the sole decision-maker. From the perspective of faith, it was God's design. When I was a student, I had many interests but I chose RO because it was challenging and the professor was tough. Many seniors went in to consult on their research project and came out with tears. I thought what's happening? But I found out she was a good professor.

ET2's affirmative experience involved visions. The first vision was received through her senior pastor who said: "God will use you in education." She responded, "I was surprised but tried to test it out . . . I went through health screening processes and others and I passed them all. However, my friend who had the same GPA as me did not pass." The second vision was received through a friend from her small group, who said, "I was in two rooms. You were happy in one room but God's hands pushed you to the other room." Finding the vision similar to her experience, ET2 asserted, "I came here not because I chose to, but it was the rector who pulled me in. I know that God has used other people to get me here and God has led me all the way."

Affirmation from authoritative figures. Some participants expressed that the wise counsel from authoritative figures, such as parents, spouses, mentors, and well known Christian leaders have played an affirmative role in their entering their calling in teaching. For example, for HS1 and DS1, approval from parents has affirmed their teaching vocation. HS1 was from a Chinese family. Being the only son, he was expected to take over the family business after his father's retirement. Surprisingly, his parents allowed him to choose. Reflecting on his experience, HS1 said, "I am grateful that I am not required to replace my father. My brother-in-law takes my place. I am grateful for my parents' support. If not I could not survive in this teaching job."

Similarly, as a son from a Chinese family, BS1 was not required to work in business but his father gave him full support by saying, "If you want to pursue the teaching career, do not expect that you would have a lot of money, but there might be an opportunity to go for graduate study." For DS1, one of the reasons that led her to apply for the teaching job at a state university was because of her father's desire. She explained, "Since I was young, my father often said, "I want you to be a civil servant. I have nine children but there is none became a civil servant." So after graduation, because of my father's influence and encouragement from my mentor, I applied to be a lecturer and I was accepted."

Affirmation to their calling in teaching for LS3 and BW1 was from their spouses. Coming back to Indonesia after more than fifteen years living abroad, LS3 was wondering what she could do. She said, "My husband encouraged me to teach but I was a practitioner. But again my husband said that I had put a lot of effort into my study and now I should put it to use by sharing with others." Little did she know that after following her husband's advice, she would find her life calling in teaching. Likewise, BW1 was grateful to have his wife's support and understanding that affirmed his decision to be a lecturer. He said, "My wife is also a lecturer, so she knows the job and supports me."

Participants such as DS1 and BS1 considered the words of encouragement and counsel from their spiritual mentors to help them to feel more confident in heading toward their calling to teach. Feeling unsure about a sudden teaching job offered by his professor, BS1 sought counsel from his spiritual mentor. He expressed, "It was sudden because I never dreamed about this but God opened the door in such a way. It's shocking . . . I then consulted my mentor, an OMF missionary . . . From there I decided to become a lecturer." DS1 has received her parents' blessing to be a lecturer, but it was her mentor she has known since she was a college student who affirmed her step to the teaching vocation. She said, "Mr. T often said that if I have the opportunity to be a lecturer, particularly at a state university, go for it because not everyone has the opportunity. For Christians to be accepted as a lecturer at a state university was not easy."

For CS3, the influential figure who helped re-affirmed his calling was a well-known Christian leader. CS3 felt called to go into teaching in higher education and he was preparing himself by taking graduate courses. However, toward the end of his program, he felt doubtful because he saw that many of his peers had high-paying jobs. Coming from a farming family with limited financial resources, CS3 felt like a wave of the sea as he was tempted to go back to his original life goal, namely to be rich. In this situation, he attended a camp, which he recalled, "At the camp, I choose education for my elective class. The speaker was Mr. JP and he shared about the condition of education in Indonesia. He reaffirmed my calling. I was convinced that I needed to be all out in education . . . God helps me to love this country."

Faith Gives Purpose and Meaning to Faculty's Work

In this second theme, many participants said that faith has given them a strong sense of purpose and meaning in their work as faculty. For these participants, being a faculty member is beyond merely fulfilling the trilogy tasks of teaching, research, and community service. As Christian faculty, they expressed that faith has shaped their view of teaching vocation as follows: (1) giving the opportunities to fulfill the gospel and cultural mandate; (2) being God's instruments; (3) pleasing and glorifying God; (4) making a positive impact on a young generation; (5) educating future leaders and agents of change; and (6) helping students in character and personal growth.

Opportunity to Fulfill the Gospel and Cultural Mandate

The first purpose and meaning of being a teacher expressed by many participants is the opportunity to fulfill the gospel and cultural mandate (e.g. CS1, TM1, RT1, AS1, CS3, SW3, CH3). For example, CS1 expressed: "Being a Christian faculty I have the opportunity to share the gospel. Besides, I have the opportunity to fulfill the cultural mandate through my field in fisheries science." In a similar fashion, TM1 who taught forestry explained, "God opens my eyes that campus is a strategic place to serve the students . . . Faith also reminds me about God the Creator and what he wants us to do, such as taking care of our forests and its resources and preventing forest destruction, which is commonly happening in Indonesia."

RT1 shared that being a Christian faculty member, he has a deep concern for student ministry on campus. He argued that "every Christian has two tasks, the gospel mandate, and the cultural mandate, and faith is the starting point for both." Thus, being a Christian faculty member, he was concerned about students' spiritual growth as well as academic growth. He expressed, "First, students need to be born again. I think revival services for new students are important. The next step is their faith growth. Also, they need to grow in understanding of the cultural mandate. But I don't want to see the good in Bible knowledge but bad in their academic performance. Both need to be cultivated." Pondering on how his faith has shaped his vocation as a faculty, AS1 confidently said, "I am doing the Great Commandment of Matthew 28 through my ministry in education. I am not called as pastor to serve in the church, but my calling is here, on campus."

The privilege and responsibility of partaking in the gospel and cultural mandate are not just cited by the aforementioned participants who are all faculty teaching at state universities. The following faculty members teaching at Christian universities also shared similar views. CS3, a faculty at a Christian university, saw plentiful opportunities to reach college students with a love of the gospel, as well as equip them for service in the workforce. CS3 said:

> The roles of a faculty are commonly understood as teaching, research, and community service. But after a long struggle back to the original vision, I see that a faculty is a person who God has placed on campus to educate the young generation with a strong Christian identity that will not fade away when they enter the world of work. Thus, for me, the guiding principle is clear, as I often share with my colleagues that every student who enters my class must hear the gospel.

Similarly CS3, who joined a Christian university ten years ago as a professor teaching theology courses, saw campus as a strategic mission field to reach out to students from all over Indonesia. He expressed:

> I have been longing to reach out to people in the regions outside Java but I do not have finance, relationship, and networking capacity. However, as I look at my institution, it reaches out to students from all over Indonesia. They are from Kalimantan, Java, Sumatra, Ambon, Papua, NTT, and so on. There are at least more than 15 provinces. This suits my desire and vision. I do not have to travel or consume my energy and money which I do not have . . . this is a one-stop institution.

To Be God's Instruments

Some participants describe that one reason to be a faculty member is to be an instrument in the hands of God. Among the terms, they used to describe this role were: "extension of God's hand," "to be salt," "to be a blessing," and "transfer godly life." To fulfill this, these participants acknowledge that how they live their lives as Christians plays a crucial role in being effective instruments for God.

WU3 explained that the institution where she taught was a Christian university but it did not mean all the students were Christians. Being a Christian faculty member, she said, "I am here as God's servant, an extension of God's hand, a role-model . . . That means I must maintain my integrity and follow Christian values, such as being honest, just, and fair in treating all my students, regardless of their race and religious backgrounds." BS1 said that his presence on campus was "to be salt and salt should not stay in the plastic bag. The fish would be rotten if kept in the bag." He explained that Christians should come out of their Christian circles in order to be witnesses for Christ. To be a witness for Christ was to be authentic; as he said, "I do not have to pretend to be a Christian [in my behavior] or pretend to be godly by citing Bible verses in the class."

Reflecting on his purpose working as a faculty member, TM said, "I want to be a blessing, especially for students whom I teach or serve. This certainly includes my teaching, behavior, and service." In addition to teaching, ET2 was also an academic leader at an institution where non-Muslim faculty and women in leadership were rare. Contemplating the purpose and meaning of why she was working in an unfriendly environment, she expressed, "I am only an instrument of God. Other people may ask for riches but I always ask God for wisdom, like Solomon . . ., that my faith would not be eroded. Instead, I have strength from God that I can transfer my godly life to others."

Pleasing and Glorifying God

A number of participants emphasized an intention to please and glorify God through their life and work as a faculty member (e.g. JS2, LI1, CS1). For example, JS2 explained, "I have been in the teaching profession for twenty-four years. It's my calling, to serve God in my field for his kingdom. What we do, like Paul says, whatever we do for the glory of God." LI1 expressed a similar intention in her work stating: "Everything I do is to glorify God . . ., include doing all my duties as a faculty member responsibly. I do not have to see the honorarium but finish all my tasks on time. To be a good lecturer for me is to glorify God with what I have."

Another participant, PK3, pointed out why she became an educator: "I choose to teach in this Christian university because I hope that I might glorify God's name by making this institution better . . ., through my attitude, works, and service. God's name is glorified." CS1 also shared a similar sentiment that he wanted to express his gratitude to God as a redeemed person through his work. Thus, he said, "I am not working to get money, nor to please my superiors, but to please God." DY3 also expressed that her motivation to become a faculty member was out of gratitude as a Christian. "Other people maybe work merely for the sake of money. But for me, Jesus has died to redeem me, and as a person who has received his love, I have to share it with others by doing good works, teaching."

Make a Positive Impact on a Young Generation

Almost one-third of participants cited the words "impact" or "influence" to describe their work orientation as Christian faculty members (e.g. EW2, DS1, HS1, YP2, JH2, DC2, WU3, SW3). For example, EW2 expressed that being a Christian faculty member at a non-faith based university was "not merely to seek money or self-actualization, but to contribute, to make an impact on students' lives." Again, EW2 emphasized, "It is always my prayer, how can I make a positive impact on them [students]." DS1 also expressed a strong awareness about her being as Christian faculty member and the influence she might have on her students.

> I am often reminded that as a faculty member I have a great influence on students. How I assess and grade, how I comment on their work, how I criticize or encourage them, all will impact on their lives. Thus, I see myself as a faculty member with great responsibility. I always thought if I gave a harsh comment to a student, the impact might last for his or her whole life. Maybe not all students, some are easy going but some are sensitive. So I need to be careful and wise. The impact I give can be permanent. I am asking myself, "Will it build the students up or destroy them?"

JH2 also shared a similar intention by saying, "from the Christian faith perspective I see my calling as a teacher to give certain impacts." In a similar fashion, HS1 pointed out his unique being as a teacher at a state university had double impacts.

> I am a Christian as well as Chinese. In this institution, it means I am a double minority. I have to show them that I have an additional value to make an impact on the students. To the Muslim students, I can change their negative perceptions about Chinese and Christians. To Chinese Christians that they can be accepted here, as proof there is a Chinese Christian faculty in this institution.

Although considering herself as a junior faculty member, YP2 stated confidently, "I try my best to make a positive impact on the young generation, although my role is only a small part because my academic rank is still low, whatever I can do I will do my best." Another similar expression was also shared by LI1: "It is always my prayer that wherever the Lord puts me, I can make an impact. It does not have to be big [impact], but at least people would feel peace and [be] motivated to be better."

Educating Future Leaders and Agents of Change

Some participants in this study described their faith-informed purpose and meaning of teaching to educate the next generation of leaders and agents of change. Three participants quoted the phrase "students today, leaders tomorrow" to describe their point (CS1, EW2, CS3). For example, CS1 said, "I remember Perkantas' motto – students today, leaders tomorrow. It means that students I teach today, later when they graduate and go back to their regions they will be leaders." Likewise, EW2 and CS3 also used the motto to express their vision to build the nation by educating students to be future leaders.

A similar intent to prepare students to be future leaders is also expressed by DC2: "I am called to be a faculty teaching in higher education . . . to educate students who one day will be business leaders or a president maybe, who will lead many people. Thus, when I teach, I serve, I demonstrate dedication to my Christian faith in my work and they [students] will see." Another participant, EW2, hoped that her students would not just become any leaders but leaders who would bring positive changes to society. Thus, she said, "I want my students to change [their mindset]. Many of them think that study is just for the sake of a degree, graduate and then get married. That's all? No, I want them to be agents of change, regardless of their religious backgrounds." Likewise, BS1 expressed his deep concern about the corruption and religious intolerance in Indonesia and saw the need to educate future ethical leaders:

> I see the need to educate students to be future leaders with integrity. Corruption is rampant in Indonesia. It has been decreasing but it is still an enormous problem. If they were not caught, they would not return the money. This is not integrity. Also, why are people from different faiths still harassing each other? Why did children shout and chant "kill Ahok,[1] kill Ahok"? Why are shaking hands or greeting Christians with "Merry Christmas" considered *haram*? There are so many questions related to social problems. Students, especially those graduated from this institution, will be future leaders. Intellectually, they lack nothing, but for me, I think they need non-cognitive elements. If we do nothing, this institution will give nothing to build this nation. It sounds bombastic when I say "building a nation's character" but the fact is that we need that.

Helping Students in Their Character Development and Personal Growth

A number of participants also emphasize an intention to help their students in character development and personal growth (e.g. CS3, AS1, JS2, JA2). The key terms often used by these participants is "change" or "transformation." For example, CS3 showed serious concern about developing students' character when he said:

> Character building has become my focus. I feel satisfied and realize that my labor is not in vain when I see my students change. On his graduation day, I remembered how one student used to be stubborn. I gave him a call and he shared about his faith now and how he brought his family to Christ . . . So, one of my roles

---

1. Ahok, whose full name is Basuki Tjahaja Purnama, was Jakarta's first Chinese Christian governor (2012–2017). He was sentenced to two years in jail for blasphemy by referencing a verse from the Qur'an when addressing his voters about non-Muslim leaders.

is to educate the younger generation to have good character. I really want to see alumni of this institution love God through their profession, particularly in the field of accounting, being knowledgeable is not enough . . ., having integrity is important.

AS1, a faculty teaching physics at a state university, also expressed similar care for character formation by weaving it together to address the students' spiritual needs. He believed that character change began from within when he said:

> I see that graduates play an important role in society. So I think it would be better, especially for Christian students, not just to bring their skills out. Skills without faith would bring damage to society. Thus some of my colleagues and I feel the need to build the students from within. In my understanding this would happen when the students accept Jesus and become born again; then the character would change from within.

A similar intent of educating students for spiritual formation was also shared by JS2 who stated:

> I want to see a transformation in the life of my students who are like caterpillars, coming out from their cocoons and turning into beautiful butterflies. I meet some of my former students; praise the Lord, many of them are successful, not in terms of their positions but in their walk with the Lord. It is God's providence that they remain faithful to God although many of them have become directors or managers . . . For me, education is important, namely to educate each student to become more like Jesus.

Another participant, JA2 expressed his central role as the faculty member teaching psychology to walk beside his students in the process of finding who they are. He explained the importance of helping students' personal growth by stating: "College students are young people who easily fall into conformity by listening to what other people consider valuable. They just go with the flow, busy with various activities, like a whirlpool, [they] do not take time for self-reflection or ask questions: Who am I? Where am I going? Where do I come from?" He added, "Faith shapes how I teach students in understanding the essence of self. Because as long as I am in my teaching journey, I think the most important part is helping students to become themselves and understand their 'big' role in this world."

Faith Provides Moral and Ethical Guidance

Another outstanding theme participants describe as one of the influences of faith in their teaching vocation is providing a moral and ethical compass to carry out their tasks. For these participants, Christian faith helps maintain their personal integrity and professional ethics against corruption and abuse of power, and being honest in money matters.

EW2, a senior and well-respected faculty member, was often nominated to be a representative by her department for television interviews. However, as a Christian and a psychologist by training, EW2 responded:

> I think I am not a person who loves to appear in front of the crowd. Actually, I do not like to be in the spotlight . . . especially if the TV interview is not related to my [academic] background. I do not want it but some of my colleagues say, "Take it, just give them any answers." I think, there is an ethical code in my profession as a psychologist. If I give information that is not in line with my academic discipline then I would have violated my professional code of ethics.

DA1 and ET2 both expressed that faith helped maintain their commitment to integrity and anti-bribery practices. DA1 stated, "Faith keeps me away from bribery, from taking or asking for bribes from students, and this is a prevalent issue. I experienced several times when students tried to approach me with bribes." Similarly, ET2, who assumed a leadership position in addition to her teaching role, explained:

> People see my life that I do not compromise. Like here too, education is not all-clean, it has dirty practices. Some of my colleagues said, "Ah, you are tough, you do not invite us to join the projects because you are honest. You are only fit for teaching." I am challenged but I know that God has led me to this situation. I am pressed from above and below. I am just six months assuming this leadership position. The previous leader was fired because of moral issues. This is a tough working condition because people have been used to the old practices.

In the case of DS1, the unethical problems she faced at her workplace were not just related to money matters, but also about misusing working hours. DS1 described her working environment where "civil servants are known for their laziness." However, as a Christian, DS1 expressed that faith helped her resist conformity, and instead, to be honest, and productive with her working hours and responsibility. DS1 firmly said:

> My responsibility is not to my boss or government, but to God. So, my motivation is different from others while I do my service as a lecturer. Civil servants in Indonesia cannot be fired and it is difficult to be reprimanded, so most of them take the job casually. But for me as a believer, again my responsibility is to God and that reminds me that once I was entrusted only with one course, but I used my time to do research.

Another response relating to faith as a moral and ethical compass is shared by WU3. For WU3, faith has guided her to use her power as a faculty member carefully and responsibly. Recognizing that abuses of power still continued in her institution since she was a college student, WU3 asserted, "I know there are many temptations for a lecturer. One of them is playing with the students' grades. This is an arbitrary action toward the students. Yes, we have the authority. But for me personally as a believer, I understand that I am here as a servant of God . . . that means I have to follow Christian values: integrity, honesty, and fairness. I treat each of my students equally regardless of their race or religious backgrounds." WU3 acknowledged that keeping integrity intact was not easy, but she said, "I am trying and learning to be a person of integrity. I know it is hard, even until this moment, I am still learning to be a role model for my students."

Other moral and ethical challenges for some participants in this study are related to money matters, particularly in the case of how to use and report research grants. For these participants, faith provides an inner compass to help decide and do what is ethical and moral in the situation. RS1 shared her experience saying, "I once received a research grant, 10 million Indonesia Rupiah. There were remaining funds after I finished my research and I wanted to return it. They said I could not return it, rather they asked me to go to any stores to ask for a blank receipt and write down any items as if I have purchased them. I knew that it was a dishonest practice. Since then, I decided

I would not join the research grant program." DY2 also expressed a similar experience with her research grant. She explained:

> I think the system is forcing us to cheat in that if I receive a grant I must use it up, if not I cannot [get] another grant in the future... For example, I wrote in the proposal that I needed to buy a camera but then in practice, I needed a handy-cam. I thought this should be fine as long as I was responsible for the money. I could show them the receipt. But strangely, in Indonesia, they did not read the results of my research instead they read the financial report and asked why I changed a camera to a handy-cam and et cetera. Sometimes, they did not approve of this kind of report and as a result, I must return all the research money. But because I have purchased the handy-cam, so my colleagues who were also in the team, suggested that I just asked the store cashier to write down "camera" instead of "handy-cam." They argued that as long as we were honest in using the money, playing around with the report was okay. This kind of practice and bureaucracy makes me struggle.

Faith Gives a Strong Work Ethos

Another major theme participants describe as the impact of faith on their vocation is a strong working ethos. Most of these participants recognize that faith permeates their being as Christian faculty members who are: (1) highly committed to their work; (2) consistent and persistent; (3) willing to give sacrificially; and (4) caring about their institutions and beyond.

Highly Committed Workers

Many participants in this study demonstrate a high commitment to their vocation. This commitment is expressed through their work ethic: "to give the best," to be hardworking, and to be disciplined and responsible faculty members.

"To Give the Best"

Participants, for example, TM1, YP2, and CS3 claim that faith makes them "to give the best" in their teaching vocation. TM1 asserted, "Definitely faith has an influence . . . in how I give the best in teaching, communicating, and serving the students . . ., including serving my colleagues. The Word of God teaches us that we should work hard, serve others, and such things." YP2 also recognized the influence of faith on her work attitude, saying: "Faith helps me understand that I am a living sacrifice. Because I am a living sacrifice, then I must give my best, not my worst. So I try to be a better faculty member. I keep learning, not out of curiosity, but I want to give my life as the best offering to God." For CS3, giving the best means setting a high bar for him to work hard and exceed the expectations as he described below:

> I have always been reminded that research, service, and teaching need to meet an excellent standard . . . I believe we as Christians have to be different. Why? Because we are already redeemed, and our life purpose is clear. Therefore when we teach, do research and community service, or interact with students, we must be different from unbelievers. Is it easy? No, it is not easy. Suppose the dean asks the faculty to do research and publish it in an international journal. For me, I must try my best not to be a stumbling block so that by the end of the semester my name is announced as a faculty member who has not published in an international journal. Maybe other faculty would not do it but I will try to meet the standard. And when I do research, I will not do it carelessly, including in teaching, 12 out of 14 meetings are okay but I will always teach 14 meetings.

Hard Working Faculty Member

A number of participants express that faith encourages them to be hard-working employers by putting extra in working hours beyond what is expected (EP1, EW2, ET2). EP1, a teaching faculty member, a lab coordinator, and a graduate program director at a state university, expressed, "All work that I can do on my own, I take them home. Work such as teaching preparation and grading student exams. But during office hours, I give all my time to the students. I try to never reject any students who want to meet me for whatever reason." A similar expression was also shared by EW2, who assumed dual roles of both faculty member and leader at a private non-faith based university, saying: "I work until night. Even I often bring my teaching and office work home because some of those works are impossible to be finished in an office room. I usually work until 5:00 or 6:00 p.m., but it doesn't finish. I must stop and go home to take care of my children first. After that, I open my laptop and continue my work." Likewise, ET2 described a similar work behavior by saying: "I work from morning until night because God has taught me. My paradigm is that it is a ministry. Ministry does not have to be at a church but it can be anywhere, including in the marketplace. So people can see Christ in me – that it is not by my strength that I can work hard."

Disciplined and Responsible Workers

Another distinctive faith-shaped work behavior described by the participants is being disciplined and responsible workers (e.g. LI1, HS1, CS3, DA1, PK3). LI1expressed:

> What can I do to glorify God? I can read the Bible, listen to sermons, and read Christian books. But I think I can do a simple thing, that is doing my job as a faculty [member] responsibly. I do not need to look at my honorarium, but finish my work on time. [Faith] makes me a more responsible person . . . I come to class on time. I teach seriously and that means I teach to help them understand. This is always my prayer and I always do it. So I won't take teaching carelessly, because I feel if I do it fullheartedly, God is pleased. This includes grading students' papers and exams that maybe many people do not care about, but I know God is pleased if I do it seriously. Although sometimes I feel tired and fail, O God forgives me, I won't do it again. Life is a struggle.

HS1 expressed a similar work attitude saying: "I am very grateful that I did join the Christian student fellowship on campus while I was a college student. From there, I gained a lot of knowledge and my faith was very much strengthened. After graduation, I became a lecturer. I try to put into practice . . ., what I have learned in concrete ways. I do what is assigned to me by the department, I teach responsibly, I come to the class on time and finish on time." Another participant, PK3 also expressed a similar work ethic: "Faith for me is not preaching the gospel in front of the class, but I do my job as well as possible so it would benefit my students. Otherwise, I would have stolen their rights."

Consistent and Persistent Workers

Another trait that participants demonstrate as a faith-shaped work ethos is being consistent and persistent workers. A number of participants express that faith gives them the inner strength to stay focused on their teaching vocation and remain productive despite working under a challenging environment (e.g. DS1, CS1, MP1, EW2). DS1 experienced a dramatic change in her teaching workload under new leadership in her department. Responding to this situation, DS1 said:

> I remain consistent and persistent. There was a time some of my colleagues and I were only assigned only one course. We could take a long sleep at home because it was only one class per semester. However, precisely that incident made me think about doing research . . . Looking back, I feel grateful because God has designed a different plan. During that incident, a colleague of mine just finished her doctoral study from Australia. She was a Christian faculty too and highly active in research. I was in the field of R.O. [Research Operation] and she asked me to co-research with her about the graph theory . . . Well, because I was given only 3 credit teaching hours per semester, I started to be involved in research and accepting many senior students to help with their research projects.

DS1 added that her consistent and persistent work attitude has brought a favorable result in which her collaborative work became the first research article from her department that ever made to an international journal publication. Further, DS1 said"

> I was surprised and grateful because this became our "additional values." Now, with the change of leadership and new rules in our department, the international publication is a requirement for those who want to be a senior faculty member . . . Many faculty members are against this rule include those who hold doctoral degrees. I was promoted as a senior faculty although I was not holding a doctoral degree. This case was used by one honorable

professor from my department to rebuke them saying, "Why are you against this new rule? Look at one of our faculty members who only hold a master's degree but she can publish in an international journal. What is your problem that you, doctoral graduates, cannot do the same?

Another participant, CS1, expressed his concern that many faculty members were competing to get a research grant to get extra income and upgrade their academic ranks. Alarmed by this situation, CS1 found that his faith has guarded him against the distractions and helped him to stay focused on his priority of work. He said, "Today, many faculty members prioritize research over teaching. For me, students are my first priority and research comes after that." This attitude towards work has led his colleagues and staff at his department to comment, "Sir, you are a consistent person." MP1, a faculty teaching microbiology at a state medical school, also expressed a positive attitude despite working in an unfavorable environment, saying:

> During lab practicum, many lecturers only come and go. They do not teach or guide the students. After signing the attendance record, they go home. They do not make time for questions or discussions. On the other hand, students today are demanding but show little responsibility. Maybe that's why the lecturers are angry with them. Also, when we meet students on the street, especially medical students entering clinical training, they just walk by without greeting us, and that hurts many lecturers. Some lecturers wonder why we should teach them seriously if once they become doctors they show no appreciation to us. But as for me, I remain [consistent]. If I have to be stern to my students then I will be stern, and when I teach them, I will teach seriously.

Sacrificial Giving Workers

The third distinctive work ethos embodied by many Christian faculty members in this study is self-sacrificial giving (e.g. CS1, TM1, LI1, EP1, AS1, DS1, CS3). These participants possess a dedication that leads them to give beyond what is expected to meet the need of the students. In addition to their trilogy tasks, these participants who mostly teach at state universities also volunteer their time and energy to teach Christian religious education, be involved in campus ministry, or both.

Teaching Christian religious education classes

Some participants who teach at state universities mentioned religious education is a core subject for all freshmen, but the institutions do not always provide faculty to teach this subject, especially for students from religious minorities, which include Catholicism and Protestantism. To fill the need, these participants, though they have no formal theological training, step up and take up the job voluntarily. For example, CS1, a faculty member with disciplinary expertise in fisheries science, but who felt compelled to teach Christian religious education, explained:

> Here, I also am involved in teaching a Christian religion class. I am an autodidact in studying the Bible. I was trained on how to do a Bible study since I was a college student. In the near future, I will be entrusted as the team coordinator of this course. There is no salary for teaching a Christian religion class. The institution does not accept any lecturers from outside to teach the course, but there are many Christian students here. So we as Christian faculty take the initiative to teach the course.

Similarly, driven by the need and desire to serve the students, LI, whose academic discipline was land resources management, decided to teach Christian religious studies in addition to her main job. She said:

> Our institution does not recruit or open a vacancy for a lecturer with this specialty; instead, it invites the existing lecturers to teach the courses. Not all Christian lecturers are willing to take this extra job, so it is offered to those who want to . . . I went home and prayed, "Lord, is this you want me to do?" I have never taught religious education before, but I also asked what else I could give . . . So, I decided to teach the class up till now. I do it without thinking about the honorarium. This is a voluntary job, purely to serve [the students].

AS1, a professor of physics at a state university, also expressed a similar sentiment saying, "Since I was a college student I have been active in

Navigators and then in 2010 there was a need for Christian lecturers to teach Christian religious education. I felt called to teach the class, so in 2011 I started to teach a Christian religious education class."

The story of EP1 is a bit different from the aforementioned participants. Inspired by her professor's exemplary life when she was a college student, EP1 right away volunteered to teach a Christian religious education class when she was accepted as a faculty at the department of agronomy and horticulture. Excitedly she expressed:

> Working here is practicing my faith in my work. When I applied to become a lecturer here, I had seen how Mr. Chambers, a missionary and a faculty teaching geology, served in campus ministry. To his teaching assistants in Christian religious education classes, he always emphasized that this ministry was very important and strategic. He said that it was a privilege that we could serve students from all over Indonesia who came here to study, and we were given a full semester to nurture them spiritually. The institution only gives one semester for this class, and further spiritual formation is through student fellowship.

Because of this urgent need and strategic ministry, she further said, "Therefore, we want to use this opportunity as well as possible, to teach the students about the importance of keeping their faith. So by next semester when they do not have the religious education class anymore, they can keep their faith and remain strong in the midst of the challenging campus atmosphere."

Involvement in campus ministry

A sacrificial-giving attitude is also reflected in the way participants take extra time and effort to supervise or mentor on-campus ministry activities. For example, TM1 described his involvement in student ministry saying, "Besides my trilogy duties, I also have additional roles such as supervising the Christian student fellowship. This unit of activity is official and registered by the institution. This additional role is voluntary. EP1 also shared a similar passion to serve the students by putting in extra hours and opening her house for the students to gather. She explained, "I am helping the student ministry by opening my house as wide as possible for students holding the fellowship as well as other faith-building activities." Likewise, CS3 voluntarily took additional responsibilities by leading a discipleship group for the students. He excitedly explained:

> Faith and character building has become my focus. So, I am involved in supervising a Christian student fellowship even though it is outside of my responsibility as a lecturer. But on this campus, I still have some freedom that I can manage to finish my tasks and have some free time to meet the students, such as leading a small group. I purposely suggest mentoring students outside my department in order to avoid subjectivity in case one day the students are going to take my class.

For CS3, his role as a mentor to help his students' faith formation continued after their graduation. He explained:

> I am longing to see the alumni remain strong in their faith. So during the graduation ceremony, I always remind them that if any alumni stray from the faith, let us correct each other. So, in the last three years, we started a small group for married couples; they are all alumni from my institution and live nearby my house. Now we have two groups, not many people, just about six families who meet monthly. Certainly, our topics now are about family-building and parenting.

Caring about Their Institutions

Another excellent work ethos demonstrated by many participants in this study is caring about their departments and institutions. These participants are not simply focused on day-to-day tasks, but also show a deep concern for their institutions by being actively involved in: (1) improving university performance; (2) achieving institutional values, vision, and mission; (3) sharing ways to improve their institutions; (4) mentoring prospective Christian faculty and leaders; and (5) fostering inter-faith harmony.

Improving university performance

One of the tangible ways the participants show their ownership and care for their institutions is to seek ways to improve their institutions' performance through academic research and publication. For example, DS1, who taught at a state university expressed her concern, saying, "We are still far behind Malaysia, and other neighboring countries. One indicator to improve the university ranking is through networking and publication at the international level. Not long ago, I found that the rank of my institution went up a bit. So in the near future, I see these two things which I can do: publishing my research papers in international journals and building international networking." In the same way, DC2, who taught at a non-faith-based university expressed a strong worker-owner attitude to improve his institution's reputation through research and publication. He said:

> I see how my existence here can bring a positive impact on my department and help improve my institution's performance. I try my best to do research that can be published in national and international journals. This is one way to increase my institution's performance. I always prioritize the interests of my department or institution, because it is like a big ship; if the ship is collapsed then we are all collapsed. I know that not many people think that way. Most people think about themselves as the most important ones.

Likewise, PK3, who taught at a Christian university also described her ownership and contribution to her institution by stating: "I want to give something that is valuable. At least I can participate in building a research atmosphere in this institution. I am one of the pioneers who started research focusing on community service. I think through this research, at least the students get to know what research is." Another participant, WU3, also expressed a similar desire to improve her institution's reputation by saying: "In the beginning, I was not proud to be a member of this institution, but now I have this attitude: I want to make this institution to be the best, at least in Jakarta and then at national and international level. That is my hope."

Achieving institutional values, vision, and mission

A number of participants, particularly those who taught at Christian universities, were concerned about the gaps between their institutional vision-mission statements and practices. Instead of criticizing, these participants showed their strong work ethos by positioning themselves as agents to bridge the gaps (WU3, CH3, SW3). For example, WU3 saw the disparity of values and practices within her institution by asserting: "Our student body is universal, not just one type of student; we have Muslim students too. We bear a capital C as a Christian university, but C does not manifest clearly in our daily activities as a "civitas academica." Concerned with this reality, WU3 tried to bridge the gaps by incorporating Christian values into her own teaching, saying:

> I feel challenged, standing in between [the institution and students]. Sometimes I feel myself moving back and forth, seeking ways to manifest the capital C, values that we believe as Christians. It is not enough to educate students with knowledge alone, but they also need values such as honesty, gratitude, etcetera. I am so eager to develop gratitude, honesty, justice, and integrity among my colleagues and students. I want students really to feel the atmosphere and take the values and pass them on.

SW3 also expressed a similar concern and hope to improve the inconsistency between the facts she found in daily practices and the ideals her institution tried to achieve. She described:

> I was surprised to find that many students in this Christian university were from Chinese and middle and upper-class backgrounds. I was educated in public schools since I was young. I was shocked to see the manner of these students here was much lower than the students in public schools, maybe because they were children of rich families. I hope my institution can be an institution of integrity, light, and salt, not a stumbling block, but can be a blessing for the society. I hope others can see us as followers of Christ through our lives. This is our calling, thus, I will start with myself by sowing the seeds of Christian values to my students.

Another participant, CH3, expressed a high appreciation for his institution's vision-mission statement but he was concerned that little understanding of the statement might lead to silos among departments and faculty members. He expressed his concern and hope for change in his institution as follows:

> I observe there is one weakness in my department. Each semester we have two meetings. I hope there will be a team of research

and development that will do research and give suggestions to improve each study program. I hope the dean and faculty members who attend the meeting from all ten study programs can work together in harmony... If not, I am afraid we will produce incompetent graduates... I hope every one of us who works here understands the vision and mission of our institution which is an excellent statement but in the application, we tend to forget and walk by ourselves.

Sharing ways to improve their institutions

A few of the participants in this study express care for their institutions by looking for and sharing ways to improve their working environment and teaching quality. EW2, a faculty teaching at a private non-faith based university, was a dedicated and hardworking faculty member who often gave extra working hours beyond what was expected. However, the institution also required her and her colleagues to work on Sundays, particularly to take care of the university-entrance exams for prospective students. Thinking this policy would not be healthy for her and the institution as a whole, she took courage to speak up and proposed an alternative. She reported:

> I spoke to the head of my department and colleagues. I said that we should have more faith in our institution. If possible do not make any event on Sundays. Please do not schedule the entrance exams on Sundays. I say honestly that I will not come because Sunday is a day for worship. We should not be afraid as if we will not gain any profits . . . I propose to them why not use Saturday and if we have other events on that day we can reschedule them.

Another participant, CH1, after returning from graduate study abroad found that the teaching resources used by most faculty members at his department were the same old material as when he was a college student. Instead of criticizing, he was actively sharing ways to improve the quality of teaching by stating:

> I subscribe to several academic journals, so I always follow the research updates. I know the frontier research in my field. If I didn't do it, I would be left far behind. This is one thing I do to

motivate my students as well as my colleagues. I also join the faculty WhatsApp group, so I can send any research updates to my colleagues. For example, the old classification for tuna fish is the Scombridae family, but now it's in a different family. Well, we can see that knowledge keeps progressing thus we should be sensitive.

Mentoring prospective Christian faculty and leaders

Some participants, especially those who taught at the state and non-faith-based universities, expressed their concerns about the continuity and regeneration of Christian faculty and leaders in their respective institutions (e.g. CH1, RT1, DC2, LS3). Responding to these concerns, CH1 made an effort to share the need, pray, and mentor potential students. He explained, "I hope in the future many Christian students would be admitted to this institution because they are the light. Our world is getting darker. I hope and pray that there would be Christian students who seriously consider being a faculty member here." Besides praying, CS1 also took an active approach to share the need when he said:

> Yesterday, I met a female Christian student. She is a Christian, Chinese, smart, and active in student ministry. I am praying for her that she would be willing to be a lecturer and I will mentor her because it is impossible for a Muslim professor to mentor a Christian . . . Here, the process of being a faculty member is by becoming an assistant lecturer first. Now, the student is a sophomore, she is doing well academically and spiritually. Yesterday, I shared with her about the need and life calling, and she said that she would think and pray about it.

RT1, who would retire in the next five years, expressed a similar concern and took steps to share the need and persuade young Christian intellectuals to consider a vocation in higher education, especially at a state university. Of Christian students who were taking his class, he said, "I had a chance to talk to my students, undergraduate and graduate students. I hope at least 30 percent of them would consider teaching but from a total of 30 Christian students, only one or two of them were willing. In my department, there are only three full professors and one of them just passed away. So, this will be a crisis. I need to ask for God's grace only."

In addition, RT1, who was also a senior academic leader in his institution, encouraged young Christian faculty to become leaders by saying: "I also try to encourage Christian faculty to be leaders in order to give a wider influence. I try to share with some Christian faculty here and encourage those who have leadership potentials to extend their teaching career because we need leaders who possess values and characters. This state institution has a big name but how many faculty here are seriously knowledgeable and high in their moral values? I don't know."

DC2, who taught at a private non-faith based university, was alarmed by the increased numbers of Muslim faculty. He responded by saying, "I am actively seeking alumni to become faculty members here, especially those who are Christians. The founder of this university was Chinese and this institution accepted a majority of Chinese students because of some historical-political reasons at that time. Until now we do not have a significant challenge yet because our previous rector was a Javanese but he was a Catholic."

Fostering interreligious harmony

Some participants in this study also described a genuine concern about the interreligious relationship among the students and faculty (e.g. BS1, DA1, RS1, ET2, RM2). Although Christian faculty members were a minority, especially those who taught at the state and non-faith based universities, they took the initiative to foster good interfaith relationships through research partnerships and attending religious events. For example, BS1, a senior faculty member at a state university, initiated a research partnership with Muslim colleagues saying:

> I have a research partnership with faculty from another department. Fortunately, seven or eight of these faculty members were my former students who had their research projects under my advising, either when they were in undergraduate or graduate studies ... It is interesting to note that all the lecturers in this department are Sundanese who start and close their activities with prayer recitations. On the one side, I do the research with

them but on the other side, I have a chance to build a friendship with my Sundanese Muslim friends.

DA1, who also found himself as a minority among the faculty members at a state university, took a proactive approach to build a relationship with his majority of Muslim colleagues rather than let himself be isolated. He explained:

> During the plenary meeting, I could see that 90 percent of the female faculty members were wearing hijabs and only a few were Christians . . . There is a tendency among the faculty to group with those who are similar to them. I try my best to be wise, to get along with the majority of Muslim colleagues. The more I distanced myself, the more they would not understand us. So, during Ramadan month, I attended their fast-breaking events to show them that I was not allergic to their faith.

ET2 is a rare case, a Christian faculty who was elected to be a program director in a majority Muslim working environment. Although it was challenging, as a leader, ET2 took serious efforts to build good interfaith relationships among her colleagues as well as students. She explained:

> It is a real challenge. In this office, the all-female staff is wearing hijabs except me. When we have gatherings, sometimes they liked to say, "Wow, only Mrs. [ET2] who doesn't wear a hijab!" I just smiled. Then sometimes they also said, "Can we use your office room for *salat* (prayers)?" I said to them, "Just go ahead, no problem with me." I also attend the gathering to break the Ramadan fast and because I was their leader they asked me to give a message. For example, during the fast-breaking yesterday, I said that success did not come from one's position, wealth, and so on and so forth. I didn't realize that some of the students paid attention to it.

RM2 also expressed a similar caring attitude for his institution by taking a proactive approach to creating interreligious harmony. He asserted, "I want to show them that I am not a hater. For example, yesterday we just had a gathering for breaking the fast, and I came and helped them. In this institution, we encourage our students to help each other. If Muslims have events, Christians should help and vice versa."

Faith Gives Strength in the Face of Adversity

The fifth theme participants describe as one of the major influences of faith in their teaching vocation is the inner strength to face and overcome challenges. The first part of this section presents major challenges facing Christian faculty, which can be categorized as institutional, personal, and student-related issues. The second part focuses on how they respond to the challenges. Instead of despair or antipathy, the participants demonstrated a positive attitude and testified that in the face of adversity faith gave them the strength to endure, to hope, and to find possible solutions.

Institutional Related Challenges

Participants in this study identified several major institutional related issues that included: discrimination, radicalism, unethical practices, lack of resources, difficult working environment, peer social interaction, navigating faith in a pluralistic workplace, and institutional identity crisis.

Ethnoreligious discrimination

"Religious discrimination is very real in Indonesia," said DS1. This issue of discrimination was most frequently cited by participants who taught at state universities (e.g. DS1, HS1, TM1, AS1, MP1, CS1) and particularly Muslim-dominant non-faith-based universities (e.g. YP2, ET2, KC2). The followings are descriptions of the participants' experiences of ethnoreligious discrimination and its impact on faculty hiring, career development, and access to campus facilities.

"Double minority." Besides religious discrimination, some participants who described themselves as "double minority" also experienced racial discrimination. For example, CS1, who taught at a predominantly Muslim-majority state university, explained:

> I am a double minority, a Batakese and a Christian. During my novice year of teaching, I could feel the way they treated me; it's kind of different. But this challenge also comes with opportunity, which means I can show them that Christians are not like the

> stereotypes they have in mind. Also, the students can evaluate me. From there, I hope they would think twice if they want to push me out. So I am like the kind of person they hate but also love because I am still needed by the institution . . . I think that God is working through all this process.

HS1 shared similarly, saying, "I am a Chinese Christian which is also known as a double minority here in this university. But I want to show them that I have additional values and give a positive impact on all students."

Faculty hiring and career mobility impediment. Some participants expressed that ethnoreligious discrimination had affected their career mobility negatively. TM1, a senior faculty member who had taught for about thirty years at a state university, explained, "There are various impacts of discrimination in this institution, including the opportunity for Christian faculty to become heads of departments or other kinds of leadership positions is very small. Such things are common because they have a belief that Muslims should not be led by non-Muslims, such as in the case of Ahok." TM1 further explained that religious discrimination also created an immense barrier for hiring professionally qualified faculty.

> The opportunity to be a lecturer in this institution is also very difficult while most senior lecturers here are nearing their retirement. If this discrimination continues, it would be difficult to have a successor. For example, there was a young Christian faculty [member] who fought hard to get into this institution. He was hired as an adjunct lecturer for many years until later he became a fulltime lecturer. He almost gave up several times. He's married with children and struggling to provide for his family with such a small salary and uncertain future. The challenge is real.

Similar religious discrimination also shared by AS1 when he went through a series of procedures for a promotion to be a full professor. Carefully he explained:

> My career promotion was slow here as compared to my colleagues here. I have been in the process of promotion to be a full professor since 2011 but until now there is no news yet. My

colleague, we are at the same level, but he is chosen because he is a Muslim. They asked me whether I still wanted to pursue it. I said, "It's up to you, sir." From this case, I observe that there is a factor of religious discrimination . . . I've fulfilled all the qualifications. Sadly, although this is a national university the issues of race and religion still exist.

In contrast to most participants who taught at a state university, BS1, a senior and double minority faculty who has taught for about thirty-one years, expressed, "I am Christian and a Chinese descendant but thankfully I do not experience any discrimination. I have a good friendship with those from different racial and religious backgrounds." However, BS1 recognized that the issue of discrimination was real for many of his Christian colleagues who taught at other state universities. He then continued by relating a discrimination issue faced by one of his friends who taught at a particular state university that has been penetrated deeply by a radical Islamist movement.

Unequal access to campus facilities. One participant expressed that religious discrimination also affected access to campus facilities for religious minority students. EP1 explained, "Until now I and some Christian faculty are still hoping to find an adequate place for the student fellowship. We hope for equal access to use the facilities as they give to the Muslim students, such as a mosque on campus and a secretariat room for their spiritual activities. What we ask is permission to use a bigger room for weekly worship but the rector says no."

Religious radicalism

The second major challenge cited by many participants is religious radicalism in higher education (e.g. EP1, DS1, TM1, HS1, BW1, MC2, JH2). "Radicalism is not a new issue," DS1 said, "It has existed long ago but recently it has been growing and becoming a serious challenge for universities." The participants expressed serious concern about the destructive impacts of radicalism on the students, religious minority faculty members, the institutions, and the nation as a whole. It seems from all types of tertiary institutions, the infiltration and impacts of radicalism in state universities are much deeper and wider than non-faith based and Christian universities.

BW1, who taught at a state university, asserted that the radical Islamic movement is aimed at college students and found its way to campus through student religious gatherings that were not well supervised by the authorities. He said, "I observe that radicalism enters campus using various doors. Mostly they use the mosques (on campus), the religious gatherings where the preachers spread their radical teachings. So it is uncontrollable. I do not see any faculty yet but mostly the students who have been influenced by these teachings." HS1, who taught at a state university, also observed that the campus has become a hotbed of Islamic extremism and posed a serious threat to the students. Cautiously he said:

> With the condition of Indonesia in the last two years, I am worried that students here, especially students in this department, would be easily influenced by radical Islamic teaching. This has infiltrated at the *mushalla*[2] level. Most speakers invited for their gatherings were from the radical Islamists. I hope the head of my department would be a moderate Muslim, so he could protect new students from getting into these radical teachings.

HS1 described further his concern about the negative impacts of radicalism on faculty and his institution saying:

> The radical Muslims do not like Christians. These Muslims support the *caliphate;* even some of my colleagues also support the Islamic caliphate. I am worried about the future of this department because many students and faculty have bought this idea. Not just this department but I am also worried about other departments, the institution as a whole. I see this institution is not brave enough to defend Pancasila[3] as our main national ideology.

Another participant, EP1 also expressed a similar tension among faculty members caused by the radicalism on campus:

> The tension is much more obvious on social media. We have a WhatsApp group so we can see an individual's views that are explicitly written on WA. Sometimes they use Arabic scripts

---

2. A room for prayer or a place of gathering on campus for Muslim students.

3. A national ideology which consists of five principles: (1) belief in one supreme God; (2) just and civilized society; (3) the unity of Indonesia; (4) democracy guided by the wisdom through the discussions and agreements of the representatives of the people; and (5) social justice for all Indonesians.

> and I can't read them. I really feel excluded as if I am nobody and my existence is not acknowledged. Especially during the Jakarta's governor election, the messages posted over the WA groups were biased and violent. It made me angry. Rather than sinning against God and having negative thinking about my colleagues, I decided to quit the group.

Worse still, EP1 recalled an incident that has alarmed the whole nation about how deeply radicalism has penetrated into higher education. This incident involved a massive group of students from all over Indonesia at a religious conference organized by the Muslim student body of her institution to pledge their allegiance to the Islamic caliphate. EP1 explained, "Actually the rector knew about this event, but somehow at the closing of the event the students made a pledge that they would be loyal to the caliphate. It's really happened and it's recorded in the video. Listening to their pledge made me feel horrified, really horrified, how deeply this institution has been infiltrated by the radicalism." Strongly rooted in her faith, EP1 responded to the situation by saying, "OK God, into this world you have sent us. I have no worry for myself, my future, and my career." However, what she worried about was that "students started to choose not to be supervised by Christian faculty for research projects."

The challenge of radicalism facing higher education is also told by participants teaching at non-faith based universities. MC2 observed radicalism found its way into campus through students' activities and sharpened the existing divisions between ethnoreligious groups among the students as well as the faculty members.

> Lately, I saw HTI[4] had started penetrating into the campus through small group gatherings. Recently, we just found a group of students that related to this movement.
>
> We also monitor their social media to find out who are the *ustazs* (preachers) they invite to preach on campus. This campus was originally founded by some Chinese but now the campus has become so racist.

---

4. HTI (*Hizbut Tahrir of Indonesia*) is a transnational Islamist organization that aims to re-establish the Islamic caliphate state.

In the midst of this working climate in her institution, MC2 did not let the radicalism and division distract her focus and responsibility as a Christian faculty. Instead, she said, "Let us prove it. It doesn't matter which religion you are from, your faith will not be useful if you are not a professional lecturer. Do not talk about religion but prove yourself that you are a good worker, and then your faith will talk."

Another participant, JA2, who also taught at a non-faith-based university, stated that he found no indication yet that radicalism has penetrated into the campus but precautions were needed. He said: "I have heard some news about the students who hid terrorists in their house. I also attended several workshops where the speakers tried to integrate psychology and their radical religious teachings. It could happen here too; thus we need to be careful and take precautionary actions."

CS3, an academic leader and faculty teaching at a Christian university, started to pay closer attention to the possibility of radicalism inside his campus after following the news about the rise of Islamic radicals in Indonesia. Expressing his concern, he said:

> Because of the news about the HTI, I began to survey my students and I found about thirty percent of them are Muslims. Strangely enough that the Muslims become more and more interested in enrolling in this campus, but the Christians become less and less. I take the positive side that this institution is attractive enough for them to study here but I also become cautious that this campus might have become "gray" in our identity. This is a challenge.

Unethical behavior and practices

Another challenge facing the participants is unethical practices in their respective institutions which involve corruption, dishonest leaders, and money related matters. DT3, who taught for nearly four decades at a Christian university, was disappointed by the systemic corruption and dishonest practices in her institution. She said, "Corruption is a great issue. There was a leader [who] took away twenty-six million rupiahs which was quite a large amount of money, but the leaders cut him loose. They said that we were Christians and needed to practice love." She explained that, "On the contrary, when the faculty members asked for a salary raise, the leaders said that our treasures were in heaven, not on earth where moths ate them." DT3 also cited another example which addressed the dishonesty practiced in her department, saying, "The department head asked one of my colleagues to lie about her working hours by putting fictional hours in a letter as he did."

For DY3 and RS1 the unethical practices facing their institutions are related to research grants. For example, RS1 shared a case in her department that might involve a research grant fraud:

> The biggest challenge here is dishonesty such as research grants that make me so angry. One of the faculty members got six grants with each grant worth 250 million rupiahs and the projects were completed in ten months. The person who could do it must be a genius, but it's unbelievable that one faculty received six grants, a total of 1.5 billion rupiahs. If I were the one who did the project it would cost lower than 250 million rupiahs. If it were one or two grants I still would believe it but six grants? Later I found out it was divided among the students. What's the money for? It's shared among them for attending seminars abroad.

RS1 also shared another unethical financial behavior among the institutional leaders which deeply upset her heart, saying: "Another struggle for me is still about money problems. The salary for deans is 60 million rupiahs, which is higher than Governor Ahok's salary. Once, some faculty members from the mathematics department were asked to teach at the engineering department. They paid us 60 million rupiahs. But what's happened? The 30 million rupiahs were shared among the deans and only left 30 million for the faculty. I was really angry."

Negative organizational culture

Some participants in this study expressed negative organizational culture as one of their major challenges, which included unequal and unfair treatment, unreceptiveness to change, and bureaucratic and politicized organizational culture.

PK3 was a biomolecular scientist teaching at a medical school who described the unequal treatment she had as a non-medical degree faculty member:

> In medical school sometimes I do not have the rights like other faculty members who hold MDs. I understand that I can only teach up to third or fourth-semester students because after that they will start their health profession classes. It's logical and it's OK for me. But I feel I am not treated or appreciated as well as the doctors. My challenge is that I want them to realize that medical school also needs pure science. I can show the contributive values of biomedical science to medical education; not to be arrogant but I want to be treated equally.

For ET2, her challenge was working under pressure in a bureaucratic and politicized environment and with unreceptive colleagues. As a Christian faculty and newly appointed academic leader in her department, ET2 described her workplace as follows:

> Because of my ethnicity and religion, it's not easy for people to accept me. Then, my second challenge is that this institution has been an extraordinary bureaucratic and politicized workplace … The bureaucratic culture is severe because we lack good human resources while the old people are difficult to change because they feel comfortable with the old culture. In addition, seniority culture is very intense. Here, your ethnicity and religion dictate your privilege. It is like the feud in the House of Representatives or other political disputes in Indonesia. So, when people say that this institution is a miniature of Indonesia, I think it's true. The representatives said they wanted to serve the people, but they lied; they aimed for money. Likewise, many aged senior leaders here do not want to step down from their positions.

DS1 also described an unfavorable workplace environment when the new department leader played favorites among the faculty members.

> Our previous leader assessed faculty members based on their performance, so the more you performed well, the more teaching responsibilities he would give. So, I got a lot of teaching hours. Many faculty members misunderstood it by thinking the more hours I taught the more money I got, but actually, I was considered trustworthy and nothing had to do with money. On the contrary, under the new leadership, my teaching hours

were reduced to three-credit hours per semester. Now the policy changed, the incentives go parallel with teaching hours. This new leader gives these incentives to his friends or those who close to him. So, besides the religious element, favoritism also plays a role here.

Peer social interaction

A number of participants found peer social interaction at work a challenging issue, particularly being an ethnic and religious minority in a Muslim dominant workplace. HS1 felt unsafe interacting with non-Christian faculty members at his department. He said:

> I need to be careful in my daily interactions. It seems to me that my non-Christian peers are not sincere. I am afraid if I open my self to them, they might use it to hit me. So, I must be careful, sincere like a dove but shrewd like a snake." HS1 added that the infiltration of religious radicalism on campus further segregated the social interactions among faculty as well as students. He said, "Many of them are not willing to mingle, both students and lecturers. Thus, my communication with them is limited to academic matters.

LI1 also described a similar experience of social exclusion from her majority of Muslim colleagues. "It is not easy working here," EP1 said, "because, like many people in this area, they tend to differentiate and excommunicate those who are different from them. This environment makes me feel uncomfortable but also encourages me to be more serious in learning that God is God."

DA1 also found himself in a lonely social world of being an ethnoreligious minority at his department, saying, "In this university, I am a minority and it's rather difficult for me to have a supportive community. For example, every Friday they go for *salat* (prayers); only I alone don't do so. And then, during this fasting month, it's only I who has lunch. If I have a colleague to eat with, it would be better."

Lack of resources

Lack of teaching and learning resources, educational facilities, equipment maintenance skills, and research funding is bringing challenges in the ways of the participants' work and development. Getting suitable teaching materials means helping students learn best, which is a real challenge for MF3 due to the limited availability of educational books written in the Indonesian language. MF3 explained:

> For students to learn better I think they should read before class. So, they have to find books in the library. However, most students cannot read in English. So I scanned a few chapters and provided some guiding questions . . . This semester I have asked a group of people to translate the books; I got them while I was studying at Calvin. Although those are excellent books and translated into *Bahasa Indonesia*, they are still in American cultural contexts. Thus, I need to make another set of guiding questions to help students understand what they are reading. My hope is that one day we can write education books in our own language and cultural contexts.

Lack of institutional support in providing research facilities is another challenge. CS1 expressed that as one of the pioneers of fish larvae science in Indonesia, he intended to continue his research and promote this discipline to the students and academics. Thus, he asked for institutional support to provide basic research equipment, but the response was explained by CS1 as follows: "My proposal was turned down. I think because this microscope was expensive, equivalent to a new SUV car, and we could not get it here but it's to be sent from Japan. This two-volume book was my professor's work. I would like to produce this kind of book with fish in Indonesia . . . So for larval research, I need a special microscope for hand drawing or sketching."

BS1 also expressed his strong interest in research and his concern about engineering research in general in Indonesia, which is not well developed due to lack of research funds and facilities, the ability to maintain research equipment, and industry relevance. In his own words, BS1 asserted:

> We have limited research funds and there should be 10 percent budgeted for facility maintenance. We may be able to purchase new equipment, but we are still weak in maintenance. It's happened that because we could not replace one component of the equipment that though it's new but has to be retired . . . Here, most research findings go to the library. From what I read in

the newspaper, only 5 percent of the research was relevant to the industry. Actually, there is a strong interest in research but because of its lack of relevance, we don't have much funding support or partnership from the industry. This is a challenge for the institution as well as for us in academics.

Institutional identity crisis

The challenge of a crisis in institutional identity is mostly described by participants who teach at Christian universities. For example, DT3 was concerned that the leaders' unethical behavior and means to engage stakeholders might lead the institution to an identity crisis. Her department leader dismissed corruption cases by misusing Christian principles of love and encouraged one instructor to write a fraud report. She also recalled the dean's decision to hire Muslim faculty in order to get more Muslim students and access to government.

> I am confused why a Christian institution is acting like this? Our dean should know that this is a Christian institution but instead of hiring Christian faculty, he hired three Muslim faculty members. He argued that this would give easy access to work with government institutions such as state hospitals. We also have MOU [a memorandum of understanding] with Malaysia institutions. Whenever the Malaysian representatives or students came, these Muslim faculty members were asked to handle all the protocols. They also knew that they have been used by the institution to get more Muslim students. What surprised me more was on one occasion the dean was asked to give a welcome speech, and our dean mentioned "Alloh"[5] instead of Allah. The identity of our institution has become confusing.

A similar concern was also shared by CS1 who observed the increasing number of Muslim students and wondered if the institution has departed from its original identity. He responded by stating: "My concern is how to help my

---

5. Both Christians and Muslims in Indonesia use the word Allah to address God, but they have different ways to pronounce it. The Christians use the Latinized pronunciation (Al-lah) while the Muslims use Arabized pronunciation (Al-loh).

institution become an inclusive, not pluralistic university. I will not interfere or minimize the faith of others but clearly hold to my faith. So, this is my struggle with my fellow leaders that we need to hold on to our original vision and purpose of our existence, and manifest it into our policies. Historically, I know that this university existed as an extension of the church. The primary vision is to share the Gospel and Christian values."

Navigating faith in a pluralistic institution

Some participants expressed that one of the challenges of working at non-faith-based universities is navigating their Christian faith in a pluralistic environment. At a non-faith-based university, all religions are welcome, and for JA2 it is challenging to teach the diverse student body with its ethnoreligious dynamic, especially with the rise of religious radicalism in Indonesia. JA2 expressed his desire to make the students felt welcome and seek common principles among diverse beliefs:

> The number of Christian and Muslim students here is almost equal. Recently the radical religious movement is rising locally and nationally. The ethnic and religious identity of a particular group of people has increasingly thickened in a negative way. So, it becomes much more difficult to find a common ground for diverse beliefs. My biggest challenge is to find common ground. I want students to feel accepted in my class although I as their lecturer have a different religion from them. I want them to feel welcome, not threatened because I am a Christian.

JA2 further explained that he could carelessly use the classroom to promote Christianity if he is not careful with his power as a faculty member. He recalled, "One of my colleagues was involved in MLM (Multi-Level Marketing). Every time he taught the class he always gave a hidden promotion that made the students feel uncomfortable. This also could happen in the context of faith because Christian faculty members bring their faith to the class and promote it, and if not careful it can make the students feel uncomfortable or even create enmity."

JS2 argued that as a Christian he was called not to isolate himself but go to the world and live among people with any kind of belief. However, living out his calling as a Christian faculty member teaching at a secular and diverse campus comes with a challenge. "My biggest challenge is keeping my faith and at the same time showing respect to other's beliefs. I try to understand their beliefs without getting too deep because it can be a sensitive area. I believe the way I live my life is much more powerful than what I say."

Student-Related Challenges

The second major challenge participants described in this study is related to large class size and students' behavioral problems and learning attitudes. Large size classes and the digital attendance system make it harder for faculty to remember their students' names, let alone know them personally. Other major challenges related to students are the learning attitude that is "instantly oriented" and the lack of self-agency, and behavioral problems related to their manner of dress, lifestyle, and the lack of respect for authorities.

Class size challenges

Many participants mentioned that teaching large classes makes it difficult for them to know and care for their students (e.g. CH3, TM1, LT2, BW1). "One of my big challenges is a big-sized class," CH1 said, "I have 50–60 students in my class and I can only pay attention to 15–20 students. Sometimes I feel guilty for not being able to care for my students sufficiently." BW1 also shared a similar challenge saying, "One class is about 80–100 students. We cannot divide them into smaller classes because it would add too much burden to the faculty and we have a shortage of faculty here."

In addition to large class sizes, the use of technology in keeping student attendance further prevents the faculty from knowing their students personally. LT2 who often taught a classroom of sixty-four students expressed, "I can't remember their names. I give up because now the student attendance system has changed to fingerprint-based. I don't call their names and mark their attendance in the attendance sheet anymore. The manual system still allows me to remember their names in one month, but now I can't remember their names anymore."

Student mindset and behavioral issues

Some participants in this study are often faced with challenging behaviors and the mindset of the students, particularly with regard to their lifestyle and manners, lack of respect to authorities, and result-orientation. SW3 stated that for the past few years, "the institution has committed to reaching out to underprivileged students from eastern parts of Indonesia, such as West Papua, Ambon, and NTT while it continues to accept students from Celebes and Kalimantan who were mostly Chinese from the middle-upper class." "The problem was," SW3 explained, "Most rich students do not care about dressing and grooming manners. The campus is surrounded by poor neighborhoods and their dress manner creates social gaps in the community. Their lifestyle also influences other students on campus. This is my challenge, how to teach them, not to become stumbling blocks, but light and salt for the surrounding campus' communities."

For RD3, "the biggest external challenge is the students who primarily aim for high scores without appreciating the learning process." "The students tend to have an instant mindset," RD3 explained, "For example, the architect studio class is 10 credit hours in one semester. It's about half from a total of 21 credit hours per semester. Well, if a student got B+ or B it would affect his or her GPA significantly. So, some of the students came to me and said, "Please ma'am, raise my grade a bit." Although they have bad scores, they like to negotiate persistently . . . I want them to appreciate the process. This is your life, God is shaping you. If you fall, get up, know your purpose and try again." ES3 also shared a similar student-related challenge asserting, "I want my students to become more motivated to do better in their study and manner. At private universities, we have second-class students. Students at state universities are easier to teach, their attitude is OK and their brain is OK. But students here at a private university, they lack good manners and motivation to learn."

Another student behavior problem expressed by DY3 is the decline of respect for authority. DY3 asserted that "the young generations are becoming more and more misbehaved and disrespectful to authorities." LI1 expressed a similar sentiment with regard to courtesy: "Students are so much getting into gadgets and sometimes I find them not polite by sending messages asking about the class quite late at night. It's a dilemma for me, I don't answer them sometimes."

Passive learners
Another student-related challenge expressed by many participants is the students' passive attitude in the learning process (e.g. LT2, MC2, DS1, TM1

DC2). LT2 expresses his disappointment with his students' passive attitude toward learning. A few days before final exams, he provided an extra optional class time for his students to review and ask questions. He said, "Some students who came were not from my class, but I welcome all students. I waited for two hours, but none of my students showed up. I thought they might have understood all the lessons." However, the test results showed otherwise, and LT2 was disappointed with his students. Showing some of his students' test sheets, he added, "Look at the scores, 30, 40, and 50! I am truly upset and sad."

Similarly, DS1 found that most of the students were passive learners and had made efforts to make her class more interactive. "I have tried to stimulate my students to be more interactive, yet like most Indonesian students in general, they tend to be passive," explained DS1. She added, "Students also do not make use of the opportunities to seek help from their lecturers after the class. It seems not natural for them, except for seniors who have to consult their supervisors about their research projects."

Likewise, TM1 explained, "Almost in all my classes, students lack in interaction. They tend to be good listeners and [at] taking notes. They do not show any critical thinking or desire to ask, debate, or challenge any ideas. I think this was the result of the education system that they received from kindergarten to higher education." MC2 also found herself frustrated with a lack of enthusiasm in learning: "Every time I teach them I get a headache. I wonder why students in Indonesia are so passive. For me, the most important thing is they must be brave to ask and try. If they are wrong, it's alright."

Personal Challenges

Another type of challenge participants describe is related to personal matters, which involve being underpaid and keeping a work-family balance. Some participants are struggling with low pay as faculty in higher education that makes it difficult for them to support their family, and for a solution they took extra work. Another personal challenge is balancing and prioritizing between work and family. In addition, some participants juggle their responsibilities with graduate study and church ministry.

Underpaid and underappreciated

Despite efforts from government and higher education institutions to increase faculty salaries, many participants found that their incomes were much lower compared to other professional jobs (e.g. TM1, DT3, CS1, HS1, RT1). Because of low pay, some participants were working extra jobs to make ends meet. For example, TM1, a senior faculty teaching at a state university, felt underappreciated and underpaid. He asserted, "The salary of a civil servant is always low, although it's been better lately. I always say this, particularly [about] my salary in the past: 'This is a contempt salary.' Although I have completed my PhD from America, the salary is still a real challenge." Due to low income, TM1 said that he had to take on extra jobs outside teaching as a consultant.

Another senior faculty member teaching at a state university, RT1, also expressed a similar sentiment, saying: "Although for the last 10 years, the salary is getting better, but compared to teaching faculty in the USA, the teaching profession in Indonesia is a volunteer job. My colleagues who teach at private universities have salaries that are far less than this institution." RT1 further explained that there was a pay disparity among faculty in the same institution. "Even among schools in this university, faculty teaching in economics receive a better payment that those who teach in pure sciences. The disparity of the salary is permissible because economics is a favorite and has many students." RT1 also said that to get extra income outside teaching, he worked as a public accountant and taught at a private institution.

HS1, a young faculty member teaching at a state university, also described his financial struggle especially during the first few years of teaching.

> The welfare of new lecturers is quite sad. At the beginning of my teaching career, I still received support from my parents by living with them and paying the water and electric expenditures. It took about five years. Those smart students, after graduating from college, aim to work in private sectors. As novice professionals, they can gain 8 million rupiahs[6], while in this institution only 2 million rupiahs[7]. So, to be a fulltime faculty in this institution will be financially challenging.

Thus, based on his experience, he proposed an external financial source to support young Christian faculty by saying:

---

6. Equivalent to US$560.00
7. Equivalent to US$140.00

If we truly hope for Christian alumni to enter teaching vocation at a state university, we need to think about financial support to help them get through during their first years of teaching. Christian alumni who are well established may think to return the favor to their campus by supporting young alumni who want to be lecturers. If not, it would be too hard for them to survive financially or they would prefer to work in the private sector, for the payment is much better.

Keeping a work-family balance

Some participants found difficulty in managing their work and family life. MC2, a fulltime faculty as well as a dentist, said, "I know that I cannot give 100 percent to the students. Because I am a dentist, I have my own practice, and I am also a mom. Thus, out of 100 percent, I can only give about 50 percent of my time and energy to teaching. When my children grow older, maybe I can give more."

For EP1, in addition to fulltime teaching in her own academic discipline and academic administrator, also volunteered to teach Christian religious education classes and supervise Christian student ministry. With these multiple roles, she said: "My personal challenge is time. Some of the activities are in the afternoon, and after working at my office, I still need to work until night at home. My body is tired." "Thankfully," she added, "I have an assistant who is my former student and still single, who helps me supervise the students' Friday fellowship and assistants' Sunday fellowship. And then, every Thursday, he helps me co-lead discussion groups." For JS2, his personal struggle included balancing work, study, church, and family life. He explained, "I pray to God that I can manage my time, work and study at the same time, also have time for family and ministry at church. I have to manage all these so I can be consistent and keep them balanced. I don't want to sacrifice any of them."

Faith and Response to Adversity

Although many participants described a strong conviction of calling in their teaching vocation, as adversities come, some of them have been tempted to quit (e.g. RS1, HS1, MC2, ET2). For example, RS1felt burdened with many rules as a faculty, such as administrative duties and paper publication every semester, and coupled with disappointments with her colleagues' unethical uses of research grants, she was tempted to leave her teaching job. She said, "I want to quit my job but because the students still need me, I keep teaching. If the students don't like me anymore, I will quit. I have applied for early retirement, but my department head said no." However, despite many adversities as listed above, all participants remained faithful to their teaching vocation. They expressed various ways faith had shaped their perception and attitude in responding to adversity which included the following: (1) perceiving challenges as opportunities for growth; (2) giving strength to endure; (3) praying in the midst of difficulties; (4) refreshing their calling and helping them "not to be afraid"; (5) giving inner stability to overcome success and failures; (5) actively seeking for solutions; and (6) aspiring to be excellent faculty members.

Faith helps faculty see challenges as opportunities

Some participants in this study found that faith helped them to accept challenges as opportunities to grow in their spiritual life as well as to do good works. DS1 asserted that religious discrimination was a real challenge at her workplace, yet she responded by saying, "the challenge provides us with an opportunity if we are to be faculty members with a quality and specific expertise for us to play our specific role." Another participant, CS1, also shared a similar response to the ethnoreligious discrimination he experienced at his workplace, stating: "This challenge also comes with an opportunity . . . I think that God is working through all this process." This perception led CS1 to transform the challenge into an opportunity to witness and change the stereotypes and prejudices his Muslim colleagues and students have against Christians through the quality of his work.

EP1 also experienced similar religious discrimination and she responded, "If I have challenges because I am a Christian, then it is a privilege because I am considered a coworker of the Lord's and that it's too lofty for me. If Christ himself experienced many sufferings, who am I then to reject all those challenges? I saw that there were some incidents that I have experienced because of my Christian faith. But at the same time, I also saw God using the challenges to mold me." Instead of becoming frustrated, DT3 also saw the challenges of unethical leadership behavior and practices at her department as God's means to wake up her spiritual life. She said, "This institution has confused many of us. But I am grateful that because these messes happened in this institution, they had made me find out more about my Christian faith."

Prayers in times of adversity

Prayer is another subtheme echoed by many participants in facing difficulties and challenges in their teaching vocation (e.g. EP1, MP1, CS3, ET2, JS3). EP1 shared that she and her team have been fervently praying in response to the need for a better space for students' weekly fellowship on campus. She approached the institution's leader to ask permission to use a larger classroom, but he did not approve of the request. The problem also involved unequal access to campus facilities where the Muslim students had their own secretariat room and a *mushallah* for their spiritual activities on campus. However, EP1 did not despair but continued to put her hope in God through prayers. She explained,

> We rent a space outside the campus for a student secretariat. For the weekly fellowship, we use campus facilities, a room with a capacity for a maximum of 70 people, while the students who come can be 150 to 180. When it's raining, my heart goes out to the students, O God have pity on them, standing under the rain thirsting for God's Word. Sometimes I think they do not get anything. We have prayed for this for a long time. I took the courage to approach the director to ask for a bigger room, but he said there was no room that had such capacity. There is a bigger room, but it's used for extension class at night, so we cannot use it. So yes, we accept it and continue to pray for this matter. I hope that in the future this institution will be better and give equal treatment, not just for Christians but also for the Hindus, Buddhists, and others.

MP1 also shared a similar attitude in overcoming adversity. She expressed that being a competent faculty member is not enough to respond to the practice of discrimination at her workplace. She also expressed that she often prayed when encountering problems at work. God's answers to her prayers had enabled her to earn respect and a reputation as a "psychic" from her coworkers. She explained,

It's inexplicable by reasons. Until now whenever these hospital labs have problems they would say, "Call [MP1], the psychic." I say to them that I am not a psychic, I am just praying . . . once the autoclave didn't work. I ask God for help, to give me wisdom. And then I just pressed the small red button and it worked. I left to go teach my class, they were all gawking. All the Muslim workers had tried hard with no results until they asked me, "MP1, please help us with your prayer." I said to them that I would pray in the Christian way. To that extent they trust me."

JS3 and CS3 also mentioned praying through challenges and receiving wisdom from God. Keeping work-study-family harmony is challenging for JS3 and she expressed, "God enables me. I pray, bring all my struggles and ask God for help. I struggle with many conflicted responsibilities in my life but God helps me. He gives me wisdom as to how to prioritize things. In the case of CS3, in addition to bringing his concerns about the institutional identity crisis to his superiors, he also prayed over them. He said, "I have prayed about it and I have conveyed this issue to my superiors that we must have policies according to the vision of this university, of why we have a Christian university in the first place."

Faith gives strength to endure

Some participants cited "God enables me," "God provides," "God's love," "God's gift," and "God's guidance," to point to the values of faith in giving strength to endure difficulties with courage and wisdom to do what is right in the face of many challenges. For example, SW3 said that to fulfill her vocational calling with all the challenges she had at her institution was "like being invited by God to a marathon race with a goal to reach a finish line. This is not easy because this is a marathon, not a sprint. There are many ups and downs." SW3 recognized that faith carried her through all difficulties by stating, "But I can survive until now because God provides me with people who love me. God's love is above all what enables me to run until I get to the finish line."

Similarly, JS3, who is undergoing a doctoral study in addition to her challenge in keeping a balance between work and family, also recognizes that "God enables" and provides wisdom to carry out her responsibilities. She asserted,

"I see my life in God's grace that cannot be separated from my work, family, and church ministry . . . Without God's guidance, I can be unbalanced in performing multiple roles, including the job that draws a lot of my energy and attention because of many responsibilities entrusted to me."

Likewise, ET2, who worked in a highly bureaucratic and politicized organizational culture, often experienced pressures from many sides as an academic leader who also found encouragement and strength to persevere in her Christian faith. She expressed, "When I talk to my superiors, I often feel stuck in between. If I did not have God, I would be stressed. The students were protesting why the institution did not provide this and that. I went to the rectorate but it didn't work. It's not easy." She further explained that she could take an easy path to join the worker strike demonstration or just quit her job, but instead she said, "But I don't do it because God wants me here. I never shared this with my small group of friends but one of them got a vision and said, "God tells you to remain silent. This is not the time yet. He tells you to pray." So, I keep persevering."

Faith "refreshes my calling" and "helps me not be afraid"

MF3 was tempted to give up her calling because the teaching job often made her feel "stressful and frustrated" but she said, "God refreshes my calling whenever I see my students at the commissioning ceremony. One of the student parents said to me, "I have nine children but we cannot send them all to school. He is the first college graduate in the family." I felt so touched because this student was under my supervision. It refreshes me again that this vision is great. This student is going back to Papua to make a change . . . This keeps my spirit alive. My journey as a lecture is like a roller-coaster; sometimes I am down but He makes me up again."

When asked about the role of faith in her teaching vocation, MC2 expressed that faith kept her focused on her calling despite limited opportunities to do her own research and better job offers. "In my journey of thirteen years of teaching, I came to understand more why I become a lecturer. And it makes me stay on my calling. Being a lecturer in Indonesia, I need to fight for my own research. Unlike institutions abroad, here I feel unsupported. In the beginnings, I wanted to move to other jobs. I had job offers here and there. But I stay and focus on my job and I know it's because of the influence of faith on me." MC2 also added that faith helped her to be unafraid in the face of religious discrimination and radicalism at her workplace. She said, "I remember a benediction by Neal Plantinga, that said, "God go before you to lead you, God go behind you to protect you, God go beneath you to support you, God go beside you to befriend you." I forget the year I received that benediction, but it did strengthen me and help me not to be afraid."

Faith gives inner stability to overcome success and failure

A few participants mentioned that faith gave spiritual power to keep them from being overthrown by either success or failure. CS1, a doctorate degree holder from abroad and actively involved in research and various academic communities, was a "rising star" at his department. With this came a temptation. He said, "I was struggling, I could be a lighthouse or a candle." But CS1 decided to remain "humble and kind" and set a good example by "giving a good work performance and following professional ethics." He also expressed that with all the success and popularity, he was tempted to make research his first priority like many of his colleagues did, but confidently he stated, "Students are my priority." Another challenge for CS1 was the unavailability of research equipment. Instead of complaining or giving up his research, he decided to use his own savings to buy the equipment. He explained:

> Praise the Lord. I still have some money left from my scholarship. I saved the money to buy a microscope with a lucida-camera attachment. I have ordered it from Japan and it will arrive next month. It's about 150 million rupiahs. There is no available budget from the department so I must use my own money. I believe this is God's calling and He will provide. Praise the Lord. My wife also supports me. She is a dentist. She said that dental equipment is a must for a dentist's job and so is the microscope for my research.

For DC2, faith helped him rise up from failures. He said, "This is my second PhD study. My first PhD study failed because I had difficulties with the research equipment." However, he added, "I didn't give up. If I had difficulties, I would think, read books, and find solutions. In the same way, when I supervise the students . . . when they fail, I would ask them to try again. They see me that I don't give up but ask God for help, and I can overcome the difficulties."

Faith leads to actively seeking for possible solutions

Besides facing difficulties with a positive attitude, the participants also actively seek solutions to the problems they have. For DS1, the change of leadership in her department also came with a dramatic change in her teaching workload. Assigned only three credit hours of teaching, she responded, "I could not do anything about the matter, so I learned to do everything I could do." DS1 demonstrated a strong inner-self motivation to turn the idle hours to productivity. Taking ownership of her work, she said, "So I started doing research and supervising many students. After some time, I offered students some courses that had not been available for a few years. They said yes without knowing that I had been busy creating my own courses for the students. I asked the department head about the courses and he approved. Finally, I have a lot of work which I have created myself."

EW2 shared that her institution had an ambitious vision to be a research university and demanded that all faculty be actively involved in research and publication in peer-reviewed journals. "What the institution wants is undisputable," EW2 said, "So I must join in. But I can't pursue publications all the time. Who is going to take care of the students, those who have problems such as premarital pregnancy and rape cases? Who is going to do the community service?" The institutional demands led some faculty members to compete for research grants, and EW2 commented, "Not all can be measured with money, like a transaction. We are only a small group of intellectuals our nation has, only 10 percent." She also observed that the competition had made some of her colleagues become "insensitive to the needs of others and fighting among themselves." Instead of being "frontal," she actively sought solutions, explaining, "I didn't want to compete like them; I chose collaboration. So I got to know faculty members from other departments, such as those at the IT department and the communication department. We did the research together. The work became lighter because we divided it among ourselves."

In response to radicalism and being a Christian faculty in a religious pluralistic institution, JH2 stated, "This is not a Christian institution but we have quite a number of Christian students and faculty. I emphasize the universal values in my class. As an institution, to counteract radicalism, we declare publicly our commitment to the unitary state of the Republic Indonesia, *Pancasila*, and *Bhinneka Tunggal Ika*."

Faith inspires Christian faculty members to be excellent

Facing students who have been influenced by religious radicalism and tended to choose Muslim faculty members as their research advisors, some participants responded by pushing themselves to be excellent and "professional" faculty members with specific expertise. DS1 argued that, "Being a minority, I am not going to be assigned with special tasks unless I am really qualified. This is a challenge. We need to be highly qualified; if not we aren't going to have any impact. For me, I don't have to be highly qualified in all areas but at least I have one expertise that I can play well." She further explained, "For example, I am studying the Ramsey theory. It doesn't matter that I don't know much about other fields, but I focus my expertise on Ramsey theory. It's enough because when students need to study about Ramsey's theorem, they have come to me. My Christian faith might be a barrier for them, but they have to come to me because I have an expertise in this area."

MC2 also shared a similar view by saying, "There are only two TMJ (temporo-mandibular joint) experts. One is me in this institution and the other at a state university. So students who have to do research in this area cannot reject me as their supervisor. They cannot press me because they need my expertise. In response to discrimination at her workplace, MP1 also did not use "confrontation," instead she said, "If we are competent; they could not do anything. There is still discrimination going on, but I don't let them step on me."

Faith Gives Desire for Personal Growth

Another aspect of a faith-shaped teaching vocation described by many participants is a desire for personal growth. The understanding of purpose and meaning of being a Christian faculty teaching in higher education and the challenges of the vocation encourage the participants to grow in various aspects, including: (1) spiritual growth; (2) character growth; and (3) academic growth. Some participants took personal responsibility for their personal development while others expressed a need for support from their family, institution, community of believers, and community of academia.

Desires for Spiritual Growth

Most of the participants described their need for spiritual growth to keep them focused on their calling and give them the strength to deal with pressure and challenges in the workplace (e.g. BS1, HS1, RM2, ET2, JA2, SW3, WU3). These participants expressed their longing to deepen their relationship with God and be faithful to God's guidance.

Personal relationship with God

To have a closer walk with God, some participants focused on reading and meditation on the Word of God. For BS1, being a Christian faculty at a state university meant to be a witness for Christ. BS1 expressed that a witness could not be "superficial" nor "pretend to be a holy person" but it must flow "naturally" out of one's being and reflect "who you are." To be that kind of witness, BS1 emphasized the importance of daily Bible reading and meditation in his life. He used the metaphors of making salted eggs and rebuilding an old house to describe the value of the Word of God on a person's head and heart.

> Why are salted eggs salty? Well, because the eggs are soaked in salt water and this involves time. The longer the eggs are soaked the saltier they will be. Likewise, my head is like a salted egg soaked in the Word of God. It also takes time, day in and day out, little by little, the Word slowly shapes my being. Or imagine my head is like an old house. This house has to be torn down, which happened during the time of conversion. But this house is not collapsed instantly. Likewise, my old thinking slowly slumped down, maybe the door is taken down first, followed by other parts, and then slowly building the new one. Change needs a transition. So, I see my daily walk with God affects me, the way I live out my life.

HS1 also expressed the importance of his daily walk with God to find strength in challenging times. He said, "I have to have my devotions every morning; if not I would not be strong to face the day. Sometimes I feel upset and angry with what is happening on this campus. But I also must think to change what I can change and to accept what cannot be changed. If not I would be stressed. So, vertically I maintain my personal relationship with God to give me daily strength."

Facing many challenges at her workplace, ET2 was reminded of her need for a deeper relationship with God and a meaningful life. She said, "God rebukes me. After taking up the structural position I have less time to read the Word of God. When I was a student I took ministries both at church and campus and had an intensive reading of the Bible. I was stable. But now I have less and less time . . . After meditating on what Paul says that after knowing Christ all things become rubbish, I want to live more meaningfully."

Working in a dominant Muslim environment, LI1 feels the need to know more about her Christian faith. In addition, she was also encouraged to learn about Islam. She said, "I want to understand the conflicts between the teachings of Islam and Christianity. But the more I learned the more I become convinced with Christianity, especially the teachings about love, the first and second commandments. There is no other teaching like ours."

Spiritual discernment and obedience to God

Some participants also expressed their longing to discern and obey God's will in their vocational journey. Having taught for almost four decades, BS1 was still constantly paying attention to God's guidance in his work. Again, he used two metaphors to describe his life and spiritual discernment. He first used "sailboat" in which he said:

> It is a sailboat, not a rowing boat. A sailboat moves because of the wind. If we sail to the wind's direction then it will move fast. But if we sail in the opposite direction by paddling the boat by ourselves, then you know the result. Likewise, I see that God's or the Holy Spirit's guidance is like a sailboat. What I need to do is to open my mainsail. God will direct my path. I think God is like a moving wind, meaning that there will be a time when the wind changes direction. If the wind changes from North to South, maybe I need to change my life direction too. I don't have to force myself to stay in the teaching profession for my whole life.

The second illustration he used was a car's headlights. BS1 was passionate about "the ministry of the word" and is approaching his retirement in the next few years. He used this metaphor to describe his searching for God's will and the possibility of a new vocation in his future.

> I would describe a car that runs through the dark whose headlights can shine on the road within 50 to 100 meters. We don't know what is ahead of us, we don't even know when to make a

turn because it's dark, but later we will know if we need to turn. Well, this metaphor reminds me of God's guidance. If the first metaphor describes that God can give direction, well this one is about God's guidance one step at a time. It means that I can't see my future. It's like in the first place God "cornered" me to be a faculty member here but later he may change his direction. Because my faith is integrated into my life, God is my shipmaster or the wind.

JS3 also shared a similar deep yearning for God's guidance in her life, especially for what she can do through her presence and teaching vocation at her current university. She expressed, "God has put me here; I want to do what he wants me to do. I have to fulfill my responsibility as a faculty member, but there are also some parts I can do within the department and beyond. I think God wants to use me in a wider scope; thus he equips me through my doctoral study. God is the source of wisdom, I need to seek his guidance about the needs and the direction of where we should go."

In the journey of her vocational life, EW2 also learned to be sensitive to God's guidance of knowing when to remain silent and when to act, and when to receive and when to give. Using an eagle as a metaphor, she explained:

I think I might be like an eagle. The Psalms describe a flying eagle but sometimes it needs to hide in a cave pulling off its feathers. And it takes time to let the feathers grow back. With new feathers, the eagle can fly stronger and higher. I think in life sometimes I need to go to my cave to learn more, such as going for a workshop or doing research . . . Sometimes there is a phase to remain silent when I don't have to appear in front of the crowd. This includes when counseling students, I think if I always give them advice they would become lazy. So, I learn to pull myself to observe and listen. Later on, I spread my wings and suggest to them this and that.

Desires for Character Growth

In addition to spiritual growth, many participants also expressed their desire for character development. Some character traits these participants wanted to improve included: (1) to be "faithful to the end"; (2) to grow in humility; and (3) to become more loving and caring for the students.

To be "faithful to the end"

Despite the fact that a teaching vocation came with many challenges and the results were uncertain, some participants expressed that they would not give up but remain faithful to work in the field they have been called to. For example, AS1 described his desire to cultivate faithfulness especially when times got difficult. Using a farmer as a metaphor, he said, "What is important for a farmer is sowing. My father used to be a tomato and chili farmer; although it was hard, he never gave up. When the harvest came, one basket only sold for 2,000 rupiahs, the basket alone was 300 rupiahs. My father was angry but the next year he would still plant tomatoes, keep sowing, keep planting." Getting closer to his retirement, AS1 hoped that he would remain "faithful to the end" to fulfill his calling.

> I want to finish well the task given to me. Maybe it's about my age too. I don't want to seek any profits nor to be something else. I just want to teach and finish it well when the Lord calls me home. I don't know if my GPA will be 2.0 or 4.0. My work performance will be different from others, but my definition of "finish" is to fulfill what I am called to. I don't want that at the end of my life I have been climbing coconut trees tirelessly but only to find out that I was called to climb areca nut trees.

In contrast to AS1, CS1 was a much young participant but he expressed a similar desire to grow in faith by being faithful. He shared that God has taught him to be faithful to his calling despite many challenges especially during the early years of teaching. He recalled,

> I worked as an adjunct faculty for seven years and I waited faithfully until I was accepted as a fulltime lecturer. Financially, my payment was very small as an adjunct lecturer. Frankly, during my sixth year of waiting, there was an offer from another state university and I almost wanted to run away at that time but the next morning during my devotions I read about Jonah. I thought that I was reprimanded by God, so I remained and the next year my appointment as a fulltime lecturer was approved. I believe

that this is God's calling. Although it's not easy to bear this cross, if I am faithful, I am sure that God would give me strength.

As a reminder, CS1 also made this as his personal motto: "Be faithful to your calling, be faithful to the end."

Growing in humility

Growing in humility is another aspect of character growth mentioned by some participants. RS1 said that she often felt upset with colleagues whose opinions and ways of doing things were different from hers and because of this she tended to isolate herself from social interaction at the workplace. However, deep in her heart, she expressed her longing to be a better person by growing in humility, saying: "I should be more humble. When I feel I am right then they must be wrong. I think they must be right in a certain sense too. So I want to be more humble and wiser to deal with the differences."

Similar to RS1, MF3 also found that social interaction and working with co-workers was challenging. Thus, she argued that learning to be humble at work was necessary, especially willing to listen and learn from peers.

> It's challenging to interact with fellow lecturers. It seems to me that everybody thinks that they know everything. Everybody walks according to his or her way, but actually, for particular classes, it would be better if he or she could work together. I think my Christian faith demands me to be humble. I need to learn to listen to others and avoid the assumption that he or she is less than me, such as she is not well-read as compared to me.

Another participant, PK3, said that humility was a characteristic she needed to keep her from being arrogant after completing her doctoral study. She expressed, "Graduating from a Ph.D. program may show that I am a smart person. But someone once said to me: 'If you are in a high position you need to bend down; if not, everybody has to look up to talk to you.' So the first thing I need to learn is to be wise and humble, and not brag about myself but to contribute something meaningful. At least it starts from my disciplinary area."

Become more loving and caring

Another area of character growth expressed by some participants is becoming a more loving and caring faculty member. EP1, a Christian faculty member teaching and serving tirelessly at a state university for almost three decades, received a birthday surprise for the first time from her students. This token of love and appreciation from her mostly Muslim students was an important affirmation that she was well accepted and esteemed. She recalled:

> A few months ago, a student said to me that I had to go to the lab. Students often ask for help if they don't understand something and I usually would respond immediately. Without knowing, I opened the door and they sang happy birthday and brought me a birthday cake. It's never happened to any faculty members before and I never had it before, either. They said, 'We love you, ma'am.' I was really surprised because they all had religious beliefs that were different from mine.

Touched by her students' love, she said, "For the next five years, I want to love my students more."

Contrary to EP1, MC2 found her students were unlikeable. "Many students in this department are coming from the "have" families. Compared to my alma mater (a state university) these kids are more spoiled, like to be spoon-fed. I tend to be impatient; if they don't ask I don't give. They have to be active. But I still need to evaluate if that's the right approach, so maybe I need to change." Reflecting on her teaching, she continued to say, "To be sure, I feel I don't love them enough so I don't make any extra efforts to guide them. I want to love them more."

Motivated by a strong sense of responsibility as a steward of God, JS3 also expressed a similar desire to be more loving and caring for her students. She asserted, "I want to care more for my students because God loves every one of them and they are sent and entrusted to me as their teacher to guide them in this short period of time and after that, they will go according to their paths. My responsibility is to equip them and touch their lives, to help them to be ready to face society and global influences. "

Desires for Academic Growth

Another area of personal growth noted by the majority of participants is academic growth. These participants cited two types of academic development: (1) academic passion, which includes research, further study, and skill development in teaching and curriculum design; and (2) academic career, which includes a desire for upgrading their academic ranks and possibilities for leadership roles.

Academic passion

Many participants in this study demonstrated a deep passion for personal academic growth by doing research (CS1, DS1, TM1, LT2, CH3), planning for doctoral studies (RT1, DS1, JH2, RM2, MF3), and improving their pedagogical and course design skills (MP1, JA2, JH2, MF3, RD3).

Academic passion for research. There are two kinds of research mentioned by the participants, namely disciplinary research and interdisciplinary research. CS1 was a young faculty member who enthusiastically shared his focus of research on Ichthyoplankton, particularly fish larvae in Indonesian waters and his desire to start a community of researchers for this area of research. He said,

> From the aspect of scholarship, I want to continue my research on fish larvae, which is relatively new in Indonesia. I was asked by many institutions to share this knowledge. In America, Australia, and Japan, this field has been well-developed. I want to start networking to make this branch of the discipline stronger in Indonesia. I am a member of the Indonesian Society of Ichthyologists, and soon I will be a board member there. I also want to make a group of researchers that focuses on fish larvae.

Another young faculty, HS1, also passionately shared his research on mathematical modeling and prediction in infectious diseases. He explained, "This is ongoing research, a two-year project. Currently, I am researching an epidemic model for SARS. For my Ph.D. research, I did modeling for malaria."

While CS1 and HS1 focused on their disciplinary research, CH3 and CS3 were interested in incorporating faith into their academic research. CS3 shared his interest in conducting interdisciplinary research when saying, "My current research is focusing on behavior and its relationship to accounting. I want to find out about the character of a person and his or her ability in making financial reports, for example, honesty in reporting taxes. So, it's about the influence of spirituality and the obligation to pay taxes." CH3 also expressed his hope to develop a model for faith-integrated learning through his research. Describing his personal academic growth for the next five years, he said: "Indonesia is a unique country which recognizes six official religions. So, I hope in the near future to develop a model of Christian education that is well integrated, without making faith as an add-on value, but naturally flows from faith. In doing so, we can give birth to holistic education."

Academic passion for further studies. Some participants who currently hold a master's degree in their discipline uttered their desire to go for further studies. Recognizing his need for academic growth, JH2 planned to take a sabbatical leave from his teaching and administrative duty from a non-faith-based university to go for his doctoral study in philosophy. He said, "Right now I am at a level when my ax needs to be sharpened. That's why I will go for a doctoral study. I think I might miss some of the details of my teaching. For example, how the methodological approach I choose helps students to understand better about universal values contained in the Pancasila. This is one reason why I want to go for further study." Further, explaining his desire to be deep-rooted in his Christian faith yet with a wide impact across religions, he expressed, "I want to understand faith existentially. We see universal figures such as Gus Dur, Gandhi, and Mother Teresa. These people came from different religious backgrounds. Thus, I want to learn more about this and how I can grow more in this area. I don't want to be a narrow-minded Christian, but to be a Christian who can give 'color' across religions."

By pursuing a doctoral degree, JS2 hoped to be a better faculty member and contribute more to nation-building. Enthusiastically he explained,

> I'll be in a doctoral program soon . . . I feel lacking in many areas and I want to learn more. In the next five years, hopefully, it's sufficient time for me to be transformed by gaining more knowledge, skills, and all sorts, especially in my disciplinary areas, English and education. I don't just want to improve in my knowledge but also research skills in a Ph.D. program, so I can contribute to nation-building, to build the Indonesian people. Taking a further study is not aimed to enrich myself, to make me smarter, but to share, to serve more people, to serve this institution and of course ultimately for God's glory.

Improving pedagogical and course design skills. As a faculty member teaching for almost three decades, the only pedagogical knowledge MP1 ever had was from a Sunday-school teacher training when she was a college student. Recognizing her need, she said:

> I need teaching skill training. I've learned from a Sunday-school teacher training when I had to write or draw on the whiteboard, I had to face the students. This kind of teaching technique, I never had it as a lecture. My class is always full. If they do not like it, they could leave the class. But I try to use OHP, LCD, and all sorts. I make animation, or video clips from old CDs to make my microbiology class attractive. For the civic education class, which I just started last semester, I tried to make a simulation. I need training for these kinds of practical skills. I've applied for a workshop on teaching skills held by the Ministry of Research, Technology and Higher Education. I am not sure whether I will be accepted or not.

RD3, a faculty member teaching architecture for almost two decades, also expressed a similar need to improve her pedagogical skills. She said, "The institution provides various venues for us to grow, such as retreats, leadership training, and chapels. But personally, what I need to learn more is technical skills such as teaching methodology, so my class will be more inspiring for students."

In the case of JH2, his institution has partnered with state agencies to provide pedagogical and course design training for all faculty members. However, he expressed: "We already had the training; what we need now is to incorporate them into our classes and to update them continuously." For JA2, his desire was to improve knowledge and skills in integrating spirituality into his classes as he expressed: "I hope to be more natural and proficient in integrating the spiritual values I believe into my classes. On the other hand, I am still in the process of digging deeper into the true values of Christianity, because in reality there are many versions of understanding and living out the Christian faith. I hope to be naturally integrating and delivering the values without creating an in-group and out-group atmosphere."

Academic career

A number of participants referred to academic rank promotion and obtaining leadership positions as their goal of personal academic development.

The current academic ranks of most participants were either lecturer or head lecturer (associate professor). The highest academic rank was professor,[8] and some participants had expressed their desire to be promoted into this rank (DA1, AS1, EW2, ET2, DC2). Compared to the academic rank promotion, fewer participants expressed their desire for personal development for leadership positions (DA1, PK3, JS3).

Academic rank promotion. AS1 shared his desire to be promoted to the rank of professor before his retirement. He said, "My academic rank promotion is so slow. Some of my close friends, mostly Muslims, have received their full professorships, but for me, I have been in the process since 2011 but until now the appointment has not come out yet . . . My prayer is that the Lord will look at the problem. I have been fighting hard for this and I pray that God is willing to grant my wish." EW2 shared a similar hope to be considered for a full professor status when she expressed: "I have the ambition to be a professor but in the context of Christian faith that being a true professor is doing research which gives benefits for others, not just for the sake of getting published."

ET2 also planned for her future academic career promotion after completing her office term as a director of the master study program. "For my future," ET2 explained, "I want to take care of my academic rank by doing more research and writing articles. And if God is willing to open the door, step by step I will apply for a professor rank."

Leadership positions. A few participants expressed their desire to engage in leadership roles. DA1, a young faculty member teaching at a state university, explained that he did not show keenness for any leadership position because he thought of himself as a minority-religion faculty member; however, his view changed after receiving some advice and encouragement from a senior Christian faculty. He said,

---

8. The academic rank structure established by the Ministry of Research, Technology, and Higher Education of Indonesia was comprised of nine levels: associate lecturer, lecturer (two levels-IIIc, and IIIb), head lecturer (associate professor) (three levels-IVa, IVb, and IVc), and professor (levels IVd and IVe, or full professor). From lecturer to full professor, a candidate should have a doctoral degree, one thousand credit points, and published two articles in peer-reviewed or internationally recognized journals (Ministry of Research, Technology, and Higher Education 2016).

> In terms of my career, I hope to be promoted to head lecturer or professor. So now I am diligently doing research and writing . . . But after talking to Mr. RT, I think it's time for us Christians to think about strategic positions either in government or bureaucratic leadership, which sometimes we think as taboo or unimportant. According to me, it's important to have Christians in the government such as in the Ministry of Education and Culture where some of the educational policies and curriculum are harmful. For us as Christian faculty members who have the opportunity, we should not be allergic to leadership positions because our neighbors (Muslim faculty members) are thinking to put their young leaders in strategic positions.

PK3 hoped to help her institution become better and for this purpose, she was thinking about the possibility of a leadership position. She expressed, "My institution needs to be improved in the areas of administration, leadership, and academics. All these areas are not maximized yet. I can't do much because I am still in my doctoral study and in a position that has no power. So, I hope to have a position that has the power to do something." JS3 also shared a similar hope to make a change in her institution by obtaining a leadership role when she said: "I am interested in leadership, such as how to give direction to the staff and leading this department in line with Christian as well as educational principles I have learned. How to serve the students better . . . So I have given a special thought of becoming a leader."

Resources and Support Needed for Personal Growth

In response to the need for their personal development, a small number of participants choose self-directed initiatives, while the majority of participants expressed their need for resources and support from family members and/or spouses, institutions, and communities of both Christians and academia.

Self-directed initiatives

Some participants preferred self-directed learning for their spiritual and professional development (DS1, CS1, BS1, LI1, CH3). These participants used terms such as "self-supply," "autodidact," and "independent study," to describe their personal agency. For example, BS1 explained, "I have my own independent studies. I read a wide array of books in addition to engineering." Besides self-study, BS1 also collaborated with his son especially on the subject of civic education in response to radicalism.

> My son is a sociology graduate from the University of Indonesia. Sometimes I discuss with him how to develop models of tolerance and intolerance. Last week I was invited by the Philippines Council of Evangelical Churches to present about the prospect and future relationship between Christians and Muslims. I am glad that my research now is not just about engineering but also related to *Pancasila* and the like. These are important topics as currently, we are facing the problems of radicalism. I don't want to be busy with engineering problems while our national ideology falls apart. This should not be happening.

DS1 also took initiative toward her need for personal spiritual growth. She explained, "I don't have the opportunity to attend Christian seminars, but I read a lot of books. So for my personal development, I preferred self-supply. I have been used to studying my own. For my spiritual growth, I set aside time to read books. I tend not to depend on others on this matter."

CH3 expressed his desire for better time management especially using the long school holidays to self-evaluate and improve teaching contents and personal skills. "So, there are two months of school holidays which I can use to review my teaching level and evaluate what I've done. I just realized this opportunity lately. I don't know why, maybe because of my ignorance in the last seven or eight years, but only for the last two years, I started to use this time. In the past, my mind was always filled with the thoughts of where to go for a vacation and spend time with family. I think I can manage the time and make better use of it."

Spouse and family support

Some participants expressed the need for support from their family members and spouses to make their personal development possible. For professional development, EW2 expressed her desires for academic rank promotion and leadership position, but to make these realities she said, "Family support is the first support I need," she explained, "because I have two children, have no housemaid, and my husband is also working out of town. Thus, it would be difficult for me but my husband is very supportive; he said he would not spend long hours on his work. Without family support, it would be hard for me as a woman to move forward."

Similarly, JS2 appreciated his wife's understanding and support for his pursuit of doctoral study and academic career development. He said, "My family is very supportive. My wife just finished her master's degree in linguistics. So, we are in the same field, same campus, and in the ministry together. It seems God has arranged everything. My target is that by 2020 I will be finished with my study because here I only need three years for doctoral study." PK3, who was currently doing her Ph.D. program for biomedical study and hoping to engage in a leadership role, also expressed the need for support from her family. "Besides self-commitment," she said, "support from my husband and children are essential to me to keep me in balance and not distracted. We need to take care of each other."

Institutional support

The role of an institution in providing support and resources is important in fostering the participants' career and professional development. The types of institutional support cited by the participants include equal opportunity, financial aid, study leave, and policies. EW2 stressed institutional support in the forms of equal opportunities for professional development and leadership roles. She asserted, "Certainly, institutional support in providing a fair opportunity for all faculty members is important. The information must also be fair, open to everybody, not a closed system of information that is only opened for a selected few."

Both JH2 and JS2 appreciated the financial support and study leave hours given by their respective institutions in completing their doctoral studies. JS2 expressed, "I am grateful to God because financially I received 100% scholarship from my institution for my doctoral study. The leaders also show their support so that I can keep working with flexible hours. Not all universities allow their faculty members to study while working because they would reduce productivity and be split in their concentration. But my institution gives full support both financially and time-wise." For JH2, in addition to financial support and permission to take study leave, he also expressed his hope for institutional support in providing opportunities to implement what he has learned from the doctoral study. "I hope," JH2 said, "to develop universal principles derived from Pancasila. I hope I could implement them in this institution. The content of Pancasila itself is excellent, but I need to think about the right methodology so people would see it as something that is valuable . . . At least I have two years to have an in-depth study about it and maybe later I will make it as my dissertation."

For DA1, faculty workload policies are the most essential support he expected from his institution. He said, "For academic career promotion, I have to write and publish in an international journal. This is an important element to get credit points. Thankfully, this institution just made a new workload policy for faculty members, 8+4, meaning that I can teach 8 credit hours and use the other 4 credit hours for writing. In the past, I had to teach 12 to 18 credit hours."

A need for a community of believers

The majority of participants expressed their need for a community of believers. Some referred to their faith community as a safe place to "release pressure," "support each other," share, pray, and study the Bible. Other participants hoped for a group of believers with similar "vision" and "passion" to form a community within the institution that could support each other at the workplace. Participants who expressed the latter type of community of believers were mostly taught at Christian universities. Some participants already had a small group of Christian friends where they belonged but others were still struggling to find one.

EP1 spoke about the importance and support she received from her small group of believers: "I have a small group of friends, four of us, who always support each other. We can share anything including private matters. I found it very helpful because in addition to a place to release stress, I also receive encouragement and they pray for me. We pray and support each other continuously." Besides a peer group, EP1 also received prayer support from her students. Gratefully she said, "I am a supervisor for the student fellowship on campus. These students, especially the committee members, often ask, 'How can we pray for you?' That's very encouraging for me." RS1 had a small group of college friends that continued to keep updating each other through social media but she hoped for more, saying: "We only contact each other using WhatsApp. If we have problems, sad or happy, we share over the WA. We pray together. But for Bible study, I don't have that kind of group. I think I need it."

MC2 shared her need for a community of believers at her workplace but unfortunately, she did not have one yet. "I used to think that I didn't need a community of Christian faculty but now it's necessary for me. At least this community will help to keep my focus, to be a better Christian faculty member. When I was in Holland, I learned to love like Him and I learned that from a community of Christian faculty. So I think I need that but sadly here that kind of community is not available." DA1 also shared a similar struggle in finding a Christian community when he explained, "In this state university where we are the minorities, it's difficult to find a supportive community… But I hope as time goes by I could meet some Christian colleagues so we may go for lunch together particularly during this Ramadan month."

Working at Christian university, JS3, LS3, and DY3 had no difficulty in finding a Christian community but they hoped for more, namely a community of believers who were liked minded in "vision" and the "passion" of building each other and carrying out the institution's values. JS3 expressed, "My institution upholds these values: 'community, care, and excellence.' I hope for a team of faculty members that share the same vision so we can be a great force to achieve the vision and mission of this institution." DY3 has found a community of Christian faculty at her institution "who had the same passion." However, she said, "All of us are busy with our own routines and find it hard to support each other in living out the same calling we have."

A need for a community of academics

The disciplinary academic community plays an important role in the participants' personal academic growth by providing opportunities for learning, discussion, literature resources, collaborative research, and co-publishing. As a novice fishery scientist, CS1 expressed his need for a "sharing partner" from outside the institution. "Because," he explained, "I can't find any here. So, in the near future, I plan to have collaborative research with scholars from Japan." MF3 who recently finished her graduate study in education from a Christian university in the U.S.A. also shared a similar need for an academic community. MF3 hoped to continue her research and write good quality articles and books that would be accessible in the Indonesian language. With limited resources, her aspirations might be difficult to be realized, thus, MF3 hoped "to able to connect with scholars" from the USA for the purposes of literature access, "partnership in research," and the possibility of co-publishing.

DC3 also shared about his struggle in finding like-minded scholars when he said, "I don't have a partner to discuss academic matters in my field. What I can do is find the latest books in my area. If I really need someone to discuss an academic issue, I will go to my department head, but for my area, I need to find somebody outside my institution. Fortunately, right now I have my doctoral promoter at Surabaya with whom I can communicate via e-mails and WA."

Another participant, ES3, had a desire to expand her knowledge and research in histology and pharmacology through short-term training. However, the lack of institutional financial support hindered her plan for this professional development. She expressed a need for a community of academics in her discipline outside her institution where she might find her solution. She said, "I hope to find scholars who have these skills and knowledge and are willing to take me in for the training. Or maybe an opportunity from companies, free of charge, to do research alongside their R & D scientists."

Section 2: The Integration of Faith and Academic Disciplines

When asked about their understanding of "the integration of faith and learning," almost two-thirds of the participants responded that they "never heard of" or "were not familiar" with the phrase. However, almost all participants said that they were familiar with "faith and knowledge" or "faith and science." Thus, these three terms are used interchangeably according to the participants' familiarity. This section is divided into two parts. The first part focuses on the approaches taken by participants to describe their conceptual understanding of the relationship between faith and their academic disciplines. The second part presents the participants' responses to conflict between faith and theories or issues found in their particular academic discipline.

Approaches to the Integration of Faith and Learning

The participants in this study display a convergent understanding of the relationship between faith and their academic disciplines. Their approach to a conceptual understanding on the topic can be divided into eight categories: (1) ontological and epistemological assumptions; (2) worldview approaches; (3) attitudinal approaches; (4) ethical and moral approaches; (5) intrapersonal approaches; (6) interpersonal approaches; (7) contribution to the Kingdom of God; (8) no integration approach. It is noteworthy that the categories do not mean that each participant holds only to a singular standpoint about the relationship between faith and learning. Some participants have more than one view that sometimes seems to contradict each other. For example, TM1 firmly believed that "God is the source of faith and knowledge" (ontological) and "faith influences our process of teaching and learning" (worldview), but when encountered with conflict between faith and knowledge such as in the case of the theory of evolution, he expressed a somewhat dualistic view when saying, "I believe that God created the earth and sky and everything in it. I learn and teach about it (theory) but I don't believe human beings come from an evolutionary process." Therefore, the presentation and the category are aimed to describe the overall participants' responses on the topic.

Figure 2. Eight Approaches to Faith-Integrated Knowing

The Ontological and Epistemological Assumption

This category contains responses the participants use to describe their conceptual understanding of the relationship between faith and learning including

"God is the source of faith and knowledge," "God reveals or gives knowledge," "two-domain one source," and "all truth is God's truth."

Both JH2 and JS2 speak about their conviction that "all truth is God's truth." Explaining his conviction, JH2 said, "I do not separate science from faith. So, sharing the truths found in science, logic, philosophy, and ethics, I think they are all in line with my faith." For JS2 this conviction acted as an anchor whenever he countered doubt. "Indeed, all truth is God's truth. It's undeniable. Whenever I was in doubt, I came back to this principle and read the Word of God. Yes, my questions were answered gradually by God." TM1, AS1, and CS3 traced the connection between faith and learning back to their origin. "God is the source of faith and knowledge," TM1 argued, "we, human beings are his creation, given wisdom and knowledge, and God gives the ability to learn and understand. Whenever we get stuck on something, it doesn't mean God is wrong, he is great. So this is the first thing we should know."

For DS1, MP1, and ES3, the assumption of the relationship between faith and learning relies on their theological belief that God is the creator and revealer of all human knowledge. Combining her faith and long-life learning in mathematics science, DS1 said, "Sometimes we see things that seemed disordered but in many of these disorderly phenomena we can find a pattern of orderliness. God created it that way." MP1 also firmly believed that human knowledge and inventions were from God. She asserted, "If God does not reveal, we human beings would not know. Until now there is no medium to culture leprae (bacteria that cause leprosy), thus I ask God if he is willing to give me (the knowledge)."

Another ontological assumption held by BS1 and MF3 is that faith and knowledge reside in two different domains yet have the same source. MF3 explained, "All knowledge and discoveries are common grace, but faith is a special grace. Both faith and learning are God's revelation." Drawing two circles on a paper, BS1 explained: "The big circle is the divine or supernatural domain and the small circle is the natural domain. For God, there is no difference between the two but for us, yes, there is a difference. Science needs proofs but faith (supernatural) needs no evidence, I just believe."

Interestingly, BS1 further explained, "The boundary of the natural domain is expanding as the scientists make new discoveries. What is considered supernatural can become natural, such as in the case of the moon landing... Both faith and knowledge are created by God. It is God who allows the discoveries."

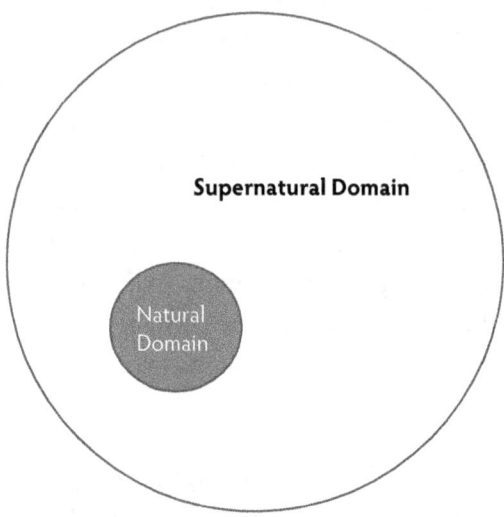

Figure 3. Two-Domain, One Source (BS1)

Worldview Approaches

More than half of the participants speak of faith that acts as a worldview to perceive and examine their academic disciplines. Some of these participants used the term "lens" to describe their worldview approach (e.g. CS1, LI1, BS1, LT2, MF3). CS1 expressed that faith provided a framework for him to view the world, including fisheries science, when he said, "Many of my researches are related to nature..., especially in fisheries science, from the smallest to the biggest creatures in the sea, they all related to each other. All are created by God and no one can imitate him. There are some people who learn science and become atheists but I see otherwise. When I see learning from the lens of faith, the more I learn the more I admire God, the more I know him through an in-depth study of his creation." MF3 also took Christian faith as a lens to question the underlying assumptions of her academic disciplines. She explained, "For example, the theory of behaviorism which emphasizes punishments and rewards. This theory thinks of human beings as robots who can only be driven by external stimuli. We are not only physical but also spiritual beings. It's still worthwhile to learn this theory but we need to be critical of who human beings are." LT2 expressed that he was aware that learning and exchanging views with other scholars would lead him to encounter diverse worldviews. For him, faith helps to uncover the assumptions behind the disciplines in the light of biblical principles. He explained, "We collaborate with faculty from UCLA. Many of them do not believe in God. It's a challenge for me when I discussed neo-liberalism, capitalism, and socialism with them. They have their own "ism" which is different from mine as a Christian. For example, capitalism is OK for them to take everything and turn it into money. As a Christian, I criticize that view. What would happen if we are led by that kind of people?"

The aforementioned participants focus faith as a lens to examine their academic discipline while the following participants emphasize faith as a basis or foundation for learning (e.g. EW2, RT1, MC2, JA2, CS3). EW2 asserted, "Faith and learning are not just related but also need to be integrated. Faith is the basis or foundation for us to develop and implement our knowledge." RT2 also affirmed that "faith should serve as a foundation for learning." He explained, "Faith is above knowledge. If faith guides learning then there will be no contradiction. Science and technological advances should not worry us if faith becomes the standard to guide learning." For JA2, faith does not just serve as a foundation but also a goal of learning. From a psychological perspective, he explained: "We are also spiritual beings and I hope that my students will be fully developed as human beings with all their sociality. For this, we need scientific means but we also need faith to serve as a guide and purpose. If not, our learning could be destructive."

Attitudinal Approaches

A number of participants view the interconnection of faith and learning from an attitudinal perspective. For these participants, faith informs their attitude and motivation toward learning. The positive attitude is expressed through learning awe and academic humility.

Learning awe

More than one-third of participants expressed their religious and aesthetic understanding as a result of their learning. To describe their amazement, they used phrases such as "the more I learn the more I admire God," "I learn the greatness of God," and "I can see the grandeur of God." BS1 expressed his awe of God when he studied the microstructure of a material. He gave an example, "I can see the signature structure of metal under the microscope. It's very beautiful, much more beautiful than the pattern of this batik I wear. Through this, I learn the greatness of God. Human beings cannot imitate this kind of structure." BS1 responded to this privilege of learning with humility when he said, "I am fortunate to be given this opportunity to learn about the material structure so I can be more observant. I can see what other people can't. Is it not grace, a gift given by God in scholarship that I can see the grandeur of God?" CS1 also affirmed the interconnection of faith and learning when saying, "Instead of contradicting my faith, I find that the more I learn the more I admire God. Like what God said in the Bible to subdue and conquer the earth, I think it includes God's command for us to study the earth and we can know him through his creation." In the same vein, TM1 spoke of his amazement of God's greatness in his forestry studies. "The more I learn the more I see the greatness of God. Look at the big trees. They come from small seeds, but they can grow into such big trees. Sometimes I stop and look at the trees. I feel how small I am and an amazed at God's greatness."

Academic humility

The faith-shaped attitude toward the participants' scholarship is also expressed through their academic humility. This attribute of scholars is manifested through their expression of "the more I learn the less I know," and the acknowledgment of the limits of human intellectual reasoning. SW2 expressed, "After finishing my doctoral degree I feel less confident because I feel that I only know a little. It makes me feel that the more I learn the less I know. I truly admire God. How incredible he is with all the knowledge and much of this knowledge has not been opened to me yet." After more than three decades studying the reproductive biology of plants, EP1 expressed her amazement and feeling of smallness in the vastness of the ocean of knowledge. "The advanced research has been using DNA and bio-molecular approaches to find which gene makes fertilization happened. Every time I read the newest finding that this gene controls this and that gene controls that, I feel so small and know very little. On the other hand, I see a strong hand that controls everything." Another participant, AS1 recognized the limitation of his own reasoning in understanding the natural and supernatural world when he explained:

> According to acid-base reactions when we add acid HCl to NaOH then it would become NaCl + H2O. But when Jesus changes water into wine, H2O turns into acid and alcohol, how can you explain? That was my struggle. But now I understand that I don't understand. What I know is science and it's only a small part of it. How can this little of me understand the greatness of God? I feel I am like an elementary school student who tries to learn calculus which is for college students.

Ethical and Moral Approaches

Another perspective taken by some participants to relate faith to their academic discipline is an ethical and moral approach (e.g. DS1, HS1, EW2, DC2, ES3). For these participants, Christian faith provides principles to guide what and how they do their research. EW2 spoke of a temptation to do psychological research about aggressive behavior but thinking from a Christian perspective she found that the methodology involved would be unethical. She explained, "I need to make the persons become aggressive before I conduct the therapy. If the therapy succeeds the persons will be fine but if it fails what would happen to them? This is crazy to play with people's brains." She finally declined to do the research and said, "I could not imagine if faith is not integrated into my research, it would be dangerous and harmful for other people." ES3 also mentioned some moral and ethical dilemmas she faced in science research: "With the progress in science there are many changes which can be positive and negative. Christian faith plays a role in guiding one's research. Some researches I find dilemmatic such as umbilical cord stem cell, test-tube baby, and other cell research."

For another participant, DC2, faith is ethically integrated into his professional work both as a teaching faculty member and as head of a laboratory testing concrete quality. This ethical integration is important especially when he faced "many contractors who like to play with price and construction quality." He responded, "Here, I and my colleagues conduct concrete testing. In some cases, we found there were mismatches between what the constructors said and the results of testing. The quality of their concrete work was low. As an independent party, we must be strict and keep our integrity intact because it's about safety and people's lives."

Intrapersonal Approaches

When asked about the relationship between faith and learning, some participants focus on themselves as the agents of integration. For them, faith permeates into their learning, living, and doing as Christian faculty. CH3 explained that as a faculty teaching biblical studies, faith made a huge difference in studying the Bible. "My discipline is biblical studies. It means that I can approach the texts from different aspects such as grammatical, structural, and linguistics. Many of these approaches have nothing to do with faith . . . If I take off my faith, then I study the Bible as merely a text like other writings. Because of faith, I do not just study the texts, but I also believe in the text. So, faith makes me live out the knowledge I gain from learning."

CS3 also shared a similar view that his thinking, being, and doing was all infused with faith. He explained, "I think there is no objectivity in teaching and learning. All are subjective. So, everything I teach and learn is influenced by my faith. A person who knows God views the stone differently from a person who doesn't know God. My faith shapes my subjectivity, the way I think, talk, judge, and so on." JS3 also took a holistic approach to the integration of faith and learning. "Faith integrated into the academic discipline is not enough," she said, "Because we are holistic persons. Integration should not be partial but must be taken as a whole that is reflected in everything we think, say, and do as we carry out our scholarship."

Interpersonal Approaches

While the intrapersonal approach focuses on the self of the educators in living out their faith, the interpersonal approach emphasizes building good relationships with the students and co-workers. For example, DS1 asserted, "Instead of directly connected to my discipline, I see faith as more connected to the way I interact with students. I value my students as God's special creation. Each of them is a masterpiece, so I appreciate and aim to build them up." Cautioned by the old image of educators who were self-distant and arrogant, ES3 stressed faculty being a servant with a posture of humility to serve the students. She explained, "Christian faith is manifested through our good attitude. In contrast to the old manner of lecturers who were crazy for respect and played with students' grades, I think to be a Christian faculty member means building a good relationship with students. Students will go back to society. We need to help build their character, not to become fearful persons but respectful individuals." For JS3, the focus of interpersonal relationships is building a good work relationship with her co-workers. Aware that a strong focus on psychological self-empowerment could be problematic at her department, JS3 said, "If our focus is how we can be powerful, to be ourselves and to do what we want, then I think that is contrary to our Christian faith. We need to humble ourselves under the authority of God in doing all these good works personally and building good relationships with co-workers and other people."

Contribution to the Kingdom of God

The final approach participants describe as a way of integrating faith and learning is applying the knowledge from their respective academic disciplines to love and care for God's world and people. CS1 argued that faith played an important role in directing his intent to use science for good. As a Christian scholar equipped with the eschatological understanding of the new heaven and earth, CS1 intended to contribute his expertise to fish and aquatic conservation. Especially with the current issue of marine pollution in the Indonesian ocean, CS1 expressed, "The new earth is started now and here. Don't damage the environment, don't throw plastic into the ocean. Plastic waste in the sea is a huge problem now. Indonesia is the biggest contributor. Plastic has killed many sea organisms. One of the most threatened is sea turtles because they eat jellyfish and plastic is like jellyfish." Informed by his Christian faith, TM1 also spoke of his intention to use his expertise in forestry science for land and forestry conservation. "Being reminded that God is the creator and commands us to take care of his creation, I think it's important for us to do something with our severely damaged forests. We need to include various stakeholders and entrepreneurs. We need also to include the element of justice for the people who live around the forest area."

Other participants intend to apply their knowledge to serve the poor and empower others. Informed by her Christian faith and expertise in urban space design, RD3 decided "to be a voice for the poor." She explained, "My latest research was about how the urban poor people saw the city space. I want the government to consider the voice of the poor in the process of designing.

Encouraged by my experience with God, I want to use my knowledge in a meaningful way." EW2 also shared a passion to serve the marginalized children with her expertise in clinical psychology. She explained, "My department has been partnering with an NGO to provide free counseling for children. This NGO operates a school for marginalized children . . . Besides counseling, we also provide a short workshop with topics related to self-esteem. That's a psychology term but actually, I incorporated the concept of imago Dei. I don't have to use the Christian jargon but all the contents are infused with Christian values."

No Integration Approach

Participants who hold to this approach assume that faith and learning are two different domains that need no integration. Included in this category are the participants' description of the relationship between faith and learning as compatible, parallel, and "uncertain."

Compatible

Participants who view the compatibility of faith and learning are mostly from the natural science disciplines (e.g. CS1, BS1, HS1, DS1, PK3). Despite identified connections between faith and science at the ontological level, these participants maintain that both are two sets of truths but compatible with each other. For them, science is "neutral" because it based on "facts" and "observations of the natural world." For example, BS1 asserted, "I am in material science, it's always honest, it never lies. What I do is observations of the natural world, so there is no conflict. For example, if I examine the microstructure of this metal table, the structure is there." PK3 also shared a similar view that science was based on facts, "not based on opinions like in the social sciences or philosophy." Thus she argued, "There is no conflict between the two." Both HS1 and DS1, whose academic discipline were in mathematics, also maintained that no integration was needed because both were "compatible with each other" (HS1) and "could function separately" (DS1).

Parallel

BW1, whose disciplinary majors were in philosophy and anthropology, expressed a conceptual understanding of faith and learning that was a bit different from the compatibilists. His view is that faith and learning should not and could not meet because they were two different realities that were mutually exclusive. He argued, "Faith and learning are parallel. There is no common ground and no conflict. For example, evolutionary theory and faith, both are parallel like railroad tracks. Both belong to different domains, they should not meet otherwise; there will be a crash."

"Uncertain"

Some participants expressed that they had no idea of how faith and learning relate to each other. Taking a long pause to ponder the question of the integration of faith and learning, YP2 finally uttered with uncertainty, "I can't see the relationship between faith and my discipline. My field is secular and capitalist. Money has the power that influences people's decision making. Faith has no influence on the market but on the contrary, the market influences faith. I am not sure." ES3 also felt unsure of how to relate faith to her discipline when she said, "Faith is believing without seeing while science is talking about facts. But I feel uncertain, sometimes it seems there is a relationship between two but sometimes there is no relationship."

Response to Conflicts between Faith and Learning

When they encounter apparent tensions or conflicts between faith and learning, the responses given by the participants varied. These responses included: choosing faith over learning, "I do not know what to do," avoiding and omitting conflicted topics, and learning and seeking alternatives.

Choosing Faith Over Learning

Some participants respond to faith-learning conflict by choosing one over the other. TM1, MC2, and AS1 expressed that as Christian scientists they were looking to faith over science. TM1 recognized that faith and science sometimes were incompatible. When he encountered the theory of evolution which he thought contradicted to his Christian faith, he responded by saying that it was "no problem" because he chose to believe what the Bible said: that God was the creator over science that claimed human beings were the result of the evolutionary process. MC2 recalled an experience she had when confronted by her classmate during her graduate study in the Netherlands about her disbelief in Darwinism. She responded: "I don't believe the theory because it's not finished yet. If in the end it's proved to be right, I would believe it but until now we cannot see the end of the process yet. I believe God, the designer of the universe, is never wrong."

A similar response is shared by AS1 that when science and faith collide, he chose faith. Using number theory, he explained: "In mathematics, we have real and complex numbers. I cannot use the real number theory to understand complex number theory. Similarly, science is dealing with the "real" world while God is above "real" or facts that we can know . . . He is beyond logic. I still believe science but when it conflicts with faith or I can't understand anything, I trust in God's authority."

"I Do Not Know What to Do"

Some participants find tensions between faith and learning but feel powerless, confused, and uncertain about what kind of response they should give. ET1 found there was a segment in her management course about moral relativism. She contended that the theory contradicted her Christian belief but she felt powerless against what was written in the textbooks. She explained, "The theory says that morality is relative because it depends on social and cultural contexts. For example, in Toraja, the dead are not buried but they are given new clothes and food. This is contrary to our faith. I also teach different levels of morality such as a person who does something because of the fear of punishment. The theory doesn't fit in my belief but I do not know what to do. I can't do anything to oppose it." YP2 also faced a dilemma when teaching a stock market trading course. She saw the similarity between stock market trading and gambling and felt uneasy about it but did not know how to respond to the issue. With a confused tone, she said, "I teach my students how to analyze the company, its financial situation, the product and selling points, market share, and all other fundamental and technical analysis. But deep in my heart, I was struggling that this is like gambling. What does my faith say about it? I have asked my colleagues of other faiths and they said that they had no problem with that. But I am still asking God whether this is right or wrong." She added, "Part of this class is that students practice buying and selling in the stock market. How about if they don't make a profit but suffer loss? I am also questioning whether a Christian can participate in forex and bond trading."

Avoiding and Omitting Conflicted Topics

A number of participants choose to resolve conflicts between faith and learning by omitting the dilemmatic topics from the course contents. SW3 found a section in her hospitality and tourism course that discussed LGBT tourism. Feeling not well equipped with biblical knowledge to address this controversial issue, SW3 decided to exclude the topic from her class. "Gay and lesbian tourism is a growing segment but it would violate my faith if I teach this subject. Besides, I am not an expert in this area. I am only a layman; if there is a controversy I don't know how to handle it. So, I choose to skip the topic." Similarly, DY3 also tried to avoid controversial topics when teaching or supervising undergraduate senior thesis projects. She explained, "It is difficult if I have to teach topics such as cultural studies, LGBT, or constructivism that advocates for no absolute truth. I also feel sad when supervising or reading a student thesis that talks about the interpersonal relationships for lesbian couples. I really struggle because it is against my conscience. I am still seeking ways how to respond to this kind of struggle."

Learning and Seeking for Alternatives

Another response expressed by participants to address the gap between faith and their academic discipline is by seeking alternative theories or views that are more in line with Christian faith. EW2 explained that some of her Christian colleagues restrained themselves from learning some theories of psychology that were not in line with the Christian faith but she chose otherwise by arguing: "How do we know the theories are wrong if we do not study about them? Of course, we must have a strong foundation of faith first so we can examine and filter which parts of the theories that we cannot use. There are many humanistic theories such as Jung, Ericson, or Freud. For example, Freud's theory of sexual drive, I don't agree with it." EW2 did not use theories that she thought problematic as a framework for her "research or community service," instead seeking alternative theories. "For example," she said, "Instead of a psychoanalytic approach, I use a cognitive-behavioral approach because I can insert Christian values in it."

JH2 also found that in his philosophy class, many philosophers criticized Christianity severely but instead of abandoning their thoughts he opted to humbly learn from them. He explained, "For example, Marx said that religion is opium or an escape. I think there is a truth in it. Because of industrialization, people feel oppressed, thus Sunday service is an escape for them." JH2 also expressed that Christian faith could provide a better alternative for the problem when he said, "Those critics are right in a certain sense but I think we can do something beyond that because we bear a task to release people from their bondage of suffering. Maybe in the business, we can encourage the owners to care more about their employees."

RD3 also encountered dilemmatic theories in her research about urban space design. She "felt uncomfortable" reading Deleuze and Guattari's thought about human freedom. Considering their ideas were "too leftist" and "afraid of being brainwashed," she said, "I try not to go deeper with this theory but find other thoughts that are more in the middle which makes me feel more comfortable." Interestingly, RD emphasized "heart" as her means to measure whether the theory is pro or contra to Christian faith. "I use my heart as the standard that if I feel uncomfortable reading the book then I would stop. I think God is speaking in my heart. It is embedded in me that God is speaking in my heart when I interpret the knowledge (readings)."

Section 3: The Integration of Faith and Educational Practices

The majority of the participants acknowledged the importance of faith in shaping their teaching and learning practices. Many of these participants speak of the integration of faith and learning, not as an intentional, but rather a "spontaneous" act of incorporating Christian values or principles into their teaching and learning practices. They also emphasize faith as guiding principles to "give the best" and "help students learn best." In addition to spontaneous integration, faith is incorporated in their educational practices in implicit ways which include: modeling an exemplary life; building positive relationships with students; and cultivating Christian values and practices. Only a small number of participants employ explicit ways of sharing their Christian faith with students through personal conversational interactions.

"Spontaneous" Integration

For most participants, faith is "internalized" (JA1), "natural" (BS1), and "ingrained" (DS1). As such, it is not in the participants' minds or plans to incorporate faith when they design a course syllabus at the beginning of the semester and/or prepare a weekly lesson plan. For them, integration is "spontaneous" (DA1, JA2, ET2) and flowing out of being (BS1, DS1). JA2 expressed that "integration was spontaneous." "Why?" he explained, "because in social psychology, it depends on the actual situation of the class in which I can incorporate a spiritual perspective when it is appropriate. For example, in personal development, faith teaches me that God creates us with a role to play in this world; the cases can be varied but the principle is there."

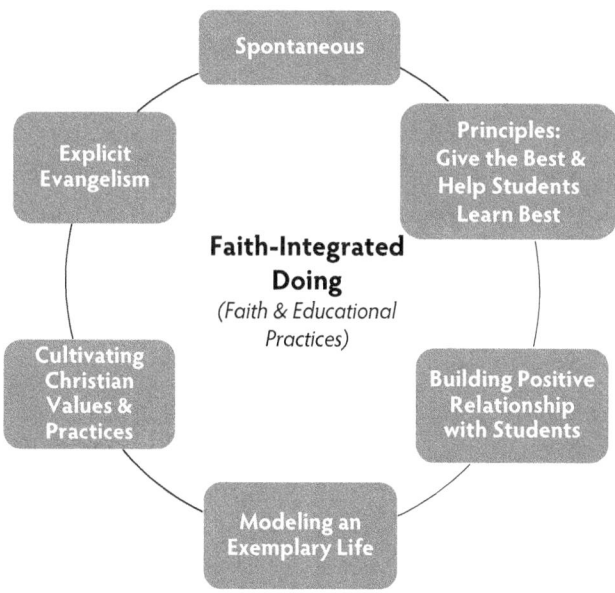

Figure 4. Six Aspects of the Integration of Faith and Educational Practices

Other participants, ET2 and DA1, also shared their spontaneous integration experiences. ET2 recalled, "Wisdom came to me suddenly when I was teaching and spontaneously, I would connect the topic to spiritual truth." DA1also expressed, "I don't make a plan, but it (the faith integration) will come out spontaneously when we discuss issues or topics that seem appropriate." For BS1, the integration of faith and learning did not have to be intentional but rather flowed out naturally from a life that has been lived by the word of God.

Actually, I do not think about it, how I might become salt and light in my classroom, I just live it out. What helps me is my daily reading of the Bible. I wake up at 4:30 a.m. or 5:00 a.m. and meditate on God's word. Because of this habit, I don't have to think of anything but to live it out naturally. So being a lecturer or when I teach I don't have to be stressed out by thinking how should I share the Gospel or how many would be converted. But just being who you are. I do not have to think, to be stressed out, or disingenuous. If I have to be angry then I would be angry or if I have to reprimand my students then I would do it. Be genuine, not superficial or pretend to be a holy person.

DS1 also shared a similar view by saying, "For me, faith is something natural, ingrained in me. It's embedded in whatever I do, so I don't have to think about how to put faith in my teaching. I see myself as a being that has been formed by Christ. He works through me, so faith influences and interconnects with whatever I do."

Faith Gives Principles to "Give the Best" and "Help Students Learn Best"

As described previously, most participants described faith integration as unplanned but spontaneously occurring during the teaching and learning process. For some participants, faith provides a guiding principle to offer their best both in preparing and conducting their teaching and the learning process. For example, desiring to reflect the character and work quality of the heavenly Father in his own teaching job, CS1 asserted, "Because the Bible teaches us to 'be perfect, therefore, as your heavenly Father is perfect.' Thus in everything I do, I give my best, including teaching and leading practicum. I am serious about my work . . . So the perspective of faith helps me to give my best." RS1 also expressed a similar principle that guided her teaching practice when she said, "God has put me here, so I must give my best. I love to tell stories, most of the time they just come up spontaneously. But every time before I teach I always prepare." For some other participants, faith directs their attitude and efforts to "help students learn best." For example, LT2 expressed that being informed by faith he took "all kinds of ways to help students learn."

In a similar fashion, DC2 also expressed, "Only one goal, that is helping students learn best, making my class easy enough for them to absorb."

The principles of giving the best and helping students learn best is reflected in the participants' efforts to create a conducive learning climate, teaching attitude and competencies, pedagogical choice, selection of student assessment methods, and prayer for wisdom.

Creating a Conducive Learning Climate

To foster a positive learning experience, some participants take strategies to create a friendly class atmosphere through interactive and relational learning. Yet, they also make sure that students know their responsibilities by setting the "rules of the game."

Relational and interactive

Coming to the class with a smiling face and friendly greetings, taking time to know each student's name, and having some casual conversations, are the means taken by some participants to establish positive relationships with their students. For example, JS3 expressed, "I will focus on my students first. Sometimes I look at them quietly, or say 'hi.' I greet them with a smile and ask them, 'How is your day?' For me, building a good relationship with students is important."

SW2 had a special ability to remember all her students' names. She found it helpful in creating a dynamic class interaction. She said, "I can memorize their names; those from new batch to old batch, every single name... Sometimes I involve them when I share a joke by calling their names, or if any of them come late or sleep in the class; I will call them by their names. So the students are cautious about cheating because they know I will call them by their names."

For HS1, RS1, and SW2, engaging students with stories and humor helps to create a positive classroom atmosphere. HS1 said, "My guiding value is that I must give the best for my students. I try to create a class environment that students can feel relaxed, because if the students feel depressed or afraid of their lecturer, then they will not be able to capture the contents. So sometimes I like to tell funny stories to make them laugh and less tense." Similarly, RS1 also liked to incorporate stories in her mathematics classes. Enthusiastically she said, "I love to tell stories, most of the time they just come up spontaneously... This is the most enjoyable activity as a lecturer. I think I can play drama in front of them. Students love it. When there are parallel classes, many students would choose my class."

In the case of EP1, key words to keep the class interesting are "improvisation" and being sensitive to the class' needs. She said, "I encourage students to raise hands if they do not understand. For me, if I cannot finish the materials that I've prepared, it's fine for me. My priority is that students understand what I teach." At other times, during the afternoon class when most students felt sleepy after lunch, she would start the class by singing together. She explained, "I need to make a lot of improvisations. Sometimes I would talk about popular issues that are still useful for them, for example, the content of caffeine in coffee beans and how it works and makes us stay awake. I try to dissolve the class atmosphere from boredom; I really love my job."

"Rules of the game"

Some participants preferred the "rules of the game" to classroom contracts, but some other participants also include course descriptions and expectations. EW2 liked to use the few class meetings to get acquainted with the students and establish the classroom contracts which included rules, rewards, and consequences. She explained, "I am an open person, sometimes I joke, and sometimes I am firm. If any of them comes late I will rebuke them. But whenever they do great, with zero absence, I will praise them and give them a snack bar. Once, they were surprised when I passed them the rewards and I encouraged them to continue to be on time, even if they would not be in my class next semester."

For SW3, the classroom contract was collaboratively created by the students and herself. She explained, "Sometimes the class agrees that there will be no compromises for those who come late. But other classes will tolerate fifteen minutes late, beyond that there will be consequences, such as singing a song or dancing in front of the class." SW2 added, "The rules of the game also include the course descriptions and objectives, what do I expect from students, assessments, lessons per each meeting, and grading components. These rules of the game apply to me as well as the students." Similarly, DY3 emphasized class discipline as a starting point to develop a conducive learning environment. She said, "The semester is always started with a classroom contract. I always emphasize to the class that to be consistent and to have integrity are also the manifestations of Christian faith. If I say A then I must act A. It is the same with the classroom contract that binds both students and me as their lecturer. Everybody must come on time. If students or I come late, the consequences will apply to both. "

Teaching Attitude and Competencies

In addition to creating a conducive learning climate, many participants embody the principles to "give the best" and "help students learn best" through their teaching attitude and competencies. These participants come to the class well-prepared, demonstrate confidence, enthusiasm, and competence, have high expectations for the students, are open to feedback, and prone to teaching and learning innovations.

Being well-prepared

Many participants expressed that coming to class well-prepared was an attitude informed by their Christian faith. Pondering on why she was called in the first place, RS1 responded by saying, "God has put me here, so I must give my best . . ., Before I come to the class, I always prepare myself. I never come to a class unprepared." A similar attitude also shared by HS1. He said, "Although I have taught the course many times, I am still obliged to prepare for the class. I browse the internet to find new information and I keep myself away from being monotone."

Well-prepared for TM1 meant coming to class on time and being ready with an updated course syllabus, teaching resources, weekly lesson plans, various means of teaching presentation, and student assessments. For DS1, planning and preparing for teaching were keys to an effective teaching and learning process. She referred to her lesson plan as a "magic book," which she followed closely when teaching the class. She said, "In the magic book, I explain to students what we will learn at the first meeting, second, third, and so on. Including what are the assignments and deadlines, group discussions, how many groups, and what topics . . . I have disciplined myself in this way for many years. So whenever I come to the class, I greet the students and am ready to start according to the agenda."

Confidence, enthusiasm, and competence

Other aspects of a faith-shaped teaching attitude and competencies expressed by some participants are teaching with confidence, enthusiasm, and competence. These three elements are interrelated. EP1 expressed that teaching with confidence and competence required good preparations. She said, "I work hard to prepare myself before I come to the class." In addition, she said, "I teach with full enthusiasm. If I am not enthusiastic, the students will not be enthusiastic either." For RM2, the contributing factor to his confidence and enthusiasm in teaching was prayer. He expressed that prayer made him teach with a "burning spirit." He explained, "I am eager to share with the students and motivate them to be more and better than me. Sometimes I look at their eyes: they seem to be without hope. I don't just teach, but I want to inspire them."

TM1, CS1, and LI3 related confidence to being knowledgeable and staying current in their field. For example, CS1 said that he "read a lot," subscribed to several scientific journals, and actively involved in the research. In addition to competence, CS1 also demonstrated enthusiasm in teaching. He explained, "Why am I so enthusiastic? Because God still gives me opportunities, thus I must give the best. Sometimes I struggle to teach the afternoon class, especially after lunch, students are sleepy. But I try to make the class atmosphere alive . . . I stay enthusiastic." Students were inspired by his teaching attitude and competencies and curiously asked how he could attain such broad knowledge, and CS1 answered, "I read a lot. I love to tell them about the books and journals that I read. I encourage them to read, so they can have a broad knowledge too."

Have high expectations for students

Another quality of the teaching attitude and competencies shown by many participants is building a culture of high expectations for their students. BS1 and JA2 cultivated a culture of high expectations by challenging their students to learn in English. For several years, BS1 had used English as a medium in his engineering class. Explaining the reason behind this practice, he said, "I have a dream that my students would continue their graduate studies abroad. I want to build their confidence from now. So, one way to show my faith is by encouraging them to be brave enough to dream for their future. So far this institution has excellent undergraduate students." In the case of JA2, he decided to use "books and slide presentations" written in English, but the medium for oral communication was still in Bahasa Indonesia. He explained that the resources in the Indonesian language were limited, and although translation efforts have been made, the quality of the translated books was not as good as the original textbooks. However, this challenge provided an opportunity for JA2 to motivate his students to go a little beyond a perfunctory effort in their learning. In addition, he also explained the following strategies to bridge their learning in English and Indonesian language: "First, students can choose additional equivalent textbooks translated into the Indonesian language; and second, I put them into groups to discuss the texts and they can use gadgets or dictionaries to help with the translations."

CS1 expected each of his students to "give the best," the same principle he applied to himself. He explained, "I motivate them to work hard, give the best. In the beginning, students were shocked but then they realized its importance. Generally, students study just to pass the exams. No one is looking for more." Similarly, LT2 expressed high academic expectations by setting a high passing grade for students who took his classes. He said, "For a building analysis class, I cannot let the students pass if they have low grades. This is basic, it's impossible to pass them because building structure is about the safety of the people. I want them to understand both the concepts and the calculations." In addition, LT2 strongly encouraged his students to pursue graduate studies at famous universities abroad. "I often motivate them to think big," LT2 said, "because there are many scholarships and opportunities . . . I hope students under my tutelage, some of them will go international and become lecturers with broad knowledge. Thus I hope they can get scholarships and study abroad. Recently, one student got accepted at Columbia University with an LPDP's scholarship. It's really surprising. Another student got accepted at Stockholm University. I am so pleased."

Open to feedback

Another quality of the teaching attitude shown by some participants is openness to feedback given by their students and/or colleagues. EP1 explained that at the end of every semester, students would give an evaluation of her teaching contents, methods, assessments, and learning tools and facilities. EP1 responded to her students' feedback by saying, "Some complained that the class was boring, the slides were not interesting, and so on. Others complained that 1:00 p.m. class was sleepy and lacked enthusiasm. I go through all the evaluations and improve. As long as it's under my authority, I would do it. However, some complaints are about the facilities such as that the lab had only six microscopes for ten students. I bring the matter to the department meeting. Generally, the department would respond positively as long as the equipment is not expensive."

For RI3, improving her teaching practices involved listening to the students' and colleagues' feedback. Regarding the student feedback, she said, "To improve my course design, first I would look at the standard curriculum from last semester or last year to find if there are any gaps. I also listen to my students' opinions and their overall evaluations." In addition, RI3 also humbly asked for feedback from her senior colleagues. "I am a person who likes to ask. Maybe I am afraid of making mistakes or maybe I like to involve other people. Once, I finished drafting a course design, I took it to my seniors and asked them what they thought about it. They told me that I should do this and that to make it better."

Prone to teaching and learning innovations

Motivated to help students better, some participants expressed their willingness to learn and try new innovations in teaching and learning. EP1 recently attended a workshop about "teaching the Y generation," in which she commented, "I feel refreshed and equipped . . . I learned how to teach the students, design the guidelines and test questions, and evaluate students' essays." To enhance better teaching and learning, EP1 also expressed her keenness to "keep up with the technology."

EW2 preferred "try and error" in seeking a better teaching approach. She explained, "Sometimes I found this method didn't work or that method also didn't make them understand. So, I like to do 'try and error' to find a way to help my students learn better." Giving an example and explaining why she was prone to try a new teaching method, she said, "In supervising students' theses, some of them are slow and others are fast. So, I need to separate them into different groups. I know it takes more effort and time as compared to other lecturers, but I think it's a part of my faith that teaching is not just for the sake of getting your work done."

LT2 observed that many of his colleagues were "narrow-minded and used a single solution approach" in teaching and learning. "Teaching students to look for a single solution," LT2 said, "is dangerous." Finding an alternative, he tried to teach students to use a multiple-angle of analysis in his urban and real estate development class. He explained, "I teach students how to observe phenomena, how to quantify those phenomena or make the simulations. Students are encouraged to find assumptions behind all those phenomena and to think "if this" or "if that" . . . So, students should not be taught that there is only one solution; this is an engineering major and we need to help them to engineer something."

Pedagogical Choice

To help students learn best, many participants employed student active learning approaches. HS1, CS1, DA2, and JH2 included group discussions, student presentations, and question and answer sessions in their student-centered pedagogical choices. For HS1, lecturing was still a good teaching method, especially when he said, "Not all the content can be learned through group discussions. Some theories are outcomes from the accumulated thoughts that take centuries to evolve. Students need a lecture type of learning to understand these kinds of theories. If not, students would be lost." RS1 preferred incorporating stories into mathematics teaching. She explained, "Behind every formula, there is a story. I said to students that if they understand the story behind each formula, they will not forget it. But if they only memorize the formula, they will forget it."

ET2 has been using the flip class approach for one semester. She expressed that this method suited millennial learners, by fostering their personal agency in learning and positively engaging them in a dynamic teaching and learning process. Explaining how the method worked, she said, "'Students must read and answer the questions prior to coming to the class. If they don't read, I would ask them to get out of the class. I also have responsibilities. I must read too, make guideline questions, and post them online. I was anxious in the beginning whether they would do their parts. But now students have become used to this method. Every time I come to the class they know that I will ask, 'Have you answered the questions which I posted three days ago?'" In addition, she said, "Whenever we learn about definitions, I would ask for their opinion first. I also use a lot of group discussions. I don't want the students to get lost in their discussions because I can't check what they say in the groups. Sometimes they are noisy but dynamic. So I will do the wrap-up after the discussions."

Understanding the nature of her students leads DS1 to exercise differentiated instruction. DS1 explained that for new students, who were still in their transitions from high school to college and did not have much prior knowledge content, the teaching method she used would be less demanding for the students. She said, "I observe that they are flooded with euphoria when admitting to this university. Secondly, they are burdened by assignments given by their seniors. So they don't give much time to study. I give them some reading assignments prior to coming to class. They're not difficult tasks but just to familiarize themselves with mathematical terms." However, for senior students who possessed some knowledge content and were ready to take more responsibilities of their learning, DS1 took "a role of a facilitator" and used a jigsaw teaching strategy. She explained how she organized the teaching and learning process using this method:

> I break the class into groups, and each group only discusses one topic. This, I call a focus group. Each member of this focus group acts as a representative and finds a new group where they will share what they have learned. They assemble the pieces into a completed jigsaw. After that, the groups will do the presentation and I will give them feedback. I observe that this method works well because each student is given a responsibility. It forces students to participate because if they don't study, then they can't share anything. But meanwhile, their friends are demanding them to share their parts otherwise they won't understand the whole topic.

In addition to student active learning, RT1 also chose a teaching approach that resembled the students' future profession as accountants. He explained, "The class presentation is either individual or in a team, but I prefer them to work in a team because in the real world, the financial auditors work in a team. I ask them to think of themselves as internal auditors who assist the CEO and imagine who will be sitting there during their presentation. So they must know what should be included in the presentation." Interestingly, RT1 ended each of his class meeting with a "CRA" approach which he explained as follows:

> C is a conclusion. Students must be able to make a conclusion using their own words. R is for reflection. What you learn is like

a mirror. Reflect on what you have learned and how would you put it into use. I believe that it can be useful in your everyday life. For example, when do you know that your girlfriend will say yes? You can gather samples of events of when you give her flowers, asking her out for a movie, etc. Equally important is the quality of the samples. Lastly, A is action. What are your follow-ups? What do you want to learn more? What actions will you take to realize the plan?

He added that the CRA method was to help students to find "the threads" and "the connections" among the lessons they have learned throughout the semester.

Student Assessment

The principles of giving the best and helping the students learn best are also reflected in the participants' perspectives and selection of student assessment methods. JH2 expressed that student assessment was "more than just testing the students' knowledge" but it was also about developing the students' character. For example, he said, "I strongly remind my students to keep themselves away from cheating and/or plagiarism, including giving or receiving answers during exams. The consequence will be a zero score on their GPA report." To help students with special needs and unique learning styles, he broadened his choice of assessment methods which included short essay assignments, class presentations, and oral or written exams. He explained, "Some students have difficulties in reading or writing, so I must consider their other strengths. Maybe they are good at talking or presentation. Because the course I teach is about values such as Pancasila, so I can adjust the assessments to their needs."

Similarly, JS2 also expressed that "learning and assessment were more than grades or scores," it was about learning to "see students as God sees us." Informed by the Christian principles of love and forgiveness he said, "The principles prevented me from quickly passing judgment on the students; labeling, stereotyping or saying other taboo things, such as 'you are hopeless,' 'you can't do it,' or 'you never change'; if the students apologize and repent, then I need to forgive them." In the case of MF3, she refused to see a student's thesis defense as merely "judging a student's work" and defending "a faculty's pride." Informed by faith, she proposed an alternative perspective saying, "I want students and colleagues to see from a perspective of grace . . . how to see a thesis defense as a thanksgiving for the process they have been through."

Connecting student assessment to ethical professional responsibility as an engineer, DC2 chose essay exams over multiple-choice question tests. He reasoned, "It's a domino effect. If they misunderstood the concepts or miscalculated the building structure, the whole building would collapse and thousands of people could die. Thus I never use multiple-choice but only essay exams. I assess how they use the formula or concepts, the step by step procedure, the parameters, and so on. If the end results are wrong I would still give them grades."

In the case of BS1, the method of student assessment can be a means for implicit evangelism. In his philosophy of knowledge course, BS1's preferred assessment method for final exams was oral examinations. BS1 explained that this three-credit hour course was compulsory for doctoral students and they came from various countries and religious backgrounds. The one-on-one oral exams had allowed him to get to know each of his students personally as well as to glean some valuable lessons. As an example, BS1 recalled his memorable encountered with a Vietnamese student who was an atheist. Quoting this student, he said, "My father was a civil servant in Vietnam, and since I was young I was taught by him from the small book of communism that there was no God. Sir, but after attending your class for a semester, now I feel that I need God." BS1 was surprised by his student's response and reflecting on this event, he said, "This is the only course that I can freely discuss religions. I learned that I don't have to be a missionary to Vietnam but God sends them here. I didn't intentionally introduce God to him, but somehow God touched his heart that he could be closer to the truth. Maybe other people will sow the seeds further." Reminded of a mission concept he learned from an OMF missionary while he was a student, he added, "Evangelism should be not understood narrowly from -1 to +1. But it's like an x-axis scales that spread from negative to positive numbers. Maybe the person is on -8 and if could bring him to -7, that's good. Other people might lead him closer to positive numbers. Maybe many students here are in the minus zone. They hate Christianity but when they know Christians are kind people, it would reduce their negative thinking. So I think a faith-integrated life is leading a person a step closer to the positive zone."

Praying for Wisdom

Many participants were aware that their desire to give the best and engage students in learning cannot merely be achieved by being well prepared or using innovative teaching approaches. They humbly expressed their needs of praying for good health, concentration, wisdom, and joy in teaching and learning. As an example, MP1 said, "Before coming to the class, I pray to God that my students won't be sleepy and distracted. For me, first of all, is prayer, and second, I must come to class prepared."

KC2 also showed his dependence on God through prayers. Expressing his need for wisdom, he said, "Before leaving home, I pray. I pray to God that I want to teach, deliver a new topic, and ask Him to give me wisdom and understanding so that I can explain it clearly. Let the glory of God be upon me, not shame or guilt; I always pray like that. So, this how I relate faith to my teaching practices." He emphasized further, "Although I have mastered the content and prepared it at home, sometimes I find myself speechless, I can't talk or sometimes when students ask questions, I know the answers but I can't explain. All these can be problems for me. So, during the preparation, I always pray, asking God for help. Truly, He is at work."

Preparing the course and syllabus at the beginning of the semester, RM2 said that the one most important thing was prayer. He said, "I pray that throughout the semester, I will stay healthy and all my students won't have any difficulty with me. So, I can start my class with peace in my heart, and teach with a joyful heart." Likewise, LI1 also emphasized the importance of prayer in preparing for her class. Although she has taught the same course for several years, she kept humbly asking God for wisdom and strength. She said. "Because I want to glorify God in everything I do; I will teach with my all strength although sometimes I fail. It is always in my prayer that I will teach responsibly, come on time, and help students understand what I teach."

Modeling an Exemplary Life

One outstanding theme echoed by many participants about how they integrate faith into their educational practices is modeling an exemplary life. For these participants, the key of integration lies in the life of faculty members as the integrators, who can be plainly seen by their students. To describe this modeling approach, participants used phrases such as "role model" (ES3, JS3, DY3, AS1), "sharing your life" (RD3, LS3), "my life is my message" (RD3), "transfer of life" (CS1, WU3, ET2), and "live out a life that has been changed by Christ" (CS1, AS1).

Teaching at a state university with predominantly Muslim students, EP1 asserted that living out her Christian faith was the best way to demonstrate faith-integrated educational practices. EP1 argued, "This is a strategic way to show how actually we live out our Christian faith. I don't have to preach out loud about my faith but what is much more important is how I can impart my Christian beliefs into the students' lives." EP1 explained that she manifested her Christian faith by "serving the students as well as possible" both as a faculty and head of the laboratory.

Likewise, CH1 also asserted, "I am here not just doing the transfer of knowledge but also the transfer of life." CS1 demonstrated "transfer of life" by "coming to class on time, prepared, teach his best, and being knowledgeable" in his field. CS1 explained that all these features were noticeable by the students and raised their curiosity. He wanted to motivate and help his students to see "a life that has been changed by the Gospel" manifested through his working ethos of "being honest" and "giving the best. BW1 also argued that faith and doing were parallel, especially being a faculty teaching class that related to "values" such as the "ideology of Pancasila and Christian religious education." Living an exemplary life is important when he said, "You can have lofty knowledge about religions but if it's not followed by works then it's a paradox; it becomes nothing."

AS1 saw the necessity of being a role model for students. He said, "Students need role models; if they don't have one they would lose track. They have knowledge and skills, but if nobody influences them, they would be lost . . . I want my students to remember me not because of much knowledge or skills that I've passed to them, but how I live my life that has been changed by Christ, as simple as that." He added that with the rise of radicalism on campus, Christian role models were needed more than ever. Thus, reminding himself of a child who had five loaves and two fish, he expressed, "This is what I wish to bring before God that although I am just a humble person who comes from a village, a child of a farmer, but I want God to use me." AS1 testified how God has used him to touch the students' lives, both Christians and Muslims alike.

> So I translated my faith in the contexts of both teaching Christian religious education and physics. And I am pleased that many

of my students, including Muslim students, know that I am a Christian. Once, a Muslim said to me: "Thank you for all your teaching. May God bless you, sir." Wow, how can this student say something like that? They mostly use words such as *rahmat* (mercy) or *berkah* (blessings) but not *diberkati* (blessed).

RD3 also emphasized the importance of the modeling approach by stating, "My life is my message. Being a lecturer is not just about sharing your knowledge, but your life. Students see my life. I can punish them when they are late but how about me? Am I coming late to the class? Am I fair enough when assessing their works? They can see my life openly, including my social life in social media."

Building Positive Relationships with Students

Another outstanding manifestation of faith-informed educational practice mentioned by many participants is building positive and supportive relationships with the students. This teacher-student relationship is demonstrated through the participants' attitude and treatment toward the students, and various caring supports that are extended beyond the classroom.

Attitude and Treatment Toward Students

Some participants talk about biblical principles that underlie their interaction and caring for the students. These principles include the concept of imago Dei, fair and just treatment, hospitality and respect, and incarnational posture.

Imago Dei

The understanding of imago Dei helps EW2 to see each student as a person created by God with the potentials to learn and grow. She asserted, "I don't look at students as incapable but as capable persons who can do anything. I hold to Genesis that teaches about the concept of imago Dei. Therefore there is no ugly person. God created us all." In the same way, DS1 also expressed that the understanding of imago Dei gave her a principle in interacting with the students. "I see my students as God's special creation. Each of them is a masterpiece. Thus, I treat them with respect and an intention to build them up. So, the way I integrate my faith into learning practice is more on how I treat my students than directly related to my academic discipline." CH3 also expressed that in the classroom interaction, he encouraged all his students to feel free to ask questions because he said, "My faith teaches me that there is no extraordinary or stupid question. For me, they ask questions because they don't know. Even if any of them asks a trivial thing, I ask the class not to laugh. This principle is influenced by my belief that every student is God's precious creation whom I must value."

Fair and just treatment

"The real practice of faith," HS1 contended, "is shown through my attitude in teaching, giving feedback, willingness to listen to what the students think and feel about the subjects, and finding the solutions. I try my best to be an objective lecturer in giving a fair assessment regardless of their ethnic and religious backgrounds." A similar fair and just attitude was also adopted by YP2 who said, "I try to be fair. Never in a case that because the students are Christians or Bataks, who I would know from their last names, that I would favor them. Never! Or because the students are Muslims, who like to write down Al-Quran verses on the top of the paper, that I would treat them unfairly. It all depends on their answers, if the answers are wrong even they are Christians, I would not give them good grades."

Hospitality and respect

BW1, AS1, and CS expressed that faith shaped their attitude in accepting and treating other people's differences with hospitality and respect. BW1 asserted that one aspect of faith in his classroom practice was showing respect for the students who had differences of opinion. "Faith for me is respecting others. I exemplify it by appreciating my students who have different opinions from mine. I am not a person in the position who knows everything. I am willing to receive feedback from my students. So, when I teach, I also learn." CS3 also referred to mutual respect and hospitality attitude as his foundation to interact with non-Christian students. He prayed for them and expressed greetings when they celebrated their religious holidays. "I pray for my Muslim students," CS3 said, "because I always hope that one day they will return to God. During Eid al-Fitr, I say my greetings to them that they may return to the true Fitr, the true and holy God . . . I reveal to them my Christian faith, but at the same time I never diminish the faith of others." For CS3, hospitality is not just an attitude, but also a practice of receiving students at his home:

"Students often come to my house, especially those in my small group . . . Sometimes they have not eaten yet, I let them cook whatever they can find in the fridge. They feel welcomed."

Incarnational posture

The incarnational posture of the participants is shown through their efforts to close the gaps in age and power distance between them and their students. AS1 expressed that one important aspect of building a good relationship with students was being friendly and authentic. Although being a senior both in age and teaching position, AS1 expressed: "Sometimes I take public transportation and meet my students. I don't feel embarrassed. Once they asked, 'Sir, why are you taking a public bus?' I jokingly said, 'Why not? The bus is not just for you, it's for everybody.' Or when I meet my students walking on the street, I would offer them a ride. I don't maintain my prestige but try to blend in with my students naturally."

"Informed by faith," MF3 said, "I see my students not as subordinates but as co-workers . . . These students will return to their hometowns and become leaders. I become more careful when interacting with them." She recalled an incident: "I got angry when I was really busy and shouted at them. I have been doing this reflective practice; I regretted what I've done to them and I apologized to them. Now I don't feel embarrassed if I have to apologize to them. And I try to find a better way to interact with them, because I realize that sarcastic words can have negative effects on the students."

SW3 realized that there was a generation gap between her and the students but she argued that she could not teach if she did not know the students. For her, to know meant taking active steps to go and come down to where the students were. Taking this incarnational approach, SW3 expressed: "If I keep a distance I can't reach them . . . I like to cangkruk (chatting) with my students at nearby street vendors. I am the only female faculty who does this. When I eat with them, they do not dare to smoke. Sometimes I just order a cup of coffee or a meal for the sake of building relationships with the students."

Caring and Support for Students

In addition to faith-informed attitudes and treatment of students, many participants also placed a strong emphasis on concrete ways to show their care and support for the students. These efforts are shown by making themselves accessible and available, providing help for students facing academic and/or non-academic issues, and reaching out to religious radical students.

Accessibility and availability

By accessibility, EP1 meant that she "gave open opportunities for students to meet with her as widely as possible." She said, "Students could reach me by phone or come to my office to discuss or ask any academic issues, research process, or problems in the field." EP1 added that she did "all teaching preparations" at home so that she could "make all her office hours available for any students who seek her help." Likewise, JH2 also expressed, "Students can ask me anything and anytime via e-mail, LINE, or module Apps." EW2 also showed a similar commitment to care for her students by making herself accessible and available in an outstanding way. Recalling a female student who came to her for counseling, she said, "This student went for a vacation and she was raped. Back in Jakarta, she didn't report to her parents but she came to me. She would wake up at 2:00 a.m. because of nightmares. I have said to her that she could contact me anytime, even 12:00 a.m. or 3:00 a.m. I gave her 24-hour access. That's how far I interact with my students."

Helping students with academic issues

For EPI, faith informed how she responded to her students' needs. She took the opportunity to assist her students' academic needs seriously when she said: "I welcome all students who need help that is related to my expertise. I have to say that whenever I am in the office, the students queue to see me for various reasons. Besides teaching, I am also the director of the study program and head of the lab." WU3 demonstrated similar care to support her students' academic success by supervising a group of twelve medical students for ten semesters or until they graduate. She provided them with routine meetings and special care for those with low academic performance. She explained, "For these students who are under my advising group, I have a regular meeting with them. Every time when they complete one block of a course, I will contact them via WAG to discuss what they have learned. I also monitor their grades. So far, most of them are good but some of them need special attention. Intensive care is given to students who have academic problems or other problems that affect their academic performance."

Similarly, RD3 expressed her faith-informed teaching practices by giving priority to students with low academic performance to do their senior research projects under her supervision. "For senior projects, students can choose their supervisors. I let the top students find their supervisors first, and am left with students who have lower grades. I think that the students will be fine with any lecturers, but students with Bs and Cs need extra help. I know to teach a C student is much more difficult than an A student. But I want these students to receive the same opportunity given to the top students."

Helping students with non-academic problems

In addition to academic support, some participants also willingly walked extra miles to help students with their non-academic issues, such as personal or family-related problems (e.g. RS1, EW2, BS1, CS3, DY3). To demonstrate her commitment to care for the students, EW2 cultivated a habit of coming early to the class in order to get to know them through informal conversations. Because of this, she said that students felt open to share and ask help for their personal problems. She recalled, "There was a student shared with me about his mentally ill mother. He has been hiding this because of fear his friend would label him as an infidel." Because of her good relationship with students, EW2 also took a proactive approach to counsel problematic students. She said, "I also dare to rebuke a student if she or he is wrong. For example, I have a female student who has a child out of wedlock and she currently lives with her partner. She was a Hindu but converted to Christianity because of her partner. I said to her that Christians should not trick people into bad things but love them. She has been asking me for advice via WA. I said to her that we needed to meet in person."

BS1 also extended his care for students beyond academic problems. He shared a story of a student whom he supervised for a senior research project, but who went missing for several months because of his involvement with an Islamic radical organization.

> Then suddenly he appeared, his body was thin and his face was messy. He asked if he could talk to me in private. I ushered him to an empty classroom and we talked. Apparently, he was a Muslim and involved in a radical Islamic movement that demanded him to do this and that. He could not bear it anymore

and wanted to get out, but they threatened and wanted to kill him. Because of that, he was scared and lied to his parents that he needed to stay overnight at a friend's house to do his assignments. He moved from one house to another for fear of being killed. He said to me, "I have no PD (self-confidence) anymore." I said to him, "It's O.K. What's you need now is PT (trust in God)." I was not sure if he listened to me. He didn't give any comment and our meeting ended.

BS1 continued that, during the graduation ceremony, the mother of one student came to him and said, "Thank you, sir, for giving my son a bit of advice about PT, because after listening to your advice my son changed." BS1 was proud of this student for completing his Ph.D. in Australia and he concluded the story by saying, "I think this is one way God uses me to serve the students. This is one example of my interaction with students outside the classroom in which I don't design it but God sends them to me."

Reaching out to religious radical students
Some participants expressed deep care for their students who were exposed to radical Islamic teachings and movements. For example, DS1, who is concerned with "the rise of radicalism among the intellectuals," took a proactive action to reach out to her Muslim students through partnership in research projects. She said, "I have a tendency to pay attention to Christian students. But I think that I should pay special attention to radical Muslim students, so they have the opportunity to interact with people who are different from them. I hope the interactions would make them less extreme." Regarding her means of interaction, DS1 said, "Certainly not through direct evangelism or indoctrination in the classroom . . . But I also don't know exactly how." One way she could think of was a partnership in doing research together. DS1 explained, "Maybe one way to reach out to the radical students is that I can invite them to do quality research. This institution provides various grants . . . These grants can be used for research, publications, and attending seminars. Hopefully, I could send some of these students to attend seminars that are related to their academic disciplines, and hope that they could interact with others who are from out of their circles."

Similarly, RM2 also expressed that instead of words, he preferred reaching out to his Muslim students through his presence and deeds. To prevent religious radicalism, RM2 encouraged students to be actively involved in interreligious interactions by helping each other in religious celebrations. Setting himself as an example, he said, "I want to show to Muslim students that I am not a hater. For example, yesterday we just had a gathering for breaking the fast, I came and helped them. I also encourage my students to help each other. If Muslims have events, Christians should help and vice versa."

EP1 also expressed deep concern about the religious radicalism at her institution. She proposed that Christian faculty could make a change by initiating an intentional interaction with these Muslim students. She appreciated her position as ahead of the laboratory which provided her opportunities to assist and personally interact with the Muslim students. She said, "Before students use the lab facilities they need to ask permission from me and if they don't know how to use the tools then I would teach them . . . I teach them one by one and this is an opportunity for me to interact with them. Especially during this fasting month, the students are highly appreciative when I assist them and wait on them if they need anything."

Cultivating Christian Practices, Values, and Character

Other implicit ways to integrate faith into educational practices mentioned by the participants were by incorporating Christian values and practices into classroom learning. First, these participants speak of Christian practices as establishing a habit of starting a class with a short prayer and devotion. Second, they emphasized cultivating Christian values by "inserting" Bible-based principles and stories in their teachings. Lastly, the participants focused on cultivating a virtuous character that included academic honesty, discipline, and the virtue of working hard.

Cultivating Christian Practices

"Starting a class with short prayers is a common practice in Indonesia," said YP2. In the contexts of state or non-faith-based universities where most of the participants are religious minorities, engaging in this practice is more challenging than rewarding. Instead of neutral and spiritual, prayer can be a means of showing the power of the majority. In the context of Christian universities, the participants have different opinions about the purpose of practicing the spiritual disciplines and the ways of doing them. Including in these spiritual disciplines are prayer, fasting, and devotion.

Prayer practices in state and non-faith-based universities

At state universities and non-faith-based universities where Muslims were the majority, often the class would start with an Islamic prayer and the participants had different responses toward the practice. YP2 expressed that as a Christian she felt unsure about the matter so she would "stay quiet" until the prayer session was over. She was also ambiguous about how to respond to the students' greeting assalaam-alaikum when she entered the class. She said, "Sometimes I greet them back by saying wa-alaikum-salaam, but I am not sure about it." In contrast to YP2, ET2 refrained herself from praying with them by saying, "I don't need to pray in front of them. I have faith that Jesus is in front of me, I just pray in my heart. I believe what God says, that he fights and goes before me."

In the case of KC2, he would "pray at home, not at school, and say good morning or good afternoon to the class." "But occasionally," he said, "I have a class with all the female students wearing hijabs, and then I would greet them with assalaam-alaikum. Sometimes they ask if I am a Muslim. I explain that assalaam-alaikum is in Arabic, that people who live in Jordan or Egypt, including the Christians, would say that greeting. So it doesn't belong to the Muslim alone."

Not all Christian faculty responded with a passive and give-in attitude. EP1 said that her colleague was courageous enough to address the issue of "only Islamic prayer was allowed" in the class. Quoting her Christian colleague, she said, "If you give an opportunity for the Muslims to say their prayers out loud in front of the class, then you should give an equal opportunity to students from other religions. It cannot be dominated by one religion only because this is a Pancasila country." "Since that," EP1 continued, "Any students who lead the prayer will come up in front of the class and say, "let us pray." And then everybody prays silently according to their beliefs."

Prayer practices in Christian universities

Some participants who taught at Christian university expressed their goals of cultivating Christian practices through morning prayers and short Bible meditations. Explaining why she emphasized starting a class with prayers, WU3 said, "I want to inculcate a sense of gratitude." WU3 recognized that it was difficult to develop this practice at the beginning. Students felt compelled and waited for each other to come forward to lead the prayer. "But now," she said, "they understand and take the microphone right away and lead the prayer." Interestingly, although it was a Christian university, WU3 also encouraged students of other religions to lead the prayer. However, this practice was confusing to some of her Muslim students. She said, "Most students who lead the prayer are either Catholics or Protestants. Only one Muslim student did come forward to say a prayer. Maybe they think this is a Christian university and they feel reluctant to participate."

For SW3, the practice of prayer was not just at the beginning of the class but also before ending the class. "The purpose is," she said, "more than just a ritual, but I want my students to know that our lives cannot be separated from God and that we are here, sitting in this class is because of God's grace." Different from WU3, SW3 only scheduled Christian students to lead the prayer. In the case of ES3 and PK3, starting a class with prayer was a mandatory practice required by their institutions and only the Christian way of praying was allowed.

In addition to prayers, other participants also cultivated the practices of fasting and devotion. Following a morning prayer led by a student, CS3 would lead the class devotion by "sharing a daily meditation" taken from the Scripture reading he had every morning. Besides prayer, CH3 added the practice of fasting to provide his students with a moment for self-reflection and addressing "the lack of seriousness toward their learning and final exams." CH3 explained, "Last year, out of 7 classes, 4 classes did fasting. Some classes I requested them to do so but one class wanted to do it voluntarily. Through fasting, we learn to humble ourselves." The impact of fasting was positive on students when CH3 said, "After fasting, they became more open, some of them shared their stories with tears. They acknowledged that they had been ignoring their study and promised to do better for their final exams."

Cultivating Christian Values

Although it was not incorporated intentionally into their course contents or lesson plans, whenever the participants found an appropriate learning topic and moment, they would seize the opportunity to integrate Christian values into classroom learning. Many of these participants used analogies, narratives, essential questions, and "provoking methods" to instill biblical truths into their teaching. Participants who taught at non-Christian universities also spoke of instilling Christian values by using a "universal language" and the "universal values" with biblical truths as the underlying principles.

Analogy

Some participants used the law of nature to teach biblical moral principles. For example, LI1 used comparisons between the "cation exchange law in soils" and sexual orientation to address the LBGT issues. She explained, "The soils contain positive and negative ions. This is a nonliving thing, but it follows the law of nature that negative ions are attracted to positive ions. How come humans, the most highly created beings by God, are attracted to their same-sex partners? So, while I am explaining the contents of a topic, sometimes I will insert moral messages from a Christian perspective." Similarly, EP, a faculty teaching technology of seeds, said that she had many opportunities to integrate her Christian beliefs in her teachings. "Because," she said, "the Bible has many passages that talk about seeds," EP1 recalled a time when she used an analogy of seeds in the Bible and the topic she was teaching, to point spiritual truths out to her students. She said, "When we plant seeds, the results may be varied. Some will grow tall. But some remain small because they fall on infertile soil, or the farmers do not give fertilizers or other factors. If the seed falls on fertile soil, it will grow into a plant and produce fruits. Likewise, our lives will bear fruit if we are planted in fertile soil." LT2 also used the correspondence between principles found in his concrete construction class and Jesus' teaching about a strong foundation to teach students about judging others. He said, "When you judge a person, do not just look at the outside appearance. In civil engineering, if the building collapsed, they would look for the engineer. Although the foundation is invisible, it takes 20% to 30% of the total building cost. Jesus also says that if we just pay attention to the appearance it would be very dangerous. Likewise, when you are looking for a boyfriend or girlfriend, don't just look at the physical appearance."

Narratives

Including in this category are accounts of characters in the Bible, personal life experiences, and contextual social issues. "I never planned specifically what I am going to give them," CS3 said, "but I share with them my morning devotion, including my life and weakness." As an example, he said:

> Once I was in the airplane from Bali to Bandung, the pilot announced that the weather was bad and would cause some disturbances. I prayed, "God, please save me that I may arrive safely in Bandung." But I was reminded of Jesus at Gethsemane who said,

"Your will be done." I did not dare to pray like that because if I said, "Your will be done," I was afraid that his will might be for the plane to go down. I was suspicious that the Lord would not help me. I asked the Lord for forgiveness when the plane landed safely. I shared this with my students in the class yesterday.

CS3 also liked to use the Bible characters to give inspiring leadership lessons for his master students while teaching his ethics and leadership course. He explained, "I always share how a boss should treat his subordinates by taking examples from the Bible, such as the stories of David. I also give them assignments to evaluate how they have treated and trained their employees for the past years." In the case of DY3, she expressed that instead of inserting Bible verses in the courses without any meaning, she preferred "to connect Christian faith to contextual issues where students might find some potential tensions to wrestle with."

Essential questions and "provoking methods"

SW1 asked essential questions both to "evangelize" his students through the classes and to "stimulate their critical thinking." He explained, "I teach two classes: religion and philosophy. I said to my students that a belief also needs minds. Animals don't have religions, but only human beings because we have minds. So, I challenge my students by asking, 'Why you believe what you believe? Are you just following the traditions? Do you believe it because it's passed down by your parents?' This is a process of evangelization by inviting students to think." Similarly, RM2, who was converted to Christianity during his young adulthood, had a deep passion to introduce his newfound faith to his Muslim students. To incorporate this passion in his Japanese linguistic class, RM2 used "provoking methods." He explained, "Yesterday, I showed the students a movie titled "Silence." It's about the Christian persecution in Japan. Some of them were cynical but I explained to them that it's a historical account. Sitting behind me was a row of students wearing hijabs. Sometimes ago, I showed them "Prince of Egypt," it's about Moses. In the two front rows were men with long beards and women with hijabs." He was not afraid of using these methods to provoke his students' thinking and beliefs, because he said, "We think that they hate Christians but actually many Muslims are seeking truth." Sometimes he would provide opportunities for students to share about themselves or their beliefs. "An example," he said, "a student came up and shared openly about her life when she was in a Madrasah junior high school. It's not about pro or contra of a belief, but they wanted to share their stories."

"Universal values" and "universal language"

Many participants who taught at non-Christian universities spoke of tailoring faith-based universal values to student learning (e.g. KC2, JS2, TM1, BS1, RT1). For example, KC2 said, "I would share with them without specifically referring to my religion. I speak about universal values. For example, as human beings, we need to remember and worship God. This would be Friday prayers for the Muslims, Sunday Sabbaths for the Christians, Buddhists worship at the temples, and so on. Whatever you do you must rely on God. I don't represent any religions because of the fear of a conflict of interest or they would think something like that. I just insert the universal principle."

Similarly, aware of teaching at a multi-religion university, JS2 used a "universal language" to carry out Christian truths to his students. He maintained, "I always relate what I teach to Christian universal truths without using any specific Christian terminology . . . I just use a universal language because I have students who are Muslims, Catholics, Christians, Hindus, Buddhists, etc." As an example, he said, "I shared with them that the world was created by God but it had fallen into sin. Everybody agrees with it. I don't have to say that it's from the Bible but I use this wisdom to lead the students that behind all this, there is a single truth, the Word of God and Jesus." TM1 mentioned that his Muslim colleagues liked to use verses from the Al-Quran in their teachings. "It was a common practice" but for TM1 he preferred "to incorporate the Bible truths into the subjects without mentioning the verses or the sources." Giving an example, he said, "There is a general principle from the Bible about the issue of corruption, which is a big problem in Indonesia. I say to them, 'What is wrong with that?' and teach them how to eradicate this problem. They need to change and this is relatively easy for me to teach them without quoting verses like my Muslim colleagues."

Cultivating Virtuous Behavior and Character

Developing ethical character virtues was also mentioned by many participants as one way to integrate faith into their teaching and learning practice. Such character development includes academic honesty and integrity, time discipline, and ethically responsible behavior. CS1, LJ2, JH2, SW3, and RD3 strongly emphasized that her students practice academic honesty. "Learn to write a good paper," CH1 said, "but plagiarism, no!" Besides provided rules, CH1 also gave encouragement and supports for the students to stay honest in their academic work. He said, "I am a strict lecturer, but I see it as a command of God to give the best and be honest with our work. Making a mistake is alright but do not lie. So, from the lens of faith, I encourage my students to give the best." SW3 also shared the importance of cultivating academic honesty when she said, "I emphasized that they must put the author's name in a citation, which is not taught in high school. If they are caught in plagiarism or cheating, they will be punished seriously . . . I like to insert this ethical practice when I teach." SW3, who taught hotel management, also focused on honesty in dealing with customers. She explained, "If you are working at the front office you need to keep the privacy of your guests. If somebody asks, you don't answer, "I don't know." But just say that it's your company policy. Not giving the information doesn't mean that you lie. So, I like to insert those things in my classes."

LT2 also set a high bar on academic honesty. He recalled two students who did not come for the exams with an excuse that they were hospitalized. Cross-checking their names with the hospital, LT2 found out that the students were lying and as a consequence, he said, "I gave them a zero. Both students came to me and apologized but I still gave them a zero and detention for one semester." Likewise, RD3 also demonstrated a firm discipline for students who violated academic dishonesty. She said, "When I found out, I crossed out both of their names. Because from the beginning of the class I have informed them that if anybody is found cheating, lying, or committing plagiarism, I would cross out their names." In a similar vein, JS2 said that "Christian faith was expressed" through his firm response to students' unethical behaviors such as cheating, coming late to the class, and being irresponsible with their studies.

For EW2, she took a step further by incorporating Christian principles to address moral and ethical behavior in the opposite sex relationship. She explained, "Sometimes I ask who among them are in a relationship. What kind of dating do you have? I often check about courtship issues because the matters are worrisome. Staying off campus many of them practice cohabitation. Sometimes they report or confess to me that they have been doing this and that, even being pregnant or getting married at a young age." When asking why she was concerned about this non-academic issue, EW2 explained, "We are proud of ourselves because we don't sin. But we forget that we often commit a passive sin. We know a person who is going that way, but we just play ignorant. That's our contribution to the person's sin. I don't want to be like that. I am not just teaching but I am educating my students."

Explicit Evangelism

Unlike the aforementioned faith-integrated educational practices that are "spontaneous" and implicit, the following few participants describe their integration of faith and learning as an explicit way of sharing the Gospel with the students. This explicit way of sharing their faith is intentional and relational. By intentional, meaning that they had planned it at the beginning of the semester and scheduled the time to meet with the students in a small group or one-on-one basis. This is also relational evangelism: the participants create the connectedness with their students, especially with the Christian students, through their classes and/or academic advisory programs.

Teaching at Christian universities, CS3 and DY3 expressed the opportunities and freedom they had to share about their faith. CS3 had a motto: "Any student who takes my class will not leave without hearing the gospel." To realize his motto, CS3 crafted his personal life experiences and/or insights from daily devotion into his classes whenever they were appropriate. In addition, he also wanted to be intentional and explicit to share Jesus Christ with the students in a personal meeting. He explained, "To students who come to see me after the class I would ask for a minute to share about what I believe. I always believe this is a good opportunity that God gives to me to share the gospel." A similar desire to explicitly share the gospel is also expressed by DY3 who admittedly said, "I have been sharing about Christ implicitly by modeling an exemplary life, but I have not explicitly shared with them that Jesus Christ is the only way to salvation." Realizing that working at a Christian university gave her "a huge opportunity" and freedom, DY3 expressed, "I just read a book about evangelism. The field before me is huge. I want to more explicitly lead my students back to Christ."

For AS1 and EP1, their additional responsibility in teaching Christian religious education classes had provided them with an opportunity to build a relationship as well as to share the gospel explicitly with the students. Passionate about evangelism, AS1 expressed, "I often share the gospel with my students. Certainly, with those who are not Christian, I would exercise caution." For students who took his Christian religious education class, he said, "I have a schedule for each student to have a 20-minute face to face meeting with me. I use this meeting to share Jesus Christ with them. Whether they accept him or not is their business with God."

Different from AS1, EP1 focused on a small group evangelistic Bible study and retreats to reach out to her students. She explained that each meeting of Christian religious education class was followed by a small group Bible study led by the upper-class students. Sensing the urgency and limited opportunity to reach out to these students who she would teach only for one semester, EP1 expressed, "This is the best opportunity to reach out to students who are not born again. If we don't get them to join the groups that semester, the opportunity would most probably be passed. So, we do our best to reach out to them during the first semester." In addition to this evangelistic Bible study, EPI also employed retreats. She explained, "At the end of the semester, I invite all my students to participate in a retreat. This will be a moment for them to make a commitment or decision to follow Jesus Christ. There are students who were brought up in Christian families but they have not personally decided to follow Christ." Extra efforts were needed to make these evangelistic strategies work when EP1 said, "Every Sunday afternoon, we have a fellowship for all assistants who help with the small groups. During this time we also prepare them for the next Thursday Bible study. Every Thursday I need to supervise the small groups and on Fridays, we have a fellowship for all Christian students . . .Thankfully I have one graduate who assists me."

In the case of MP1, she focused the explicit evangelistic approach on Christian students under her academic advising program. She explained, "I approach the students using the one-on-one meetings. I ask them about their relationship with God. I have nine students in my advising group and five of them are Christians. I check on them one by one whether they have accepted Jesus Christ in their lives. If they have then I would encourage them to grow in their new lives."

Summary of the Findings

The first section of the findings focused on faith-integrated *being* of the participants that described their response to the value of faith in their teaching vocation. The participants expressed that faith has shaped their vocation in several ways. First, faith gave a strong sense of calling, which manifested in their discerning process and subsequently led them to a conviction of their calling as teaching faculty. Second, faith gave purpose and meaning to their work, that their lives were God's instruments to fulfill the gospel and cultural mandate as well as making a positive impact on young generations. Third, faith provides moral and ethical guidance in carrying out their tasks. Fourth, faith gave a strong work ethos that helped the participants to be highly committed to their work, consistent and persistent workers, willing to give sacrificially, and caring about their institutions and beyond. Fifth, faith gave strength in the face of adversities. Lastly, faith gave a desire for spiritual, character, and academic growth.

The second section focused on faith-integrated *knowing* of the participants that described their conceptual understanding about the relationship between faith and their academic discipline. The participants' responses were divided into eight categories. First, the ontological and epistemological approach, which viewed faith and knowledge as originating from the same source, namely God, but the two had different ways of knowing. Second, the worldview approach, that faith provided a lens and foundation for learning. Third, the attitudinal approach in which faith informed the participants' attitudes and motivations toward learning. Fourth, the ethical and moral approach in which faith provided principles to guide what and how the participants did their research. Fifth, the intrapersonal approach, which emphasized participants as the agents of integration in how they lived out their faith. Sixth, the interpersonal approach in which faith led participants to build good relationships with students and colleagues. Seventh, contribution to the Kingdom of God approach in which faith informed the application of learning to make positive impacts on the world and humanity. Lastly, the "no integration" approach that viewed faith and learning as either compatible with each other or mutually exclusive, thus no integration was needed.

The third section focused on faith-integrated *doing* of the participants that described how they integrated faith in their teaching and learning practices. The majority of the participants described their integration of faith and educational practices as unintentional, implicit, and spontaneous. For these participants, faith was expressed through guiding principles of giving the best and helping students learn best, modeling an exemplary life, building positive relationships with students, and cultivating Christian values and practices. A few of the participants practiced explicit and direct evangelism with their students through a one-on-one approach.

Faith-Integrated Being	Faith-Integrated Knowing	Faith-Integrated Doing
Faith and Vocation/Life • Faith gives a strong sense of calling • Faith gives purpose and meaning of work • Faith provides moral and ethical guidance • Faith gives a strong work ethos • Faith gives desire for personal growth: spiritual, character, academic • Faith gives strength in the midst of adversities	**Faith and Academic Discipline** • Ontological & epistemological assumption • Worldview approach • Attitudinal approach • Ethical and moral approach • Intrapersonal approach • Interpersonal approach • Contribution to the kingdom of God • No integration	**Faith and Educational Practices** *Spontaneous Integration* *Implicit & indirect of sharing Christian faith:* • Principles: give the best and help students learn best • Modeling exemplary life • Cultivating Christian practices and values *Explicit & Direct Evangelism*
Response to Challenges • View challenges as opportunities • Prayers in times of adversity • Faith gives strength to endure • Faith "refreshes my calling" and "helps me not to be afraid"	**Response to Conflicts between Faith & Learning** • Choosing faith over learning • "I do not know what to do" • Avoiding and omitting conflicted topics • Learning and seeking for alternatives.	

⬆ ⬆ ⬆

CHALLENGES

Institutional	Student-Related	Personal
Ethno-religious discrimination Religious radicalism Unethical behavior and practices Negative organizational culture Peer social interaction Lack of resources Institutional identity crisis Navigating faith in a pluralistic workplace	Class size challenges Passive learners	Underpaid and underappreciated Keeping a work-family balance Needs: Institutional support & family support Community of Believers Community of Academics

Figure 5. Summary of the Findings

CHAPTER 5

Discussions and Implications

The purpose of this research was to explore the perceptions of faith-integrated being, knowing, and doing among Christian faculty in Indonesian higher education contexts. Participants' responses give insights into the following questions: How do Indonesian Christian faculty describe the value of faith in their vocation (*being*)? How do Indonesian Christian faculty describe the relationship between faith and their educational discipline (*knowing*)? How do Indonesian Christian faculty describe the influence of faith in their educational practices (*doing*)?

This chapter begins with a discussion of the findings in the light of relevant literature and followed by the implications of the research and suggestions for further research on the integration of faith and learning.

Discussions
Faith-Integrated Being
The Centrality of Faith and Authentic Living
The powerful current culture of secularization has "created dualism of every kind,"[1] including separation of faith from the profession. Particularly in the West, faith has become a personal and private matter. However, the findings in this study indicate contrary facts. Faith plays a central role in the life and vocation of Christian faculty in Indonesia. Faith permeates the participants' lives from the beginning of their discernment process to the conviction of their calling. Some of their experiences are expressed as follows: "I see God's

---
1. Dockery, "Integrating Faith," 1.

guidance along the way" (JS3); "I see the process that God has been leading me through"; and (JS2); "I believe that God's calling for me is to be a faculty member" (CS1).

The word vocation has its root in Latin, *vocare* which means "to call"; whether called by God or by human society, vocation denotes a strong feeling, an invitation, "a strong persistent and disposition to be of service to others."[2] The contemporary culture regards teaching as merely a professional job. In North America, by the end of the nineteenth century, teaching had been fully "professionalized."[3] Similarly, in Indonesia, the government launched a comprehensive Teacher Law which attempts to professionalize teaching through the certification program.[4] Taking teaching as simply a professional activity has reduced the profession to "a set of methods and techniques."[5] Against the odds, for most participants, being a faculty member is not just a profession but a vocation which they believe was given by God. They faithfully embody the calling through their presence and work as Christian faculty members in their respective work contexts. Farnsworth conceptualized this kind of embodiment of faith as *intrapersonal integration*[6] and Bouma-Prediger calls it *faith-praxis*.[7]

For most of the participants, the conviction of calling is not instantaneous, but a process that involves a series of formative, directive, and affirmative experiences. During the discerning and decision-making process, most participants refer to their college years as the most crucial phase (e.g. EW2, CS1, BS1, DS1, HS1, ES3). Participants who did not experience this phase of vocational development tend to struggle in finding meaning and making a connection between their faith and work. DT3, for instance, who had taught more than three decades and almost came to her retirement, expressed: "Honestly, I tried to avoid being sent to rural areas by the government as a new doctor, so the only way was to teach in higher education. I just teach

---

2. David T. Hansen, "Teaching and the Sense of Vocation," *Educational Theory* 44, no. 3 (September 1994): 259.

3. Mark R. Schwehn, "Teaching as Profession and Vocation," *Journal of Theology Today* 59, no. 3 (October 2002): 396.

4. Chang et al., *Teacher Reform*, 97.

5. Schwehn, "Teaching," 401.

6. Farnsworth, "Conduct of Integration," 308–319.

7. Bouma-Prediger, "Task of Integration," 27–28.

and try to make the students understand, without involving God. I did not understand what calling was all about at that time . . . Only recently, because I faced many struggles that forced me to get to know more deeply about my faith." In addition, other important factors that convince the participants to enter a teaching vocation are interventions from God, family members, and mentors (e.g. HS1, BS1, LS3, BW1, DS1, CS3). Particularly, the role of mentors is significantly important; its influence continues through the participants' career as they become mentors themselves (e.g. CH1, RT1, DC2, LS3). These research findings affirm works done by Parks and Harjanto that the formation of vocational development is significantly established during college years and the importance of mentors and mature persons who serve as role-models.[8]

The strong sense of calling gives meaning and purpose to the lives and work of the participants. The participants view themselves as an "extension of God's hand," "to be salt," and "to be a blessing." This desire to be faithful witnesses to Christ in their workplace is shown through their authentic and organic relationship with students, a good reputation as highly committed workers, and peculiar moral-ethical behaviors that do not submit to the culture of corruption and power abuse. In short, the faith-integrated *being* is evidently demonstrated in the participants' lives as they summarize it succinctly in the following phrases: "my life is my message," flow naturally "out of being," and reflect "who you are." Bouma-Prediger identifies this type of integration as *experiential integration* where orthopraxy is shown through a person's authentic life.[9]

Living an authentic, undivided life is an act of counterculture. Palmer asserts that "we live in a culture that tells us a divided self is sane but an undivided life is foolish at best and irresponsible at worst."[10] It is foolish because "if you let others know what is going on inside, they may reject and injure you" and irresponsible because "if you reveal your inner truth, you can no longer perform your duties dispassionately" but teach from a "detached and

---

8. Sharon D. Parks, *Big Questions, Worthy Dreams: Mentoring Emerging Adults in Their Search for Meaning, Purpose, and Faith* (San Francisco, CA: Jossey-Bass, 2011); Sutrisna Harjanto, "The Development of Vocational Stewardship among Indonesian Christian Professionals," PhD diss., (Trinity International University, 2016).

9. Bouma-Prediger, "Task of Integration," 28–29.

10. Palmer, *Courage to Teach*, 178.

'objective' stance."[11] Opposed to this culture, the participants in this study bravely embrace a wholeness of their faith, being, and vocation. For instance, BS1 expresses that to be a witness for Christ is to be an authentic self who is "genuine, not superficial – what is inside is different from the outside; so I serve who I am without pretending to be a godly person." Even in unfavorable work environments and ethnoreligious discriminations, these participants do not shy away from their cultural and faith identity or detach work from their faith because they fear rejection and hurt, but boldly embody an undivided life through their presence and relationships with students and colleagues and work attitude, ethos, and productivity. This exemplary life and vocation echo what Palmer views as "an integral state of being central to good teaching"[12]; a kind of teaching that arises from educators who live authentic lives because "we teach who we are."[13]

Sharing the Good News and Doing Good Works

One effect of sin is a tendency to devote our work to "serve an entirely wrong end."[14] However, as renewed creations in Christ, the participants view their life as God's instrument and devote their vocation to fulfill the gospel and cultural mandate. Bavinck asserts that like Jesus, we are called to bring "tidings to the afflicted, to bind up the broken-hearted, to proclaim liberty to the captive and the opening of prison to those who are bound, to proclaim the year of the Lord's favor, and to comfort those who mourn" (Isa 61:1–2).[15] To fulfill this calling, Bavinck insists that everyone "remain in the vocation to which he has been called (1 Cor 7:17–23)" as opposed to "drop his natural vocation and dedicate himself to the work of the kingdom in the narrower sense."[16] Initially, some participants were thinking to be a fulltime minister; a vocation which is commonly considered to be a high calling. However, after a series of discerning processes, they chose to embrace the call of sharing good news and good works into one framework and weave it into their teaching vocation. For example, BS1 expressed, "This is the only course that

---

11. Palmer, 178.
12. Palmer, 16.
13. Palmer, 2.
14. Plantinga, *Not the Way*, 40.
15. Bavinck, "Common Grace," 62.
16. Bavinck, 63.

I can freely discuss religion. I learned that I don't have to be a missionary to Vietnam but God sends them here." Similarly, AS1 said, "I am doing the Great Commandment of Matthew 28 through my ministry in education. I am not called as pastor to serve in the church, but my calling is here, on campus." The participants respond to their "earthly calling" with gratitude to please God (JS2, LI1, CS1) and faithfully perform it with new sets of virtues, such as *hard-working, disciplined, responsible,* and *integrity*.[17]

It is worth noting that the participants embrace the duty of sharing the good news and doing good works as equally important. CS1, for instance, expressed: "Being a Christian faculty I have the opportunity to share the gospel. Besides, I have the opportunity to fulfill the cultural mandate through my field in fisheries science." They are passionate about fulfilling the cultural mandate through their teaching vocation and academic disciplines. For instance, TM1, whose expertise is in forestry, asserts: "Faith also reminds me about God the Creator and what he wants us to do, such as taking care of our forests and its resources and preventing forest destruction, which is commonly happening in Indonesia." However, they are even more passionate about carrying out the gospel mandate. For example, CS3 said: "Any student who takes my class with not leave without hearing the Gospel." Similarly, AS1 expressed, "I often share the gospel with my students." They seek opportunities to share the gospel with students through personal one-on-one meetings, leading class devotion, teaching Christian religious education class, evangelistic Bible study, and retreats (e.g. EP1, CS1, AS1, TM1, CS3, MP1). In addition, their zeal for students' spiritual regeneration and formation is also shown through their sacrificial giving of their time and energy to teach Christian religious education classes and be involved in campus ministry (e.g. CS1, TM1, LI1, EP1, AS1, DS1, CS3).

Quite the contrary, Calvin Van Reken observes that the priority and necessity of sharing the gospel has been de-emphasized in the West.[18] He explains that the Western culture has been deeply permeated by "the worldview of evolutionary naturalism" which makes heaven and the afterlife a distant reality; even Christians "find it harder and harder to believe that people are

---

17. Bavinck, "Common Grace," 63.
18. Calvin P. Van Reken, "Christians in This World: Pilgrims or Settlers?" *Calvin Theological Journal* 43, no. 2 (November 2008): 234–256.

sinners, deserving of eternal punishment."[19] Sadly, the idea of "saving souls" has now been replaced with social works.[20] Nonetheless, this study shows that Christian faculty in Indonesia are still strongly committed, both to their calling to spread the gospel in word and live it out in their teaching, service, and research.

Cultural Engagement, Conformity, and Counterculture

Mouw criticizes that "some Christian circles choose for evangelism and against engagement in social action."[21] Christian faculty members in Indonesia are zealous in their efforts to share the gospel with the students without any signs of withdrawal from their responsibility to society. In fact, faith helps them to tie the ideal of gospel and cultural mandate with the real contextual needs of the society. Living and serving in predominantly Muslim contexts and cultures of corruption and discrimination, the participants "see the needs" (e.g. EP1, CS1, DS1, MC2, CH3) to "make positive impacts on young generations" (e.g. EW2, DS1, HS1, YP2, JH2) by educating them to be "future leaders and agents of change" (e.g. CS1, EW2, CS3, DC2) and helping them in their character development and personal growth (e.g. CS3, AS1, JS2, JA2). As Mouw, Wolterstorff, Wolters, and Plantinga strongly advocate for Christians to engage the culture, these participants who view themselves as agents of change and agents of integration, demonstrate their cultural formation and transformation through their teaching vocation in Indonesian contexts.[22]

In cultural engagement, Christians are called to live *in* the world but not *of* the world (John 15:19; Rom 12:2; 1 John 2:15). The participants work in cultures where "civil servants are known for their laziness" (DS1), money, working hours, and power are easily misused (e.g. WU3, ES3, TM1, RS1, DY3), and bribery is a common practice (e.g. DA1, ET2). However, this study shows that they live and act counter-culturally. Faith gives an inner gyroscope and moral compass for them to stay focused on their calling, work honestly and

---

19. Van Reken, "Christians in This World," 248.
20. Van Reken, 247.
21. Richard J. Mouw, *Called to Holy Worldliness* (Philadelphia: Fortress, 1980), 8.
22. Mouw, *Called to Holy Worldliness*, 37; Nicholas Wolterstorff, *Until Justice and Peace Embrace* (Grand Rapids: Eerdmans, 1983), chap. 1; Albert M. Wolters, "The Nature of Fundamentalism," *Pro Rege* 15, no. 1 (September 1986): 2–9; and Plantinga, *Engaging God's World*, 96.

diligently, and maintain integrity and professional ethics. Instead of playing with power and students' grades, these participants treat their students with respect and fairness. Due to the contexts where they are, it is understandable that most participants place a strong emphasis on being a witness for Christ through their intrapersonal and interpersonal integration approaches.

That being said, cultural engagement is not without risks. As we influence the world, the world also influences us that we may no longer think of its danger but slowly conform to its worldview.[23] Wolfe also observes that in the fight between faith and culture, most often "culture has triumphed."[24] At an individual level, for example, research is mandatory to fulfill the trilogy roles of a faculty member and upgrade their academic ranks. However, with teaching and administrative workloads, many participants have difficulty finding time to do research. To solve the problem, some participants think about co-authorship of their students' research. For instance, RT1 says, "I try to translate the works of my students into English, and I can put my name as a co-author. As their thesis advisor, I can do that. That is being encouraged now." Although this is a widespread practice, automatic co-authorship without significant contributions to the research, but only by being a mentor or advisor for the student's work is a questionable practice. At an institutional level, market-driven education and unethical policies and practices have led Christian universities to an identity crisis (e.g. DT3, WU3, CS3). In a more subtle manner, some participants follow the trends to address pluralism and radicalism issues by promoting a state ideology as part of their faith-integrated learning (e.g. BS1, HS1, JS2, JA2). The universal values carried by the state ideology such as love, respect, and justice seem similar to Christian values but they are not the same. This is not a new phenomenon; because of their subtlety these Christian-like values had misled many Christian educators and leaders in history to voluntarily replace Christian teaching with secularism.[25] Thus, Van Reken warns Christians about the triumphalistic attitude in engaging culture.[26]

---

23. Van Reken, "Christians in This World," 245.

24. Alan Wolfe, *The Transformation of American Religion: How We Actually Live Our Faith* (Chicago: University of Chicago Press, 2003), 3.

25. Marsden, "Soul of the American University," 35; Glanzer and Carpenter, "Conclusion," 279.

26. Van Reken, "Christians in This World," 234–256.

Being aware of this, some participants show a dependency on God and a desire for continuous renewal and personal growth. The participants demonstrate their dependence on God through prayers. They pray during the decision-making process of becoming a teaching faculty (e.g. ET2, LI1, BS1), in the midst of difficulties (e.g. EP1, MP1, CS3, ET2, JS3), and before preparing a course or coming to the class (e.g. MP1, KC2, RM2, LI1). They express their longing to discern and obey God's will and know God deeper. For example, BS1, who has taught for almost four decades, exercises daily meditation of the Bible, sensitivity to the work of the Holy Spirit that is like a sailboat that needs to follow the wind and is patient with God's "one step a time" leading. In addition to maintaining personal holiness, the participants also need to critically examine their own experiences, beliefs, practices, and assumptions under the light of the Scripture. For this, they need to equip themselves with biblical and theological foundations and critical reflective skills.[27]

Challenges and the Need for a Community of Believers

The participants face multiple challenges which include workplace ethics and integrity issues, ethnoreligious discriminations, institutional crisis, peer social interactions, lack of resources, passive learners, big size classes, being overworked yet underpaid, and work-life imbalance. Most of these challenges are closely related to the intrapersonal (calling and moral-ethical) and interpersonal (relational) issues, which are consistent with what concerns the participants the most in their aspects of faith-integrated being. For example, corruption and dishonesty in money matters are challenges for the participants to live out their faith-informed moral-ethical lives (e.g. DY3, RS1, DT3, ET2); and social interactions and large size classes pose challenges for the participants in building meaningful relationships with students and co-workers (e.g. DA1, CH3, TM1, LT2, BW1). Reacting to workplace challenges, some participants are tempted to quit (e.g. RS1, HS1, MC2, ET2), but the majority remain faithful in their teaching vocation. What makes many adversities tolerable to the participants is their faith and hope in God. For them, faith

---

27. See, e.g. Stephen Brookfield, *Becoming a Critically Reflective Teacher* (San-Francisco: Jossey-Bass, 1995); Donald A Schön, *Educating the Reflective Practitioner: Toward a New Design for Teaching and Learning in the Professions* (San Francisco: Jossey-Bass, 1987).

gives strength to pray, endure, and seek for solutions, and helps perceive challenges as opportunities for spiritual, character, and academic growth.

In addition to this personal stance, the participants also express their need for institutional and faith community support. However, in facing the above faith-related challenges, the participants receive little or no support from their institutions, including those who work at Christian universities. Some faith-related seminars they received were from parachurch organizations that discussed leadership, Christology, character building, and preaching skills (e.g. ET2, CS3, LT2, JA2, DK3). Many participants express their need for a community of believers as a safe place to "release pressure," "support each other," share, pray, and study the Bible (e.g. EP1, MC2, RS1, DA1). A few participants have a small group of fellow Christians whom they met during college and continue to meet with after graduation, but almost none receive faith community support from their church. This problem is not unique to the participants in this study. Studies conducted by Miller in North America and Harjanto in Indonesia also show that most Christian professionals experience a lack of church support to help them integrate faith and work.[28] To remain faithful and fruitful in teaching vocation, Christian faculty members in Indonesia need a company of saints (1John 1:7; Eph 5:19; Col 3:16). The faith community, both church, and parachurch need to extend their hands to support and care for Christian faculty who are called to a teaching vocation in their respective institutional contexts.

Faith-Integrated Knowing

Semantic Ambiguity

In responding to the question about their conceptual understanding of the relationship between faith and their academic disciplines, most participants were not as articulate as they were in their response to questions pertaining to faith-integrated being. It is noteworthy that participants are unfamiliar with the phrase "integration of faith and learning." However, they suggest that they are familiar with the phrase "faith and knowledge" or ""aith and science." In addition, the findings also demonstrate that there is no single conceptual approach to integration. Participants vary in their conceptual understanding

---

28. David W. Miller, *God at Work: The History and Promise of the Faith at Work Movement* (Oxford: Oxford University Press, 2007), 21; Harjanto, "The Development of Vocational," 206.

of the terms. Some speak of "the integration of faith and learning" as *connecting* or *relating* faith to their academic disciplines, others perceive it as *the role* or the *influence* of faith in their professional practices. The unfamiliarity as well as the variation of terms and perceptions about the "integration of faith and learning" is understandable, because the term is highly philosophical abstract.[29] This finding also suggests that the semantic ambiguity of the "integration of faith and learning" is not just an issue faced by Christian scholars in North America in which the movement has spanned more than five decades,[30] but is also faced by Christian scholars in Indonesia where the movement is still relatively new.

The current terminology "the integration of faith and learning" implies and encourages a habit of dualistic thinking.[31] Other terminologies have suggested, such as "integration of faith and professional practice,"[32] "the integration of faith and academic discipline,"[33] and "creation and redemption of scholarship."[34] However, all these terms primarily emphasize either the cognitive (*knowing*) or professional practice (*doing*) aspect of a person. The new terminology is needed to describe a holistic aspect of the integration of faith and learning. This new terminology will be further discussed in the implication section.

An Ontological Approach with a Dualistic View

The responses participants give to the research question about the relationship between faith and learning are convergent. Out of eight categories of their responses, only two are directly related to substantial integration of faith and academic disciplines (i.e. the ontological and epistemological approach,

---

29. Wolfe, "Line of Demarcation," 4–5; Hasker, "Faith-Learning Integration," 234–236; Downing, "Imbricating Faith and Learning," 33–44; Jacobsen and Jacobsen, *Scholarship and Christian Faith*, 22–29.

30. See, e.g. Kenneth R. Badley, "Clarifying "Faith-Learning Integration": Essentially Contested Concepts and the Concept-Conception Distinction," *Journal of Education and Christian Belief* 13, no. 1 (March 2009): 7–17; Jacobsen and Jacobsen, *Scholarship and Christian Faith*, 22–29; Glanzer, "Why We Should," 41–51.

31. Glanzer, "Why We Should," 41–42.

32. Morton, "Description of Deliberate Attempts," 240.

33. Monte Vaughan Cooper, "Faculty Perspectives on the Integration of Faith and Academic Discipline in Southern Baptist Higher Education," *Religious Education* 94, no. 4 (Fall 1999): 380–395.

34. Glanzer, "Why We Should," 43–49.

worldview approach), the rest are leaning toward faith-integrated being aspects (i.e. inter-and-intrapersonal approach, attitudinal approach). This suggests that most participants are more articulate and familiar with the practical aspects than the conceptual abstract relationship between faith and learning.

None of the participants speak of learning as *against* faith[35] or an *enemy* of faith.[36] Nor do they follow the *reconstructionist* view that all learning is anti-Christian[37] or the inability of non-Christians to understand truths.[38] Instead, the participants believe in the ontological presupposition that all truths, either gained through general or special revelation, are originated in God. This is in line with Reformed traditions on common grace[39] as shown by the participants in their efforts to educate Christian and non-Christian students alike and to initiate research partnerships with both Christian and non-Christian scholars (e.g. BS1, EP1, DS1).

At first glance, the ontological presuppositions held by the participants suggest that they subscribe to the one-realm approach. However, a closer look reveals many of the participants practice a modernist dualistic approach to faith and their academic discipline as shown through their expressions, such as "science needs proofs but faith (supernatural) needs no evidence" (BS1) and "faith is believing without seeing while science is talking about facts" (ES3). In line with the modernist approach,[40] the participants view faith and learning as two separate realms. Although holding to ontological presuppositions of truth, the participants assert that there is no need for integration because faith and learning (science) are compatible with each other (*compatibilist*) or mutually exclusive (*parallelist*).

This dualistic view is against Augustine, Kuyper, and Polanyi. Basing his argument on Augustine, Polanyi said, "He [Augustine] taught that all knowledge was a gift of grace, for which we must strive under the guidance of

---

35. John D. Carter and Bruce Narramore, *Integration of Psychology and Theology: An Introduction* (Grand Rapids: Zondervan, 1979), chap. 4.

36. Entwistle, *Integrative Approach*, chap. 2.

37. Nelson, "Faith Discipline," 324–327.

38. Van Til, *Junior Systematics*, 22.

39. See, e.g. Bavinck, "Common Grace," 35–65; Calvin, *Institutes*, II.iii.3; Abraham Kuyper, "Common Grace," in *Abraham Kuyper: A Centennial Reader*, ed. James D. Bratt (Grand Rapids: Eerdmans, 1998), 165–201.

40. See, e.g. Dockery, "Integrating Faith," 45; "Dimensions of the Integration," 24; Van Zanten, *Joining the Mission*, 109.

antecedent belief: *nisi credideritis, non intelligetis*."[41] Polanyi asserts that unless a person first believes, he or she will not understand. Against the positivist-modernistic view of science, Polanyi maintains that knowledge possesses a personal and tacit dimension.[42]

Similarly, Kuyper asserts that "every science to a certain degree starts from faith."[43] He continues, "Every science presupposes faith in self, in our self-consciousness; presupposes faith in the accurate working of our senses; presupposes faith in the correctness of the laws of thought . . .; which signifies that all these indispensable axioms, needed in a productive scientific investigation, do not come to us by proof, but are established in our judgment by our inner conception and given with our self-consciousness."[44] Kuyper refers to faith, not to soteriological faith, but to a "formal function of life of our soul which is fundamental to every fact in our human consciousness."[45] Opposed to "empirical or demonstrative proof," faith here denotes an epistemological belief that is "immediate" and held with "certainty."[46] For example, we believe that our sense-perceptions are reliable. Without this belief, Kuyper says, "there is no other bridge to be constructed from phenomena to noumena; and scientifically all the results of observation hang in air."[47]

To conclude, the modernist-dualist approach has deeply influenced the participants' view about faith and their academic disciplines, yet total separation of the two has not occurred. Faith still plays important roles in the participants' professional practices by serving as moral-ethical guidance and shaping their attitude and application of their scholarship pursuits. These phenomena might describe that Christian faculty in Indonesia embrace *methodological secularization* but not *ideological secularization*.[48] Another explanation will

---

41. Michael Polanyi, *Personal Knowledge: Towards a Post-Critical Philosophy* (1958; repr. London: Routledge, 2005), 280, https://bibliodarq.files.wordpress.com/2015/09/polanyi-m-personal-knowledge-towards-a-post-critical-philosophy.pdf.

42. See Polanyi, *Personal Knowledge*; Polanyi, "Tacit Knowing," in *Knowledge and Society: Forms of Knowledge*, eds. Nico Stehr and Reiner Grundmann (Abingdon, OX: Routledge, 2005), 101–114.

43. Kuyper, *Lectures on Calvinism*, 131.

44. Kuyper, 131.

45. Kuyper, *Sacred Theology*, 125.

46. Kuyper, 131.

47. Kuyper, 133.

48. Marsden, "Soul of the American University," 37.

be that the participants are stepping in two boats – following the inherited colonial westernized educational systems that practice dualism and secularization on one foot[49] and holding to Christian faith on the other foot.

A Worldview Approach without Transformative Action

Many participants affirm this ontological assumption by taking a worldview approach in which faith provides a lens and basis for learning. Harris defines worldview as "a comprehensive and unifying way of looking at all life, a means of bringing coherent meaning to one's experiences, thoughts, feelings, and so on."[50] Interestingly, although the participants hold to the worldview approach, when they encounter conflicts between faith and learning, no attempt was shown to bring the two into a *coherent meaning*. Instead of identifying areas of conflicts that need to be examined and transformed from a Christian perspective, the participants simply choose faith over learning, "I do not know what to do," or avoid the controversial areas. However, this does not mean that the participants do not wrestle with the dilemmatic issues. The reasons they do not practice a *transformationalist* strategy[51] is because they are not trained and equipped with knowledge and skills to address the issues, both the philosophical aspects of their academic disciplines and biblical-theological foundations (e.g. SW3, DY3, YP2, ET2). Almost all participants reported that they do not receive any professional development related to the integration of faith and learning.

That said, both Kuyper and Wolterstorff encourage Christian scholars to examine the foundational assumptions of their academic disciplines under the scrutiny of the Scriptures.[52] But first, the Christian's thinking should be "*already* permeated by Christian attitudes and beliefs, by Christian ways of seeing God's world."[53] As Christians, the participants do demonstrate their theistic interpretation of science (*see the ontological approach and attitudinal approach*). Kuyper asserts that the experience of *palingenesis* (regeneration)

---

49. Altbach, "Twisted Roots," 27.
50. Harris, *Integration of Faith*, 77.
51. Nelson, "Faith Discipline," 327.
52. Kuyper, *Lectures on Calvinism*, 120; Wolterstorff, *Reason within the Boundary*, 70.
53. Hasker, "Faith-Learning Integration," 246.

renews a person's consciousness and worldview, makes a decisive way of interpreting the "cosmos from different points of view" and motive of study.[54]

Evidently, faith does permeate in the lives of the participants as shown in their faith-integrated beings. Faith also makes a difference in the participants' academic pursuits, particularly in selecting teaching content (SW3, DY3) and research methodology (EW2, RD3) and shaping their motive, attitude, and application of their studies. However, faith has not influenced substantially the participants' *worldview foundations* that provide fundamental principles and insights to examine and transform their academic disciplines.[55]

The Neutrality of Science and Variability Effects of Sin

When asked about the potential conflicts between faith and learning, most participants from mathematics and natural science backgrounds answer that there is no conflict between the two because science is based on "facts" and "observations of the natural world," thus it is "neutral" and objective (e.g. ES3, PK3, HS1, AS1, BS1). According to them, social science and humanities are more likely to have conflicts with faith because they are based on human opinions or values. The participants are in line with Brunner and Kuyper, but against Moroney that mathematics and natural science are least or not affected by sin.[56] In other words, the participants view sin as affecting the areas of knowledge in various degrees. This view is in accord with Brunner's principle of "closeness of relation" that "the more closely a subject is related to man's inward life, the more natural human knowledge is 'infected' by sin; while the further away it is, the less will be its effect."[57]

However, the idea that science is neutral and objective is flawed in at least in three aspects. First, the participants are holding to a modernist view of science by treating their research or study as an object and keeping themselves distant and detached in order to ascertain the objectivity and neutrality of their observations. Polanyi criticizes this view by arguing that "any act of knowing is based on indwelling."[58] For Polanyi, indwelling is using our

---

54. Kuyper, *Sacred Theology*, 154.
55. Hasker, "Faith-Learning Integration," 244.
56. Brunner, *Christian Doctrine*, 27; Kuyper, *Lectures on Calvinism*, 157, 164.
57. Brunner, *Christian Doctrine*, 27.
58. Polanyi, "Tacit Knowing," 112.

physical senses and mental awareness to observe the world. In other words, "our body is the instrument by which we know the world."[59] Thus, it is impossible to separate the knower from the known.

Second, in line with Polanyi, Palmer asserts that scientists are not just observers but also participants in the world they study.[60] Both as observers and participants, scientists subscribe to their particular worldviews, underlying assumptions, or control beliefs.[61] Thus, scientists and science cannot be purely objective and neutral. In addition, science cannot be reduced to the collection of facts by excluding the comprehension of those facts. The methodologies, interpretations, and purposes that encourage a person to embark on the research in the first place, all possess subjective elements that are influenced by learners' worldviews.

Lastly, there is a trace of *self* involved in the study. Theologically, this *self* is a fallen creature. Moroney asserts that sin affects both the object of knowledge (all areas of academic disciplines) and the knowing subject (the learners, both individual and communal).[62] Consequently, human senses and the measurement tools used in the "observations" of the facts could be tricky and imperfect. Human and methodology errors could influence our perceptions and color the facts.

In short, knowledge is never objective and neutral but has a personal and tacit dimension.[63] We can claim a certain degree of certainty in knowledge, yet because the knower and the process of knowing are inherently flawed, human knowledge possesses a possibility of errors.

Learning Awe and Academic Humility

Holmes in his theoretical models to the integration of faith and learning includes the "attitudinal approach."[64] This approach describes Christian scholars' positive attitude toward learning that "in God's creation every area of life

---

59. Richard Gelwick, *The Way of Discovery: An Introduction to the Thought of Michael Polanyi* (Eugene, OR: Wipf & Stock, 1977), 70.

60. Palmer, *Courage to Teach*, 100–102.

61. For control beliefs, see Wolterstorff, *Reason within the Boundary*, 15–20; and for worldview, see James W. Sire, *The Universe Next Door: A Basic Worldview Catalog* (Downers Grove, IL: InterVarsity Press, 1997), 15–24.

62. Moroney, *Noetic Effects*, 35.

63. See Polanyi, *Personal Knowledge*; Polanyi, "Tacit Knowing."

64. Holmes, *Christian College*, 47.

and learning is related to the wisdom and power of God."[65] Unfortunately, in practice, this aspect of integration has been little explored by Christian scholars in North America.[66] On the contrary, Christian faculty members in Indonesia demonstrate that faith has shaped their aesthetic understanding and attitude in scholarship.

Learning awe and academic humility are distinct Christians' attitudes that are counter-culture to the contemporary academia that keeps religion out of scholarship on the ground that religion is irrational.[67] The absence of these positive attitudes is due to the dominant contemporary cultures that "treat texts and works of art autonomously"[68] and a consumerist learning attitude that treats the texts merely for practical information.[69] This malformation of the habits of heart and mind has depersonalized learning by taking out the creator from his or her creation. In the same way, scholarship has disconnected and lost the sense of awe and reverence to the Creator.

Fortunately, the academic world in the East, particularly Christian faculty in Indonesia, still ties scholarship closely to their faith. They show that the study of nature has led them to glimpse God's divine wisdom in creation with expressions such as "I learn the greatness of God," and "I can see the grandeur of God." They also demonstrate academic humility by recognizing how little they know as compared to God's vastness of knowledge and the limitation of human reasoning. This appreciation of God's general revelation is in accord with the Scripture that says: "How many are your works, Lord! In wisdom you made them all; the earth is full of your creatures" (Ps 104:24), and "By wisdom, the Lord laid the earth's foundations, by understanding he set the heavens in place; by his knowledge, the watery depths were divided, and the clouds let drop the dew" (Prov 3:19–20). This aspect of integration goes beyond the cognitive domain; it touches the affective domain of the learners. It also shows that integration is a two-way process by which faith shapes

---

65. Holmes, 47.

66. To the best of my knowledge, the Kuyers Institute of Calvin College has spearheaded faith-shaped educational practices since the last few years. The institute also explores the areas of learning awe in its "What If Learning" website (http://www.whatiflearning.com/).

67. Nicholas Wolterstorff, "Fides Quaerens Intellectum," in *Christian Scholarship in the Twenty-First Century: Prospects and Perils*, eds. Thomas M. Crisp, Steve L. Porter, and Gregg A. Ten Elshof (Grand Rapids: Eerdmans, 2014), 1–17.

68. Wolterstorff, "Fides Quaerens," 6.

69. Griffiths, *Religious Reading*, 42; Smith, "Reading Practices," 43–60.

learning and in return, learning deepens the participants' understanding and relationship with God.[70]

Faith-Integrated Doing

Self-Trained for Spontaneous Integration

For most participants, the integration of faith and educational practices is spontaneous and occasionally occurs during the teaching and learning process. They do not explicitly nor intentionally incorporate faith into their course design, teaching content, and pedagogical choice. For them, Christian faith is indirectly and implicitly integrated into their educational practices through cultivating the following: Christian practices, such as prayer, fasting, and devotion; Christian values, which use an analogy, narratives, and essential questions related to the Bible; and virtuous character and behavior, which emphasize academic honesty and integrity. These findings suggest that the approaches taken by Christian faculty in Indonesia are not so different from the majority of Christian faculty in North America. Alleman, Glanzer, and Guthrie in their empirical study of 2,309 faculty teaching at CCCU-affiliated colleges and universities in North America reveal that their faith-integrated educational practices include the following: helping students' development of their spiritual disciplines, Christian worldview, theological formation, and ethical thinking and action.[71] They also incorporate Bible references into courses, and a faith-tradition interpretive approach to teaching and learning objectives, curriculum design, and pedagogical selection.

From the perspective of Hasker, these Indonesian Christian faculty members' practices of integration of faith and learning that are reduced to personal pietism are considered superficial integrations.[72] Likewise, according to Wolfe, these integration practices are pseudo-integrations.[73] These might be due to their insufficient practical knowledge and experience of how to do the integration of faith and learning as shown from their reports that they had received no professional development relating to this area (e.g. HS1, TM1, RS1, ET2, ES3, DT3). Considering various dynamics of the working

---

70. Harris, *Integration of Faith*, 224.
71. Alleman, Glanzer, and Guthrie, "The Integration," 103–124.
72. Hasker, "Faith-Learning Integration," 235.
73. Wolfe, "Line of Demarcation," 4.

context of the participants, such as pressures under a predominantly Muslim environment (participants teaching at state and non-faith based universities) and lack of institutional supports (participants teaching at Christian universities), the *superficial* level of integration might be the wisest approach they could have taken so far.

Although there is no direct and substantive integration, yet the participants' intention and efforts in integrating faith to their educational practices are by no means superficial. In contrast, they teach by the principles to "give the best" and "help students learn best." These principles are manifested in their efforts to create a conducive learning environment, teaching attitude and competencies, pedagogical choice, and assessment selection. Their earnest desire to give the best is also shown through their willingness to learn new teaching and learning innovations, listening to students' and colleague's feedback, and praying for God's wisdom in designing and delivering the lessons. After all, there is no single approach or locus to practice the integration of faith and learning.[74] For Christian faculty in Indonesia, the main form of integration of faith and learning is their own lives. Interestingly, this is consistently shown in their responses throughout the three research questions. For them, the integral relationship between faith and learning is practiced through the following: modeling an exemplary life (intrapersonal); building positive relationships with students and colleagues (intrapersonal); cultivating a pietistic life (moral and ethical); incarnational posture in teaching, learning, and serving (attitudinal); and making a positive impact on the younger generation and God's creation (contribution to the Kingdom of God).

In addition, practicing a *spontaneous* integration of faith and learning does not mean the participants are arbitrary or irresponsible. Like the martial arts athletes who are trained for life to achieve spontaneous reflex actions, the participants faithfully train themselves in daily meditation on God's word and prayer (BS1, HS1, ET2, LI1) and sensitivity to the work of the Holy Spirit (BS1, AS1, JS3, EW2). In addition, they also make serious efforts in character and academic growth in accordance with their vocation. For them, faith is more than just a conceptual set of beliefs. It is "internalized" (JA1) and "ingrained" (DS1), and integration naturally flowing out of being. Thus, for the participants, spontaneous integration is practiced by carefully *discerning*

---

74. Hasker, "Faith-Learning Integration," 243.

the appropriate contexts and moments, and then seizing the opportunities to incorporate faith into their teaching and learning practices. This knowledge of *how* and *when* to do the spontaneous integration is constructed during the *moments* of actual teaching or student-teacher interacting, which in Schön's term is known as *reflection-in-action*.[75]

Faith-Shaped Pedagogical Choice

Many participants find that the majority of their students are passive learners. They recognize that their teaching skill is outdated and they need professional training to improve in this area. For example, MP1, a senior lecturer, said that the only teaching training she ever received was from a Sunday-school teaching training about three decades ago. Few participants have employed student-active learning approaches, such as the jigsaw method (DS1) and the flip-flop approach (EW2). Most participants do not speak of pedagogical choice as directly informed by their faith, but it is more guided by a common principle to "help students learn best." For instance, RS1 prefers to incorporate stories into her mathematics course to help the students understand and remember the mathematical formulas.

Overall, the findings of this study show that the integration of faith and pedagogical choice among Christian faculty in Indonesia is weak. The lack of faith-shaped pedagogical choice is also experienced by Christian faculty in North America as shown by Smith and Smith's study.[76] Even among Christian educators who practiced a high level of faith and learning integration in their teaching contents, Jang found that the teaching methods are teacher-centered and not informed by faith at all.[77]

The pedagogical choice is important. It is not merely about teaching techniques to help students to achieve better exam grades, but it reflects the educators' underlying assumptions about the nature of learners and knowledge. Smith and Smith argue that "we are formed by the practices in which we participate, and not merely by the ideas we exchange."[78] In other words, the formation of being, knowing, and doing of both teachers and learners are not

---

75. Schön, *Educating the Reflective Practitioner*, 25–26.
76. Smith and Smith, *Teaching and Christian Practices*, 192.
77. Jang, "Analysis of the Integration of Faith," 157.
78. Smith and Smith, *Teaching and Christian Practices*, 6.

merely influenced by the teaching contents, but also by the teaching methods we are using. Therefore, substantial integration of faith and learning is not just important in the educators' lives and academic discipline, but also in their teaching and learning practices. Because of this, Christian faculty members in Indonesia need to improve in this area of integration.

Being a Role Model and Building Positive Relationships with Students

Among various educational practices, most participants place a strong emphasis on being role models and building positive relationships with students. They do not focus on faith-integrated educational practices as an impersonal way of *teaching*, but they emphasize *living* and *showing* care and love for students by which the messages of faith are conveyed in an implicit yet personal way. Again, the participants place a strong emphasis on intrapersonal and interpersonal approaches in their integration of faith and learning. In order words, for the participants, faith-integrated learning is not about an academic exercise, but more on making "a transformational and lasting impact on students' minds, beliefs, and actions."[79] For the participants, the best means to touch the lives of the students is through their own lives by being a "role model" (ES3, JS3, DY3, AS1), "sharing my life" (RD3, LS3), and "living out a life that has been changed by Christ" (CS1, AS1). They themselves have firsthand experience of being inspired and influenced by the exemplary lives of their mentors and college professors (e.g. CS1, BS1, TM1, EP1, SW2).

In building relationships with students, the participants are rooted in the conviction that all students are created in the image of God, and treat them with respect, kindness, and fairness regardless of their ethnic and religious backgrounds. These convictions and attitudes are peculiar to the cultures where ethnoreligious discriminations and hegemony are commonly practiced in the social and academic circles (e.g. HS1, MP1, YP2, KC2, WU3). While it is also common for faculty to distance themselves from the students because of their seniority and superiority, the participants close the gaps of age, status, and degree by showing humility and servant leadership. For example,

---

79. Calvin G. Roso, "Faith and Learning in Action: Tangible Connections Between Biblical Integration and Living the Christian Life Justice," *Journal of Spirituality and Education* 3, no. 1 (November 2015): 60.

SW3 takes an incarnational posture by coming down from her "high chair" to meet and eat with her students at street vendors. Many participants are earnestly making themselves accessible and available for students to discuss their academic concerns and consult about their personal or family-related problems. What the participants show here is in line with Matthias's study that to be humble and servant-leaders are not merely personal traits but require a volitional and intentional pursuit.[80]

It is noteworthy that some participants express deep concern and desire to reach out to students who are involved in religious radicalism. Some of their means include civic education (BS1), Pancasila education (JH2), interfaith relationship (DA1, RM2, ET2), and research partnership (BS1, DS1). However, the participants observe that the positive responses they receive from their majority Muslim students are not from the aforementioned means, but from their genuine relationship and the love shown to the students. For example, EP1 received a birthday surprise from her students which was a rare treat for a faculty member. This token of love and appreciation from most of her Muslim students is an important affirmation for EP1 that her presence, love, and care for the students is well accepted and valued. Similarly, BS1 surprisingly found that God has used his sincere care and advice to help change one of his students who went missing from class because of his involvement with an Islamic radical organization.

The above experiences affirm for the participants that modeling an exemplary life and showing sincere care and love for students are non-offensive yet intriguing ways to witness for Christ in an unfavorable working environment. Their authentic being and relationship with students are effective means for their impactful teaching ministry. This is in accord with Clinton who asserts that "effective spiritual ministry flows out of being."[81] Similarly, studies were done by Sherr, Huff, and Curran, and Sites et al. that also reveal that some main indicators for effective faith-integrated learning are including

---

80. Laurie R. Matthias, "Professors Who Walk Humbly with Their God: Exemplars in the Integration of Faith and Learning at Wheaton College," *Journal of Education & Christian Belief* 12, no. 2 (September 2008): 145–157.

81. J. Robert Clinton, *The Making of a Leader* (Colorado Springs, CO: NavPress, 2012), 13.

the faculty's authentic lives and genuine interpersonal relationships with students and colleagues.[82]

Implications for Practice

Based on research findings and insights of the discussion, this section will explore some implications for educational ministry and practices to equip Christian faculty in Indonesia to better carry out their faith-integrated being, knowing, and doing: first, proposing a new terminology as an alternative for current phrase of "the integration of faith and learning" which is ambiguous, abstract, and cognitive-sided; second, developing a series of professional development formation lessons for the integration of faith and learning in Indonesia contexts; third, developing a structure of support for Christian faculty to face multiple challenges in their respective teaching contexts. I concluded by briefly discussing what Christian faculty members in North America can learn from their counterparts in Indonesia based on this study.

Proposing a New Terminology: "Faith-Integrated Being-Knowing-Doing"

A new terminology is needed to address current semantic use of "the integration of faith and learning," which overemphasizes the cognitive domain and creates ambiguity and dualistic thinking. Following this study of the integration of faith and learning among Christian faculty in Indonesian higher education contexts, I would like to propose the phrase "faith-integrated being-knowing-doing." If the terminology "integration of faith and learning" is still favorable because of its historical precedent and familiarity among Christian scholars, especially in North America, then I would suggest that the operational definition should broaden its scope to include the *being, knowing, and doing* aspects of integration. The phrase "faith-integrated being-knowing-doing" reflects a holistic view of human beings as God's image-bearers in the substantial, relational, and vocational aspects of human nature (see figure 6). Also, it takes into account that the whole of human beings was corrupted

---

82. Sherr, Huff, and Curan, "Student Perceptions," 15–33; Sites et al., Phenomenology of the Integration of Faith," 33–35.

after the fall and through the redemption in Jesus Christ, every aspect of human beings is renewed and will be fully restored at the *parousia* of Christ.

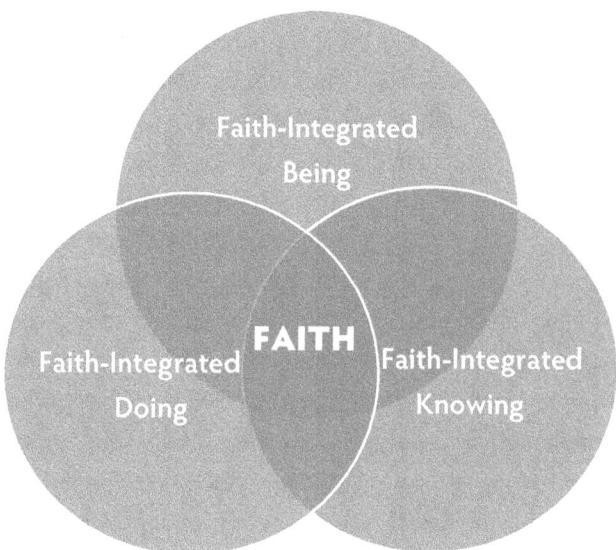

Figure 6. Model of Faith-Integrated Being, Knowing, and Doing

Why being? Unlike the aforementioned phrases that primarily focus on the academic disciplines or works of the educator, this phrase focuses on the person, the self of the educator as the agent and locus of integration. Although there are various loci of integration, teachers are the center and the most important locus for the integration of faith and learning. From a biblical perspective, first, learning entails general revelation and common grace, whereas faith is founded on special revelation and special grace. Second, the task of integration of faith and learning is a Christian's participation in God's redemptive work in this distorted and fragmented world; or in other words to "conscientiously build the kingdom of God."[83] Thus, in line with Gaebelein who argues that there is "no Christian education without Christian teachers,"[84] here I maintain that there is no integration of faith and learning without teachers who first are regenerated and sanctified by Christ through the work

---

83. Plantinga, *Engaging God's World*, 123.
84. Gaebelein, *Pattern of God's Truth*, 37.

of the Holy Spirit (John 3:1–10; Rom 10:9–10; 1 Pet 1:3; 2 Cor 5:17). The task of integration starts with *being*, the faculty member's self as an integrator, whose life and vocation are infused with faith. This embodiment of integration allows faculty to serve as a living model and teach from an authentic self that was strongly demonstrated by the participants in this study. Second, *knowing* entails the integration of faith into the faculty member's academic disciplines. This aspect of integration has been explored by many Christian scholars. In fact, it is the main focus of the integration of faith and learning in North America for the last fifty years.[85] This aspect of integration is still weak among Christian faculty in Indonesia and we need to humbly learn from our counterparts from the West. Third, *doing* refers to faith in shaping the faculty's educational practices. This aspect of integration has not been as much developed among Christian faculty in North America as in Indonesia. Thus, more attention and effort needs to be given to this area of integration.

Taken altogether, *faith-integrated being-knowing-doing* is a holistic and integrated approach to faith and learning that includes the cognitive, affective, spiritual, relational, and vocational aspects of human nature. The integration of faith and learning is more than just *scholarly tasks* to relate or unify faith and learning, but it is also about the *formation* of a Christian perspective in all areas of life, thoughts, and practices.

Professional Development Formation

This study reveals that most participants have a strong emphasis on the aspect of faith-integrated *being* but less on the aspects of faith-integrated *knowing* and *doing*. Throughout their responses to all three research questions, the participants focus on the intrapersonal authentic living, genuine intrapersonal relationship with students, and moral-ethical aspects of their vocation, scholarship, and teaching. However, Christian faculty in Indonesia should not limit the integration of faith and learning to pietistic lives and activities, but broaden it by being willing to be equipped with biblical-theological, philosophical, and educational foundations; in order to bring Christian faith into their respective academic discipline and educational practices. For this

---

85. See, e.g. Coe, "Interdependent Model of Integration," 111; Harris, *Integration of Faith*, 4; Helminiak, *Religion and the Human Sciences*, 35; Wolfe, "Line of Demarcation," 9; Nelson, "Faith Discipline," 317–319; Hasker, "Faith-Learning Integration," 234.

purpose, I would like to propose a series of basic professional development lessons which include at least three areas for a holistic integration of faith and learning (see figure 7).

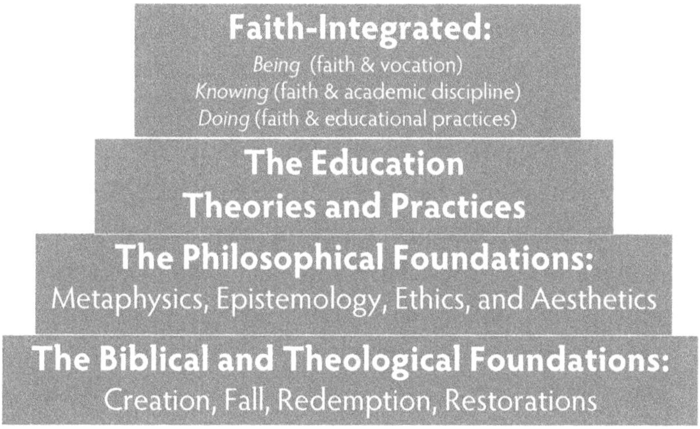

Faith-Integrated:
Being (faith & vocation)
Knowing (faith & academic discipline)
Doing (faith & educational practices)

The Education Theories and Practices

The Philosophical Foundations:
Metaphysics, Epistemology, Ethics, and Aesthetics

The Biblical and Theological Foundations:
Creation, Fall, Redemption, Restorations

Figure 7. Basic Professional Development for the Integration of Faith and Learning

a. **Developing biblical and theological foundations**: the biblical story of Creation-Fall-Redemption-Restoration as a framework to understand the nature of human beings, the nature of knowledge and reasoning, general and special grace, and calling and vocation. The biblical story provides knowledge of "who we are, what has gone wrong with the world, what God has done to redeem and restore His broken creation, and what the future holds for His people, those who accept His offer of salvation."[86] It also provides a basis to understand the *missio Dei* for our participation in the gospel mandate and cultural mandate.[87] This foundation of biblical and theological foundations will serve as the formation for Christian faculty members in Indonesia, both in the sanctification journey of growing to maturity (Rom 6:18; 8:29; 1 Cor 6:11; 2 Cor 5:17), and

---

86. Trevin Wax, *Counterfeit Gospels: Rediscovering the Good News in the World of False Hope* (Chicago: Moody Publishers, 2011), 24.
87. Wright, *Mission of God's People*.

in shaping their calling to be light and salt in this predominantly Muslim country.

b. **Developing philosophical foundations**: to go beyond superficial or pseudo-integration,[88] Christian faculty in Indonesia need to address basic philosophical questions which include aspects of metaphysics, epistemology, ethics, and aesthetics; explore some major philosophical streams in education and academic disciplines; and learn to pose philosophical questions and identify contemporary philosophies or worldviews which influence the educational systems and academic disciplines.[89] Combined with biblical-theological foundations, Christian faculty in Indonesia will be equipped to examine the ontological and epistemological foundations of their academic discipline and to find an integral relationship between the disciplines and Christian faith.

c. **Developing faith-shaped pedagogical practices**: Smith asserts that "behind every pedagogy is a philosophical anthropology."[90] He goes further by saying that humans are not just rational creatures, but also "loving, desiring, affective, and liturgical" creatures.[91] Thus, in developing a faith-shaped pedagogy, Christian faculty need to take into consideration the following aspects: the nature and contexts of the learners, the nature of their academic disciplines, educational theories, and teaching approaches. The next steps are to examine all these variables through a biblical lens, and then offer critiques and alternatives to their pedagogical practices. It is a complex scholarly activity that requires metacognitive knowledge, skills, and strategies. Here, metacognition is understood as a critical reflection – attitudes and professional habits of thinking developed by Argyris and Schön and introduced to education by Stephen D. Brookfield – as a means for educators to study their

---

88. Hasker, "Faith-Learning Integration," 235; Wolfe, "Line of Demarcation," 4.

89. George R. Knight, *Philosophy and Education: An Introduction in Christian Perspective*, 4th ed. (Berrien Springs, MI: Andrews University Press, 2006), chs. 1 and 2.

90. James K. A. Smith, *Desiring the Kingdom: Worship, Worldview, and Cultural Formation*, Cultural Liturgies (Grand Rapids: Baker Academic, 2009), 27.

91. Smith, *Desiring the Kingdom*, 34.

own teaching practices and analyze what works best to improve their student learning.[92]

Our beliefs and practices are not value-free. Naugle asserts that "Faith is always integrated with learning . . . the real question is *which* faith is integrated with learning."[93] Thus, the biblical and theological foundations serve as a basis and lens to examine other worldviews, direct motives and purposes of teaching and learning, and select what values and practices to instill in the faith-integrated being, knowing, and doing.

Developing a Support Structure

In facing multiple challenges, Christian faculty in Indonesia need a support structure that includes personal growth, a community of believers, and a community of academics (*see 8*).

This study shows that most participants have strong self-directed initiatives for their personal growth which include spiritual, character, academic, and career aspects. One aspect that can be added to this personal growth is a critical reflection. For Schön and Brookfield, professional growth begins when a person critically examines his or her current assumptions and actions.[94] Similarly, in their efforts to manifest faith through their vocation, academic discipline, and educational practices, Christian faculty need to constantly reflect and discern their assumptions, beliefs, and practices in the light of the Scripture. For an in-depth study about reflective thinking, Christian faculty can learn from Schön's *Educating the Reflective Practitioner*, Brookfield's *Becoming a Critically Reflective Teacher*, and Kolb's learning cycle.[95]

---

92. Argyris and Schön, *Theory in Practice*; Brookfield, *Becoming a Critically Reflective Teacher*.

93. David Naugle, "Models of Faith and Learning in Higher Education," Summer Institute in Christian Scholarship, accessed February 1, 2016, https://www3.dbu.edu/naugle/pdf/institute_handouts/general/models_faith_learning.pdf.

94. Schön, *Educating the Reflective Practitioner*, 22–40; Brookfield, *Becoming a Critically Reflective Teacher*, 1–20.

95. Schön, *Educating the Reflective Practitioner*; Brookfield, *Becoming a Critically Reflective Teacher*; David Kolb, *Experiential Learning: Experience as the Source of Learning and Development* (Englewood Cliffs, NJ: Prentice Hall, 1984).

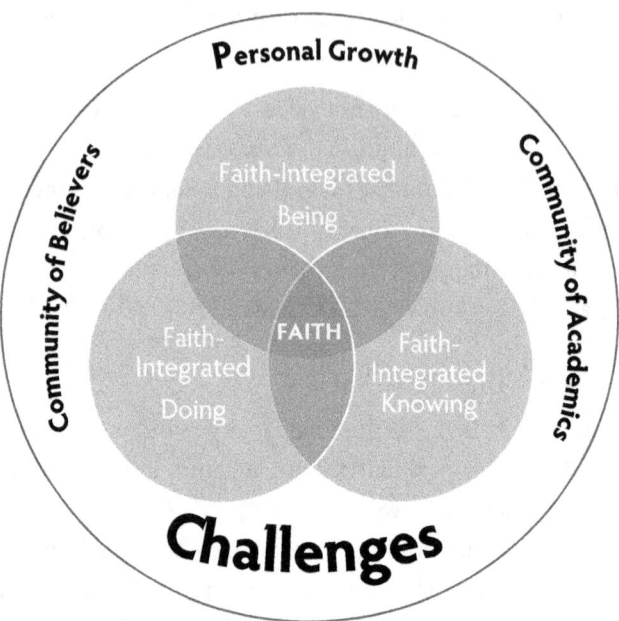

Figure 8. Support Structure for Christian Faculty

Another source of support is from the community of believers, which might include local churches, parachurch organizations, and fellow Christians at their workplace. Many participants found campus fellowships, particularly small groups, were significantly helpful during their college formative years in searching and decision-making about their calling. Christian faculty members are encouraged to continue this type of group support or form a new group among the graduates. Church and parachurch can facilitate this type of group, which provides a deep learning of the Bible as well as a supportive relationship among the group members. In addition, large group meetings such as seminars, workshops, monthly fellowships, and annual retreats can empower and refresh the weary souls of the faculty in the midst of adversities to carry out their teaching vocation.

Lastly, many participants also hope for support from a community of academics. In addition to an academic growth purpose, Christian faculty in Indonesia can learn from their Christian counterparts in North America who have more experience in the integration of faith and learning. Individual or departmental partnerships will help Christian faculty in Indonesia who are new to the concepts and practices of the integration of faith and learning, with collaborative research, literature resources, and idea exchange. In return, Christian faculty in North America can learn about the integration of gospel and cultural mandate and teaching vocation through the interpersonal and intrapersonal approaches from Christian faculty in Indonesia.

Suggestions for Further Research

This study focused on the faith-integrated being, knowing, and doing among Christian faculty in Indonesian higher education contexts. The research finding contributed to filling the gaps in the literature, especially regarding the understanding and practices of integration of faith and learning outside North America. This research is considered a pioneering study in the area of the integration of faith and learning in Indonesia contexts and is very much open for multiple further research.

First, Christian faculty teaching at Christian universities are supposed to have more freedom to integrate faith in their teaching vocation, academic discipline, and educational practices, compared to Christian faculty teaching at state and non-faith based private universities. However, this study indicates no difference between Christian faculty teaching at Christian and non-Christian universities in their understanding and practices of the integration of faith and learning. To have a comprehensive understanding of these intriguing phenomena, a qualitative study with similar topics to this study but specifically focused on Christian universities can be conducted from the perspectives of various stakeholders, such as students, individual faculty, administrative leaders, board members, and alumni.

Second, this study focuses on Christian faculty who teach at universities centered in Java Island, which is the most developed area in Indonesia. To have a broader picture of the understanding, practices, and challenges of the integration of faith and learning, a similar study can be done with Christian faculty who teach in the east and the west parts of Indonesia. These two regions of Indonesia have more Christian population but are poorer in their social-economic conditions compared to residents of Java Island.

Third, research can be done on how the implementation of a series of basic professional development courses (as suggested in this study) impact two or three focus groups of Christian faculty in Indonesia. The findings of the study will help to better tailor a curriculum for professional development in the area of faith-integrated being, knowing, and doing among Christian faculty in a broader context in Indonesia.

Conclusion

The purpose of this qualitative study was to explore the perceptions of faith-integrated being, knowing, and doing among Christian faculty in Indonesian higher education contexts. This study focused on three areas of integration: faith and vocation, faith and academic disciplines, and faith and educational practices. The findings of this study suggest that Christian faculty in Indonesia have a strong emphasis on their faith-integrated being but less on their faith-integrated knowing and doing.

Faith plays a central role in the life and vocation of the participants. Faith-integrated being is manifested in the participants' conviction of their calling as teaching faculty; the purpose and meaning of their work; work attitude, ethics, and performance; desire for personal growth; and resiliency in the face of adversities. Faith is the internal motivation that drives participants to engage in their zeal to share the Gospel in words and do the good works of cultural formation and transformation through their teaching, service, and research with a distinctive set of principles and values. The participants demonstrate that the works of evangelism and cultural engagement start with personal sanctification; and not by their might to transform cultures and the lives of people but by dependence on God's wisdom and obedience to God's direction.

In the areas of faith-integrated knowing, the modernist-dualist view that keeps faith away from learning does influence the participants' view about the neutrality and objectivity of natural science, particularly natural science and mathematics; yet the separation has not totally happened in the areas that directly touch their lives. The findings reveal that the integration of faith and learning does not occur substantially in the academic discipline of the participants. However, faith does make a difference in their scholarship pursuit by providing ethical and moral guidelines, shaping their attitudes and inter-and-intrapersonal relationships, and directing the purpose and application of their academic studies.

The integration of faith and educational practices do not occur at substantial levels. Faith is integrated into classroom practices through spontaneous integration and cultivating Christian practices and values. For most participants, living out exemplary Christian lives and building authentic relationships with students are the two most impactful faith-integrated educational practices.

In sum, for Christian faculty in Indonesia, the focus of the integration of faith and learning is on cultivating pietistic lives and practices. For them, *intrapersonal* approaches of living out an authentic and moral-ethically Christian life and *interpersonal* approaches to building genuine relationships with students are central to their integration of faith and learning. For a substantial and foundational integration to occur, this study suggests Christian faculty members in Indonesia need to be willing to be equipped with biblical-theological and philosophical foundations and educational theories and practices; and need to critically examine their assumptions and practices in the light of Scripture. In addition, Christian faculty also need a structure of support which includes personal growth, a community of believers, and a community of academics, to empower them to face multiple challenges in their respective teaching contexts.

APPENDIX 1

Informed Consent Form

Thank you for your willingness to participate in this study. Your contribution in this study is very much appreciated!

The research in which you are about to participate is designed to explore the perceptions of faith-integrated *being, knowing,* and *doing* among Christian faculty in Indonesian higher education contexts. This research is being conducted by Sarinah Lo, a PhD student in the Educational Studies program at Trinity International University, Deerfield, Illinois.

In this research, you will be asked to share your life stories in an hour-long interview pertinent to the topic. Your response will be recorded for analysis purposes. Upon completion of this study, your recorded responses will be deleted.

Please be assured that as a researcher, I will do my utmost to protect your confidentiality and anonymity. At no time will your name be reported along with your responses. Please understand that your participation in this research is completely voluntary. You may withdraw from this study at any time.

"I acknowledge that I have been informed of, and understand, the nature and purpose of this study, and I freely consent to participate."

Name: _____

Signed: _____ Date: _____

APPENDIX 2

Interview Protocol

Part I: Background Information

Thank you for your willingness to be interviewed. Please take a few minutes to answer these demographic-related questions before we start the interview.

1. What is the highest degree or level of school you have completed? (If currently enrolled, highest degree will be received).
   _____

2. Teaching experiences:
   a. Total years of service: _____ years.
   b. Rank: _____
   c. Type of Institution: _____

3. Please tick the statement that applies to you:
   ( ) I am a Christian.
   ( ) I am currently an active member of a local church.
   ( ) I attend worship service regularly.

4. Please list any professional development you have received in the last five years that related to faith.
   _____
   _____
   _____

Part II: Interview Questions

The following questions will be served as the interview questions. Bulleted questions will be used for prompts and follow-ups if the initial interview questions do not sufficiently clear for the interviewees.

RQ1: How do Indonesian Christian faculty describe the value of faith in their vocation?

> (The first part of this interview will focus on your being as a faculty. Please feel free to share your experiences, feelings, and thoughts about your personal calling and life as a faculty).

1. Please briefly describe your job as a faculty.
2. Tell me about how you become a faculty.
    - What prompted or motivated you to choose a teaching profession?
    - What consideration or circumstances have led you to teach at this institution?
3. In what ways has Christian faith shaped your vocation as a faculty?
    - How faith has helped you to see your role, identity, mission, and students?
    - How faith has influenced your principles and attitudes in living out your vocation?
4. What words or metaphor would you use to describe your being as a Christian faculty in your teaching context? Please explain.
5. Imagine yourself five years from now: What aspects of personal growth do you hope to see in yourself as a better Christian faculty?
    - What do you want to know or do more/better?
    - What kinds of support or resources do you need in order to achieve your aspirations?

RQ2: How do Indonesian Christian faculty describe the relationship between faith and their educational discipline?

(The second part of this interview will focus on your knowing or cognitive understanding about the relationship between faith and your discipline).

1. What is your understanding of "the integration of faith and learning?"
    - What does come to your mind when you hear this term? (How do you define it?)
2. What do you think about the relationship between faith and your discipline/subject?
    - Do you find any tensions between the two? If yes/no, please explain.
    - What role does faith play in the understanding of your discipline/subject?
    - How does your disciplines/subject inform your Christian faith?

RQ3: How do Indonesian Christian faculty describe the influence of faith in their educational practices?

(The last part of this interview will focus on your doing or teaching activities).

1. Please describe how your teaching and learning activities look like in your classroom.
2. In what ways has Christian faith influenced your educational practices?
    - Tell me the process of how you prepare your syllabus, teaching materials/textbooks, student assignment and teaching approach selection?
    - Interaction with students inside and/or outside the class?
    - What are some classroom practices that you consider to be Christian?

Closing Question: What challenges and hopes do you have as a Christian faculty in your service context?

Bibliography

ACSI (The Association of Christian Schools International). "About ACSI and Membership." Accessed December 15, 2015. https://www.acsi.org/about-acsi-and-membership.

ACSI Indonesia. "Christian Educator Certification." *ACSI Indonesia*. Posted on March 12, 2018. Accessed April 2, 2018. https://acsi.id/programs/cec?o=terbaru.

ADB (Asian Development Bank). "Sector Assessment (Summary): Education. Country Partnership Strategy: Indonesia, 2012–2014." Accessed February 15, 2018. https://www.adb.org/sites/default/files/linked-documents/cps-ino-2012-2014-ssa-02.pdf.

Akers, George H. "The Measure of a School." *Journal of Adventist Education* 40, no. 2 (December 1977): 7–9, 43–45.

Alleman, Nathan F., Perry L. Glanzer, and David S. Guthrie. "The Integration of Christian Theological Traditions into the Classroom: A Survey of CCCU Faculty." *Christian Scholar's Review* 45, no. 2 (Winter 2016): 103–124.

Altbach, Philip G. "Twisted Roots: The Western Impact on Asian Higher Education." *Higher Education* 18, no. 1 (February 1989): 9–29.

Argyris, Chris, and Donald A. Schön. *Theory in Practice: Increasing Professional Effectiveness*. San Francisco: Jossey-Bass, 1974.

Arnett, Jeffrey J. "A Congregation of One: Individualized Religious Beliefs among Emerging Adults." Journal of Adolescent Research 17, no. 5 (September 2002): 451–467.

———. "Emerging Adulthood: A Theory of Development from the Late Teens through the Twenties." *American Psychologist* 55, no. 5 (May 2000): 469–480.

Augustine. *Teaching Christianity: De Doctrina Christiana*. Translated by Edmund Hill. Edited by John E. Rotelle. Hyde Park, NY: New City Press, 1996.

Azra, Azyumardi. "Indonesian Higher Education: From Public Good to Privatization." *Journal of Asian Public Policy* 1, no. 2 (June 2008): 139–147.

Badan Pusat Statistik. "Jumlah Penduduk Menurut Wilayah dan Agama yang Dianut" [Population by Regions and Religions], Sensus Penduduk 2010 [2010

Census]. Accessed October 3, 2017, http://sp2010.bps.go.id/index.php/site/tabel?tid=321&wid=0.

———. "Penduduk Indonesia menurut Provinsi" [Indonesian Population by Provinces]. Accessed September 13, 2017. https://www.bps.go.id/linkTabelStatis/view/ id/1267.

Badley, Kenneth R. "Clarifying 'Faith-learning Integration': Essentially Concepts and the Concept-Conception Distinction." *Journal of Education and Christian Belief* 13, no. 1 (March 2009): 7–17.

———. "The Faith/Learning Integration Movement in Christian Higher Education: Slogan or Substance?" *Journal of Research on Christian Education* 3 (Spring 1994): 13–33.

Bavinck, Herman. "Herman Bavinck's 'Common Grace.'" Translated by R. C. Van Leeuwen. *Calvin Theological Journal* 24, no. 1 (1989): 35–65.

Beck, Albert R. "All Truth Is God's Truth: The Life and Ideas of Frank E. Gaebelein." PhD diss., Baylor University, 2008.

Birbili, Maria. "Translating from One Language to Another." *Social Research Update* 31 (Winter 2000). Accessed April 6, 2017. http://sru.soc.surrey.ac.uk/SRU31.html.

Bouma-Prediger, Steven. "The Task of Integration: A Modest Proposal." *Journal of Psychology and Theology* 18, no. 1 (March 1990): 21–31.

Boyer, Ernest L. *Scholarship Reconsidered: Priorities of the Professoriate*. Princeton, NJ: Carnegie Foundation for the Advancement of Teaching, 1990.

Bremborg, Anna D. "Interviewing." In *The Routledge Handbook of Research Methods in the Study of Religion*, edited by M. Stausberg and S. Engler, 310–322. Abingdon, UK: Routledge, 2011.

Brookfield, Stephen. *Becoming a Critically Reflective Teacher*. 2nd edition. San Francisco: Jossey-Bass, 2017.

Brunner, Emil. *Christian Doctrine of Creation and Redemption*. Translated by Olive Wyon. Philadelphia: Westminster Press, 1952.

Brycko, Dariusz M. "Steering a Course between Fundamentalism and Transformationalism: J. Gresham Machen's View of Christian Scholarship." In *Christian Scholarship in the Twenty-First Century: Prospects and Perils*, edited by Thomas M. Crisp, Steve L. Porter, and Gregg A. Ten Elshof, 80–96. Grand Rapids, MI: Eerdmans, 2014.

Bunduki, Kwany Honore. "A Phenomenological Reflection on Integrated Learning at a Christian University for Community Transformation in the Democratic Republic of the Congo." PhD diss., University of South Africa, 2016.

Burtchaell, James T. *The Dying of the Light: The Disengagement of Colleges and Universities from Their Christian Churches*. Grand Rapids, MI: Eerdmans, 1998.

Burton, Larry, and Constance C. Nwosu. "Student Perceptions of the Integration of Faith, Learning, and Practice in an Educational Methods Course." *Journal of Research on Christian Education* 12, no. 2 (Fall 2003): 101–135.

Byker, Gaylen J. "Calvin College: Institutional Positioning and Marketing Summary." Accessed October 3, 2016. https://www.calvin.edu/admin/public_relations/minds /pdf/ipms_pages_1to20.pdf.

Call, Carolyn. "The Rough Trail to Authentic Pedagogy: Incorporating Hospitality, Fellowship, and Testimony into the Classroom." In *Teaching and Christian Practices: Reshaping Faith and Learning*, edited by David I. Smith and James K. A. Smith, 61–79. Grand Rapids, MI: Eerdmans, 2011.

Calvin, John. *Institutes of the Christian Religion*. Edited by John T. McNeill. Translated by Ford Lewis Battles. Louisville: Westminster John Knox Press, 1960.

Carpenter, Joel A. "Introduction: Christian Universities and the Global Expansion of Higher Education." In *Christian Higher Education: A Global Reconnaissance*, edited by Joel Carpenter, Perry L. Glanzer, and Nicholas S. Lantinga, 1–23. Grand Rapids, MI: Eerdmans, 2014.

Carter, John D., and Bruce Narramore. *Integration of Psychology and Theology: An Introduction*. Grand Rapids: Zondervan, 1979.

CCCU (Council for Christian Colleges & Universities). "Our Mission." Accessed November 19, 2015. http://www.cccu.org/.

Chang, Mae Chu, et al. *Teacher Reform in Indonesia: The Role of Politics and Evidence in Policy Making*. Washington, DC: World Bank, 2014.

Clinton, J. Robert. *The Making of a Leader*. Colorado Springs, CO: NavPress, 2012.

Coe, John H. "An Interdependent Model of Integration and the Christian University." *Faculty Dialogue* 21 (Spring-Summer 1994): 111–137.

Cooper, Monte Vaughan. "Faculty Perspectives on the Integration of Faith and Academic Discipline in Southern Baptist Higher Education." *Religious Education* 94, no. 4 (Fall 1999): 380–395.

Cosgrove, Preston B. "Variations on a Theme: Convergent Thinking and the Integration of Faith and Learning." *Christian Higher Education* 14, no. 4 (August 2015): 229–243.

Creswell, John W. *Qualitative Inquiry and Research Design: Choosing Among Five Approaches*. Thousand Oaks, CA: Sage, 2012.

DeKoster, Lester. *Work: The Meaning of Your Life*. Grand Rapids: Christian's Library Press, 2010.

del Granado, Arze, et al. "Investigating in Investigating in Indonesia's Education: Allocation, Equity, and Efficiency of Public Expenditures." The World Bank, Policy Research Working Paper, No. 4329. Washington, DC: World Bank, 2007. Accessed February 15, 2018. http://hdl.handle.net/10986/7280.

Department of Education of Seventh-Adventist Church. "Mission and Scope." Accessed December 15, 2015. http://education.gc.adventist.org/.

Dewey, John. *Democracy and Education: An Introduction to the Philosophy of Education*. New York: Macmillan, 1916.

Dockery, David S. "Integrating Faith and Learning: An Unapologetic Case for Christian Higher Education." Faith and Mission 18, no. 1 (Fall 2000): 44–56.

———. *Shaping a Christian Worldview*. Nashville: Broadman & Holman, 2002.

Downing, Crystal L. "Imbricating Faith and Learning: The Architectonics of Christian Scholarship." In *Scholarship and Christian Faith: Enlarging the Conversation*, edited by Douglas Jacobsen and Rhonda H. Jacobsen, 33–44. New York: Oxford University Press, 2004.

Eck, Brian E., Scott A. White, and David N. Entwistle. "Teaching Integration to Postmodern and Millennial Students: Implications for the Classroom." *Journal of Psychology & Christianity* 35, no. 2 (Summer 2016): 125–136.

Ellis, Erin M., "Faculty Interpretations of Faith-Integration in Classroom Practices." Master's thesis, Baylor University, 2014.

Entwistle, David N. *Integrative Approach to Psychology and Christianity: An Introduction to Worldview Issues, Philosophical Foundations, and Models of Integration*. Eugene, OR: Wipf & Stock, 2004.

Faber, Riemer. "Martin Luther on Reformed Education." *Clarion* 47, no. 16 (August 1998): 376–379.

Fahmi, Mohamad. "Indonesian Higher Education: Gaps in Access and School Choice." Working Papers in Economics and Development Studies (WoPEDS) 201414. Department of Economics, Padjadjaran University. Revised Oct 2014. Accessed February 15, 2015. https://ideas.repec.org/p/unp/wpaper/201414.html.

Farnsworth, Kirk E. "The Conduct of Integration." *Journal of Psychology and Theology* 10, no. 4 (December 1982): 308–319.

Freire, Paolo. *Pedagogy of the Oppressed*. New York: Continuum, 1970.

Gaebelein, Frank E. *The Pattern of God's Truth: Problems of Integration in Christian Education*. Chicago: Moody Press, 1954; repr. 1968.

Gaff, Jerry G., and Ronald D. Simpson. "Faculty Development in the United States." *Innovative Higher Education* 18, no. 3 (March 1994): 167–176.

Gall, Meredith, Joyce Gall, and Walter Borg. *Educational Research: An Introduction*. New York: Longman, 1996.

Gelwick, Richard. "Polanyi: An Occasion of Thanks." *Cross Currents: Religion and Intellectual Life* 41, no. 3 (Fall 1991): 380–381.

———. *The Way of Discovery: An Introduction to the Thought of Michael Polanyi*. Eugene, OR: Wipf & Stock, 1977.

Gill, Jerry H. "Faith in Learning: Integrative Education and Incarnational Theology." *The Christian Century* 96, no. 33 (October 1979): 1009–1013.

Glanzer, Perry L. "Why We Should Discard 'the Integration of Faith and Learning': Rearticulating the Mission of the Christian Scholar." *Journal of Education and Christian Belief* 12, no. 1 (March 2008): 41–51.

Glanzer, Perry L., and Joel A. Carpenter. "Conclusion: Evaluating the Health of Christian Higher Education around the Globe." In *Christian Higher Education: A Global Reconnaissance*, edited by Joel Carpenter, Perry L. Glanzer, and Nicholas S. Lantinga, 277–305. Grand Rapids, MI: Eerdmans, 2014.

Glanzer, Perry L., and Todd C. Ream. *Christianity and Moral Identity in Higher Education*. New York: Palgrave Macmillan, 2009.

Glanzer, Perry L., Joel A. Carpenter, and Nick Lantinga. "Looking for God in the University: Examining Trends in Christian Higher Education." *Higher Education* 61, no. 6 (June 2011): 721–755.

Greidanus, Sidney. "The Use of the Bible in Christian Scholarship." *Christian Scholars Review* 11, no. 2 (1982): 138–147.

Griffiths, Paul J. *Religious Reading: The Place of Reading in the Practice of Religion*. New York, NY: Oxford University Press, 1999.

Griswold, Eliza. *The Tenth Parallel: Dispatches from the Fault Line Between Christianity and Islam*. New York: Farrar, Strauss, & Giroux, 2010.

Hall, Gene E., and Susan F. Loucks. "A Developmental Model for Determining Whether the Treatment Is Actually Implemented." *American Educational Research Journal* 14, no. 3 (May 1977): 263–276.

Hansen, David T. "Teaching and the Sense of Vocation." *Educational Theory* 44, no. 3 (September 1994): 259–275.

Hardin, Joyce, John Sweeney, and Jerry Whitworth. "Integrating Faith and Learning in Teacher Education." Paper presented at the Extended Annual Meeting of the Association of Independent Liberal Arts Colleges for Teacher Education, Abilene, TX. February 24, 1999. Accessed December 7, 2015. http://files.eric.ed.gov/fulltext/ED429044.pdf.

Harjanto, Sutrisna. "The Development of Vocational Stewardship among Indonesian Christian Professionals." PhD diss., Trinity International University, 2016.

Harris, Robert A. *The Integration of Faith and Learning: A Worldview Approach*. Eugene, OR: Wipf & Stock, 2004.

Hasker, William. "Faith-Learning Integration: An Overview." *Christian Scholar's Review* 21, no. 3 (March 1992): 234–248.

Heie, Harold. *Learning to Listen, Ready to Talk: A Pilgrimage Toward Peacemaking*. New York, NY: Universe, 2007.

———. "Mathematics: Freedom within Bounds." In *The Reality of Christian Learning*, edited by Harold Heie and David L. Wolfe, 206–230. Grand Rapids, MI: Eerdmans, 2004.

Helminiak, Daniel A. *Religion and the Human Sciences: An Approach via Spirituality*. Albany, NY: State University of New York Press, 1998.

Henry, Carl F. H. *The Uneasy Conscience of Modern Fundamentalism*. Grand Rapids, MI: Eerdmans, 1947; repr. 2003.

Hesselbein, Frances, Erik K. Shinseki, and Richard E. Cavanagh. *Be-Know-Do: Leadership the Army Way*. San Francisco: Jossey-Bass, 2004.

Hick, John. *Faith and Knowledge: A Modern Introduction to the Problem of Religious Knowledge*. Wipf & Stock, 2009.

Hoekema, Anthony A. *Created in God's Image*. Grand Rapids: Eerdmans, 1986.

Hoitenga, Dewey. "The Noetic Effects of Sin: A Review Article." *Calvin Theological Journal* 38 (2003): 68–102.

Holmes, Arthur F. *All Truth Is God's Truth*. Grand Rapids, MI: Eerdmans, 1977.

———. *The Idea of a Christian College*. Revised edition. Grand Rapids, MI: Eerdmans, 1987.

Huber, Mary T., and Pat Hutchings. *The Advancement of Learning: Building the Teaching Commons*. San Francisco: Jossey-Bass, 2005.

Hughes, Richard T., and William B. Adrian, eds. *Models for Christian Higher Education: Strategies for Survival and Success in the Twenty-First Century*. Grand Rapids, MI: Eerdmans, 1997.

INCHE (International Network for Christian Higher Education). "What is INCHE?" Accessed June 6, 2020. https://inche.one/what-is-inche.

Jacobsen, Douglas, and Rhonda H. Jacobsen. *Scholarship and Christian Faith: Enlarging the Conversation*. New York: Oxford University Press, 2004.

Jandt, Fred E. *An Introduction to Intercultural Communication: Identities in a Global Community*. 5th edition. Thousand Oaks, CA: Sage, 2007.

Jang, Kyumin. "The Administrative Role of the Academic Dean in the Integration of Faith and Learning in Christian Higher Education." PhD diss., Southwestern Baptist Theological Seminary, 2016.

Jang, You Jung. "An Analysis of the Integration of Faith and Learning Implemented by Christian Elementary School Teachers." PhD diss., Southern Baptist Theological, 2011. Accessed December 5, 2015. http://hdl.handle.net/10392/3735.

Kementerian Keuangan [Ministry of Finance Indonesia]. Anggaran Pendidikan 2010–2017. Direktorat Penyusunan APBN – Direktorat Jenderal Anggaran. Accessed May 17, 2018. http://www.data-apbn.kemenkeu.go.id/Dataset/Details/1007.

Knoema. "Indonesia: Public Spending on Education as a Share of Gross Domestic Product." Accessed February 15, 2018. https://knoema.com/atlas/Indonesia/topics/Education/Expenditures-on-Education/Public-spending-on-education-as-a-share-of-GDP.

Knight, George R. *Philosophy and Education: An Introduction in Christian Perspective*. 4th edition. Berrien Springs, MI: Andrews University Press, 2006.

Kolb, David. *Experiential Learning: Experience as the Source of Learning and Development*. Englewood Cliffs, NJ: Prentice-Hall, 1984.

Korniejczuk, Raquel I., and Jimmy Kijai. "Integrating Faith and Learning: Development of a Stage Model of Teacher Implementation." *Journal of Research on Christian Education* 3, no. 1 (Spring 1994): 79–102.

Korniejczuk, Raquel B. "The Teacher as Agent in Integrating Faith and Learning: The Process of Deliberate Teacher Implementation." Papers presented at International Faith and Learning Seminar held at Union College, Lincoln, NE. June 1993. Accessed December 12, 2015. http://christintheclassroom.org/vol_10/10cc_239-255.htm.

Kusumawardhani, Prita N. "Does Teacher Certification Program Lead to Better Quality Teachers? Evidence from Indonesia." *Education Economics* 25, no. 6 (July 2017): 590–618.

Kuyper, Abraham. "Common Grace." In *Abraham Kuyper: A Centennial Reader*, edited by James D. Bratt, 165–201. Grand Rapids: Eerdmans, 1998.

———. *Encyclopaedia of Sacred Theology: Its Principles*. Translated by J. H. de Vries. New York: Charles Scribner's Sons, 1898.

———. *Lectures on Calvinism*. Grand Rapids, MI: Eerdmans, 1931.

Lawrence, Terry Anne, Larry D. Burton, and Constance C. Nwosu. "Refocusing on the Learning in Integration of Faith and Learning." *Journal of Research on Christian Education* 14, no. 1 (Spring 2005): 17–50.

Lessard-Clouston, Michael. "Faith and Learning Integration in ESL/EFL Instruction: A Preliminary Study in America and Indonesia." In *Christian Faith and English Language Teaching and Learning: Research on the Interrelationship of Religion and ELT*, edited by Mary S. Wong, Carolyn Kristjansson, and Zoltan Dornyei, 115–135. New York: Routledge, 2013.

Lincoln, Yvonna S., and Egon G. Guba. "Paradigmatic Controversies, Contradictions, and Emerging Confluences." In *Handbook of Qualitative Research*, edited by N. K. Denzin and Y. S. Lincoln, 163–188. Thousand Oaks, CA: Sage, 2000.

Lockerbie, D. Bruce. *The Way They Should Go*. New York: Oxford University Press, 1972.

Logan, Jerry, and Janel Curry. "A Liberal Arts Education: Global Trends and Challenges." *Christian Higher Education* 14, nos. 1–2 (2015): 66–79.

Lyon, Larry, Michael Beaty, James Parker, and Carson Mencken. "Faculty Attitudes on Integrating Faith and Learning at Religious Colleges and Universities: A Research Note." *Sociology of Religion* 66, no. 1 (Spring 2005): 61–69.

Marsden, George M. *Fundamentalism, and American Culture*. New York: Oxford University Press, 2006.

———. "The Soul of the American University." *First Things* 9 (January 1991): 34–47.

———. *The Soul of the American University: From Protestant Establishment to Established Nonbelief*. New York: Oxford University Press, 1996.

Masselink, William. *Common Grace and Christian Education or a Calvinistic Philosophy of Science*. Grand Rapids: Heritage Hall, 1951.

Matthews, Lionel, and Elvin Gabriel. "Dimensions of the Integration of Faith and Learning: An Interactionist Perspective." *Journal of Research on Christian Education* 10, no. 1 (Spring 2001): 2–38.

Matthias, Laurie R. "Professors Who Walk Humbly with Their God: Exemplars in the Integration of Faith and Learning at Wheaton College." *Journal of Education & Christian Belief* 12, no. 2 (September 2008): 145–157.

Meeter, H. Henry. *The Fundamental Principle of Calvinism*. Grand Rapids: Eerdmans, 1930.

Merriam, Sharan B. *Qualitative Research: A Guide to Design and Implementation*. San Francisco, CA: Jossey-Bass, 2009.

Milacci, Frederick A. "Moving Towards Faith: An Inquiry into Spirituality in Adult Education." *Christian Higher Education* 5, no. 3 (2006): 211–233.

———. "A Step Towards Faith: The Limitations of Spirituality in Adult Education Practice." PhD diss., Liberty University, 2003. Accessed December 10, 2015. http://digitalcommons.liberty.edu/fac_dis/2.

Miller, David W. *God at Work: The History and Promise of the Faith at Work Movement*. Oxford: Oxford University Press, 2007.

Miller, Kevin D. "Reframing the Faith-Learning Relationship: Bonhoeffer and an Incarnational Alternative to the Integration Model." *Christian Scholar's Review* 43, no. 2 (January 2014): 131–38.

Miller, Deborah J. "Keeping Faith with the Mission: A Case Study of Faith and Learning Integration in Graduate Programs at George Fox University." PhD diss., George Fox University, 2006. Retrieved from ProQuest Dissertations and Theses database (UMI No. 3215154).

Moeliodihardjo, Bagyo Y., et al. "University, Industry, and Government Partnership: Its Present and Future Challenges in Indonesia." *Social and Behavioral Sciences* 52 (December 2012): 307–316.

Moroney, Stephen K. *The Noetic Effects of Sin: A Historical and Contemporary Exploration of How Sin Affects Our Thinking*. Lanham, MD: Lexington, 2000.

Morton, C. Harrison. "A Description of Deliberate Attempts of the Integration of Faith and Learning by Faculty Members at Colleges Affiliated with the Southern Baptist Denomination." PhD diss., University of South Carolina, 2004. Retrieved from ProQuest Dissertations and Theses database (UMI No. 3157171).

Mouw, Richard J. *Called to Holy Worldliness*. Philadelphia: Fortress, 1980.

Muller, Richard A. *Calvin and the Reformed Tradition*. Grand Rapids, MI: Baker Academic, 2012.

Naugle, David. "Models of Faith and Learning in Higher Education." Summer Institute in Christian Scholarship. Accessed February 1, 2016. https://www3.dbu.edu/naugle/pdf/institute_handouts/general/models_faith_learning.pdf.

Nelson, Ronald R. "Faith Discipline Integration: Compatibilist, Reconstructionist, and Transformationalist Strategies." In *The Reality of Christian Learning: Strategies for Faith-Discipline Integration*, edited by Harold Heie and David L. Wolfe, 317–339. Grand Rapids, MI: Eerdmans, 1987.

Niebuhr, H. Richard. *Christ and Culture*. San Francisco: Harper Collins, 1951.

Noll, Mark A. *Between Faith and Criticism: Evangelicals, Scholarship, and the Bible in America*. Vancouver, BC: Regent College, 2004.

———. "Common Sense Traditions and American Evangelical Thought." *American Quarterly* 37, no. 2 (Summer 1985): 216–238.

Nwosu, Constance C. "Integration of Faith and Learning in Christian Higher Education: Professional Development of Teachers and Classroom Implementation." PhD diss., Andrews University, 1999.

———. "Professional Development of Teachers: A Process for Integrating Faith and Learning in Christian Schools." Paper presented at the Annual Meeting of the Michigan Academy of Arts, Science, and Letters, Alma, MI, February 27, 1998. Accessed December 10, 2015. http://files.eric.ed.gov/fulltext/ED422326.pdf.

Ogunji, James A. "Fostering the Identity and Mission of Christian Education in Africa." *Journal of Research on Christian Education* 21 (2012): 46–61.

Palmer, Parker J. *The Courage to Teach: Exploring the Inner Landscape of a Teacher's Life*. San Francisco: Jossey-Bass, 2007.

———. *To Know as We Are Known: Education as a Spiritual Journey*. San Francisco: HarperOne, 1993.

Parks, Sharon Daloz. *Big Questions, Worthy Dreams: Mentoring Emerging Adults in Their Search for Meaning, Purpose, and Faith*. San Francisco, CA: Jossey-Bass, 2011.

Patton, Michael Q. *Qualitative Research and Evaluation Methods*. Thousand Oaks: Sage, 2002.

Plantinga, Cornelius, Jr. *Engaging God's World: A Christian Vision of Faith, Learning, and Living*. Grand Rapids: Eerdmans, 2002.

———. *Not the Way It's Supposed to Be: A Breviary of Sin*. Grand Rapids: Eerdmans, 1995.

Plantinga, Alvin. "On Christian Scholarship." In *Christian Scholarship in the Twenty-First Century: Prospects and Perils*, edited by Thomas M. Crisp, Steve L. Porter, and Gregg A. Ten Elshof, 18–33. Grand Rapids: Eerdmans, 2014.

Polanyi, Michael. *Personal Knowledge: Towards a Post-Critical Philosophy*. London: Routledge, 1958; repr. 2005. Accessed June 5, 2018. https://bibliodarq.files.wordpress.com/2015/09/polanyi-m-personal-knowledge-towards-a-post-critical-philosophy.pdf.

———. "Tacit Knowing." In *Knowledge and Society: Forms of Knowledge*, edited by Nico Stehr and Reiner Grundmann, 101–114. Abingdon, OX: Routledge, 2005.

Pressnell, Claude O., Jr. "Assessing Faith/Learning Integration Among Alumni at Taylor University." *Research on Christian Higher Education* 3 (January 1996): 1–32.

Ramm, Bernard. *The Christian View of Science and Scripture*. Grand Rapids, MI: Eerdmans, 1954.

Rasi, Humberto M. "The Integration of Faith and Values with Teaching and Learning: A Definition and Applications." *The Institute for Christian Teaching*, 2006. Accessed December 15, 2015. http://ict.aiias.edu/ifl_definition.html.

Rasmussen, Jay B., and Roberta H. Rasmussen. "The Challenge of Integrating Faith-Learning-Living in Teacher Education." *Journal of the International Christian Community for Teacher Education* 1, no. 1 (2009): 1–10. Accessed December 5, 2015. http://icctejournal.org/issues/v1i1/v1i1-rasmussen-rasmussen/.

Ream, Todd, Michael Beaty, and Larry Lyon. "Faith and Learning: Toward a Typology of Faculty Views at Religious Research Universities." *Christian Higher Education* 3, no. 4 (October-December 2004): 349–372.

Reese, William F. "The Origins of Progressive Education." *History of Education Quarterly* 41, no. 1 (Spring 2001): 1–24.

Reichard, Joshua David. "From Indoctrination to Initiation: A Non-Coercive Approach to Faith-Learning Integration." *Journal of Education & Christian Belief* 17, no. 2 (September 2013): 285–299.

Reuben, Julie A. *The Making of the Modern University: Intellectual Transformation and the Marginalization of Morality*. Chicago: University of Chicago Press, 1996.

Roso, Calvin G. "Faith and Learning in Action: Tangible Connections Between Biblical Integration and Living the Christian Life Justice." *Journal of Spirituality and Education* 3, no. 1 (November 2015): 60–72.

Sands, Paul. "The Imago Dei as Vocation." *Evangelical Quarterly* 82, no. 1 (January 2010): 28–41.

Saucy, Robert L. "Theology of Human Nature." In *Christian Perspective on Being Human: A Multidisciplinary Approach to Integration*, edited by J. P. Moreland and David M. Ciocchi, 17–53. Grand Rapids, MI: Baker, 1993.

Schön, Donald A. *Educating the Reflective Practitioner: Toward a New Design for Teaching and Learning in the Professions*. San Francisco: Jossey-Bass, 1987.

Schwehn, Mark R. "Teaching as Profession and Vocation." *Journal of Theology Today* 59, no. 3 (October 2002): 396–407.
Seidman, Irving. *Interviewing as Qualitative Research*. 4th edition. New York: Teacher College Press, 2013.
Sherr, Michael, George Huff, and Mary Curran. "Student Perceptions of Salient Indicators of Integration of Faith and Learning (IFL): The Christian Vocation Model." *Journal of Research on Christian Education* 16, no. 1 (March 2007): 15–33.
Shin, Kuk-Won. "Korean Christian Higher Education: History, Tasks and Vision." In *Christian Higher Education: A Global Reconnaissance*, edited by Joel Carpenter, Perry L. Glanzer, and Nicholas S. Lantinga, 90–110. Grand Rapids: Eerdmans, 2014.
Shipton, Warren A., Elainie Coetzee, and Rajdeep Takeuchi. *Worldviews and Christian Education: Appreciating the Cultural Outlook of Asia-Pacific People*. Singapore: Trafford, 2013.
Sire, James W. *The Universe Next Door: A Basic Worldview Catalog*. 3rd edition. Downers Grove, IL: InterVarsity Press, 1997.
Sites, Elizabeth C., et al. "A Phenomenology of the Integration of Faith and Learning." *Journal of Psychology and Theology* 37, no. 1 (Spring 2009): 28–38.
Smith, Christian, et al. *Lost in Transition: The Dark Side of Emerging Adulthood*. New York: Oxford University Press, 2011.
———. *The Secular Revolution: Power, Interests, and conflict in the Secularization of American Public Life*. Berkeley: University of California Press, 2003.
Smith, David I. "Reading Practices and Christian Pedagogy: Enacting Charity with Texts." In *Teaching and Christian Practices: Reshaping Faith and Learning*, edited by David I. Smith and James K. A. Smith, 43–60. Grand Rapids: Eerdmans, 2011.
Smith, David I., and James K. A. Smith. *Teaching and Christian Practices: Reshaping Faith and Learning*. Grand Rapids: Eerdmans, 2011.
Smith, David I., Joonyong Um, and Claudia DeVries Beversluis. "The Scholarship of Teaching and Learning in a Christian Context." *Christian Higher Education* 13, no. 1 (February 2014): 74–87.
Smith, James K. A. "Beyond Integration: Re-Narrating Christian Scholarship in Postmodernity." In *Beyond Integration: Interdisciplinary Possibilities for the Future of Christian Higher Education*, edited by Todd C. Ream, J. Pattengale, and David L. Riggs, 19–48. Abilene, TX: Abilene Christian University Press, 2012.
———. *Desiring the Kingdom: Worship, Worldview, and Cultural Formation*. Cultural Liturgies. Grand Rapids: Baker Academic, 2009.
Sorenson, Randall Lehmann. "Doctoral Students' Integration of Psychology and Christianity: Perspectives via Attachment Theory and Multidimensional

Scaling." *Journal for the Scientific Study of Religion* 36, no. 4 (December 1997): 530–548.

Spradley, Joseph L. "Changing Views of Science and Scripture: Bernard Ramm and the ASA." *Perspective on Science and Christian Faith* 44, no. 1 (March 1992): 2–9. Accessed October 28, 2019. https://www.asa3.org/ASA/PSCF/1992/PSCF3-92Complete.pdf.

Suratno, Tatang. "The Education System in Indonesia at a Time of Significant Changes." *Revue Internationale d'éducation de Sèvres* [Online], Education in Asia in 2014: What Global Issues? (12–14 June 2014). Online since 21 May 2014. Accessed on 30 April 2019. http://journals.openedition.org/ries/3814.

Suryadinata, Leo, Evi N. Arifin, and Aris Ananta. *Indonesia's Population: Ethnicity and Religion in a Changing Political Landscape*. Singapore: Institute of Southeast Asian Studies, 2003.

Susanti, Dewi. "Privatisation and Marketisation of Higher Education in Indonesia: The Challenge for Equal Access and Academic Values." *Higher Education* 61, no. 2 (February 2011): 209–218.

The Institute for Christian Teaching 2006. "About Us." Accessed December 15, 2015. http://ict.aiias.edu/about_us.html.

The Kuyers Institute. "What If Learning." Accessed July 16, 2018. http://www.whatiflearning.com/.

Thelin, John R. *A History of American Higher Education*. Baltimore: Johns Hopkins University Press, 2004.

Umakoshi, Toru. "Private Higher Education in Asia." In *Asian Universities: Historical Perspectives and Contemporary Challenges*, edited by Philip. G. Altbach and Toru Umakoshi, 33–49. Baltimore: Johns Hopkins University Press, 2004.

UNESCO. "Gross Enrolment Ratio, Tertiary, Both Sexes (%)." 2015. Accessed February 15, 2018. https://data.worldbank.org/indicator/SE.TER.ENRR?locations=ID.

Valance, Marie, Jaliene Hollabaugh, and Thu Truong. "St. Augustine's Learning for the Glory of God: Adapting 'Faith-learning Integration' Terminology for the Modern World." *Journal of the International Christian Community for Teacher Education* 4, no. 2 (2009). Accessed December 10, 2015, https://digitalcommons.georgefox.edu/cgi/viewcontent.cgi?article=1053&context=ictej.

Van Nes, Fenna, et al. "Language Differences in Qualitative Research: Is Meaning Lost in Translation?" *European Journal of Ageing* 7, no. 4 (December 2010): 313–316.

Van Reken, Calvin P. "Christians in This World: Pilgrims or Settlers?" *Calvin Theological Journal* 43, no. 2 (November 2008): 234–256.

Van Til, Cornelius. *Junior Systematics*. Glenside: Westminster Theological Seminary, 1940.
Van Zanten, Susan. *Joining the Mission: A Guide for (Mainly) New College Faculty*. Grand Rapids: Eerdmans, 2011.
Wax, Trevin. *Counterfeit Gospels: Rediscovering the Good News in the World of False Hope*. Chicago: Moody Publishers, 2011.
Weber, Max. *The Protestant Ethic and the Spirit of Capitalism*. Translated by Talcott Parsons. New York: Charles Scribner's Sons, 1930.
Welch, A. R. "Blurred Vision?: Public and Private Higher Education in Indonesia." *Higher Education* 54, no. 5 (October 2007): 665–687.
Wicaksono, Teguh Y., and Deni Friawan. "Recent Developments in Higher Education in Indonesia: Issues and Challenges." Paper prepared for discussion at the DPU/EABER Conference on Financing Higher Education and Economic Development in East Asia, Bangkok, July 16–17, 2008. Accessed February 15, 2018. http://aber.eaber.org/system/tdf/documents/WPS_DPU_2008_45.pdf?file=1&type=node&id=21949&force=.
Wingren, Gustaf. *Luther on Vocation*. Translated by Carl C. Rasmussen. Eugene, OR: Wipf & Stock, 2004.
Wolfe, Alan. *The Transformation of American Religion: How We Actually Live Our Faith*. Chicago: University of Chicago Press, 2003.
Wolfe, David L. "The Line of Demarcation Between Integration and Pseudo-Integration." In *The Reality of Christian Learning Strategies for Faith-Discipline Integration*, edited by Harold Heie and David L. Wolfe, 1–12. Grand Rapids: Eerdmans, 1987.
Wolfe, David L., and Harold Heie. *Slogans or Distinctives: Reforming Christian Higher Education*. Lanham, MD: University Press of America, 1993.
Wolters, Albert M. "The Nature of Fundamentalism." *Pro Rege* 15, no. 1 (September 1986): 2–9.
Wolterstorff, Nicholas. *Educating for Shalom: Essays on Christian Higher Education*. Edited by Clarence W. Joldersma, and Gloria G. Stronks. Grand Rapids: Eerdmans, 2004.
———. "Fides Quaerens Intellectum." In *Christian Scholarship in the Twenty-First Century: Prospects and Perils*, edited by Thomas M. Crisp, Steve L. Porter, and Gregg A. Ten Elshof, 1–17. Grand Rapids: Eerdmans, 2014.
———. *Reason within the Boundary of Religion*. Grand Rapids, MI: Eerdmans, 1984.
———. *Until Justice and Peace Embrace*. Grand Rapids: Eerdmans, 1983.
World Bank. "2017 World Development Indicators." Accessed February 15, 2018. https://openknowledge.worldbank.org/bitstream/handle/10986/.../9781464809507.pdf?

Wright, Christopher J. H. *The Mission of God's People*. Grand Rapids, MI: Zondervan, 2010.

Wright, N. T. *Simply Christian: Why Christianity Makes Sense*. New York, NY: Harper One, 2010.

Yudhoyono, Susilo B. *Undang-Undang Republik Indonesia Nomor 14 Tahun 2005*. "Tentang Guru dan Dosen." *Lembaran Negara Republik Indonesia Tahun* 2005 Nomor 157. December 30, 2005. Accessed February 6, 2017. http://luk.staff.ugm.ac.id/atur/UU14-2005GuruDosen.pdf.

Langham Literature, with its publishing work, is a ministry of Langham Partnership.

Langham Partnership is a global fellowship working in pursuit of the vision God entrusted to its founder John Stott –

> *to facilitate the growth of the church in maturity and Christ-likeness through raising the standards of biblical preaching and teaching.*

Our vision is to see churches in the Majority World equipped for mission and growing to maturity in Christ through the ministry of pastors and leaders who believe, teach and live by the word of God.

Our mission is to strengthen the ministry of the word of God through:
- nurturing national movements for biblical preaching
- fostering the creation and distribution of evangelical literature
- enhancing evangelical theological education

especially in countries where churches are under-resourced.

Our ministry

Langham Preaching partners with national leaders to nurture indigenous biblical preaching movements for pastors and lay preachers all around the world. With the support of a team of trainers from many countries, a multi-level programme of seminars provides practical training, and is followed by a programme for training local facilitators. Local preachers' groups and national and regional networks ensure continuity and ongoing development, seeking to build vigorous movements committed to Bible exposition.

Langham Literature provides Majority World preachers, scholars and seminary libraries with evangelical books and electronic resources through publishing and distribution, grants and discounts. The programme also fosters the creation of indigenous evangelical books in many languages, through writer's grants, strengthening local evangelical publishing houses, and investment in major regional literature projects, such as one volume Bible commentaries like the *Africa Bible Commentary* and the *South Asia Bible Commentary*.

Langham Scholars provides financial support for evangelical doctoral students from the Majority World so that, when they return home, they may train pastors and other Christian leaders with sound, biblical and theological teaching. This programme equips those who equip others. Langham Scholars also works in partnership with Majority World seminaries in strengthening evangelical theological education. A growing number of Langham Scholars study in high quality doctoral programmes in the Majority World itself. As well as teaching the next generation of pastors, graduated Langham Scholars exercise significant influence through their writing and leadership.

To learn more about Langham Partnership and the work we do visit **langham.org**

www.ingramcontent.com/pod-product-compliance
Lightning Source LLC
Chambersburg PA
CBHW051538230426

43669CB00015B/2639

Much scholarship and many research studies have emphasized the integration of faith and learning in the Western context. Dr. Sarinah Lo's study meets a relevant need to present an Asian perspective on how the integration of faith and learning should be interpreted to make an impact on the educational theories and practices in Christian higher education institutions in Indonesia. Should the teacher or the student be responsible to do the work of integration? Leaders and educators are invited to think afresh on her passionate and diligent exploration of the unchanging task of integration to meet the changes facing Christian mission schools and theological education institutions in Asia.

Ng Peh Cheng, PhD
Former Associate Secretary, Accreditation & Educational Development,
Asia Theological Association

The integration of faith and learning has been challenging Christian educators for decades. Sarinah Lo not only identifies the contributing factors to this challenge but also proposes a holistic approach that Christian faculty members and institutions would do well to consider. Her approach moves the faculty members and their systems toward a robust "faith-integrated being-knowing-doing" model that includes everything from personal formation to learning community participation. I highly commend Sarinah's thoughtful and creative work. It is much needed.

Donald C. Guthrie, EdD
Executive Director, Center for Transformational Churches
Director of the PhD in Educational Studies Program,
Trinity Evangelical Divinity School, Deerfield, Illinois, USA

Dr. Sarinah Lo's original research explores the practice of the know-be-do paradigm among Indonesian Christian higher education faculty. While study participants affirm a faith-informed vocational calling, Dr. Lo challenges the reader to a greater depth of knowing and doing to buttress the integration of faith and learning. Framing a broader paradigm as "faith-integrated being-knowing-doing" she argues for a holistic approach that includes cognitive, affective, spiritual, relational, and vocational aspects of the scholar-practitioner. Faith and learning becomes more than a scholarly task; it becomes a formational task engaging the Christian perspective in all areas of life, thought, and practice. Opportunity is present in the Indonesian context for faculty professional development to enhance biblical-theological understanding, philosophical foundations, and educational theories and practices critically examined in the light of Scripture toward this broader paradigm. Global higher education administrators must reckon with Dr. Lo's careful examination of the faith and learning task we all espouse in Christian higher education.

James R. Moore, PhD
Associate Professor of Educational Ministries,
Trinity Evangelical Divinity School, Deerfield, Illinois, USA

A time-honored trope in writing on the integration of faith and learning asks what Athens has to do with Jerusalem – but what about Jerusalem and Jakarta? Christian education research that is by and about Western Christians cannot give us the whole picture in a world where Christian education is shaping and being shaped by a broad array of contexts and cultures. Sarinah Lo's pioneering research on how Indonesian faculty practice Christian education stretches our horizons in important ways as it connects weaknesses in Western models with the challenges of appropriation in Indonesia. Her study points the way to important dialogue.

David I. Smith, PhD
Director, Kuyers Institute for Christian Teaching and Learning
Coordinator, Institute for Global Faculty Development
Professor of Education, Calvin University, Grand Rapids, Michigan, USA
Editor, *International Journal of Christianity and Education*